LEGAL METHOD
AND WRITING II
TRIAL AND APPELLATE ADVOCACY, CONTRACTS, AND CORRESPONDENCE

Aspen Coursebook Series

LEGAL METHOD AND WRITING II
TRIAL AND APPELLATE ADVOCACY, CONTRACTS, AND CORRESPONDENCE

EIGHTH EDITION

CHARLES R. CALLEROS

PROFESSOR OF LAW
ARIZONA STATE UNIVERSITY

KIMBERLY Y.W. HOLST

CLINICAL PROFESSOR OF LAW
ARIZONA STATE UNIVERSITY

Wolters Kluwer

Published by Wolters Kluwer in New York.

Wolters Kluwer Legal & Regulatory U.S. serves customers worldwide with CCH, Aspen Publishers, and Kluwer Law International products. (www.WKLegaledu.com)

To contact Customer Service, e-mail customer.service@wolterskluwer.com, call 1-800-234-1660, fax 1-800-901-9075, or mail correspondence to:

Wolters Kluwer
Attn: Order Department
PO Box 990
Frederick, MD 21705

Printed in the United States of America.

1 2 3 4 5 6 7 8 9 0

ISBN 978-1-4548-9715-6

Library of Congress Cataloging-in-Publication Data

Names: Calleros, Charles R., author. | Holst, Kimberly Y.W., author.
Title: Legal method and writing II : trial and appellate advocacy, contracts,
    and correspondence / Charles R. Calleros, Professor of Law, Arizona
    State University; Kimberly Y.W. Holst, Clinical professor of Law,
    Arizona State University.
Description: Eighth edition. | New York : Wolters Kluwer, 2018. | Includes
    index.
Identifiers: LCCN 2017056129 | ISBN 9781454897156
Subjects: LCSH: Legal composition. | Law--United States--Methodology.
Classification: LCC KF250 .C345 2018b | DDC 808.06/634--dc23
LC record available at https://lccn.loc.gov/2017056129

About Wolters Kluwer Legal & Regulatory U.S.

Wolters Kluwer Legal & Regulatory U.S. delivers expert content and solutions in the areas of law, corporate compliance, health compliance, reimbursement, and legal education. Its practical solutions help customers successfully navigate the demands of a changing environment to drive their daily activities, enhance decision quality and inspire confident outcomes.

Serving customers worldwide, its legal and regulatory portfolio includes products under the Aspen Publishers, CCH Incorporated, Kluwer Law International, ftwilliam.com and MediRegs names. They are regarded as exceptional and trusted resources for general legal and practice-specific knowledge, compliance and risk management, dynamic workflow solutions, and expert commentary.

Dedications

In loving memory of our wonderful mother,
Emily Calleros,
1922-2016
Charles and James Calleros

With special thanks to Alice Silkey, my original
writing teacher, my mentor, and my friend
Kimberly Holst

In honor of Marjorie D. Rombauer
1927-2016
A pioneer in our field,
and a modest master of many things
Charles Calleros and Kimberly Holst

SUMMARY OF CONTENTS

CONTENTS

TABLE OF CHARTS AND SAMPLE DOCUMENTS

PREFACE

The activities of practicing attorneys speak volumes about the importance of legal writing classes in law school. Although analytic skills and a general knowledge of legal principles form the intellectual foundation of the practice of law, legal analysis is only as effective as the quality with which it is expressed. In your practice, you undoubtedly will devote a substantial proportion of your time and effort to drafting legal documents such as office memoranda, letters, pleadings, motions, briefs, contracts, and wills. Moreover, techniques of expression are closely linked to the underlying substantive analysis; indeed, problems in writing style often betray confusion in the analysis.

Unfortunately, as a first-year law student, you might have difficulty seeing the relationship between your efforts in legal writing classes and your short-term objectives for success in law school. With this book, we hope to reassure you that the work in your first-year legal writing courses will directly contribute to your success with law school exams as well as with legal documents that you draft in a summer clerking position or in post-graduate employment. We hope to demonstrate in Volume I that the skills you develop in analyzing a client's legal problem and drafting an office memorandum are directly transferable to your task of analyzing an essay exam and writing the exam answer.

Volume II examines techniques of advocacy and client representation that should appeal to a broad spectrum of readers: participants in a first-year moot-court program, students in an advanced writing seminar, student law clerks, and practicing attorneys. For example, Volume II Parts I through III examine written advocacy in the context of pleadings, pretrial motions, and appellate briefs. Moreover, they thoroughly examine principles of writing and persuasion that apply generally to any litigation document. Part IV provides a step-by-step approach to drafting simple contracts, advice letters, and demand letters. Finally, the extensive citations in footnotes, most of which first-year law students can pass over, will provide attorneys with a valuable source of authorities.

Volume I addresses matters of style at Chapters 1 and 8-10. These chapters use problems and examples to outline a general approach to style that focuses on the policies underlying conventions of composition. They encourage you to adopt the following philosophy: We should not memorize and mechanically apply rules of composition any more than we would mechanically apply "black letter" rules of law. Instead, we must understand the goals and purposes of the conventions of legal writing, and we should apply them flexibly to satisfy those goals and purposes. Much the same can be said about persuasive writing style, addressed in Volume II at Chapter 3.

Of course, this book reflects our own style quirks and biases, especially those of the sole author for the first seven editions: He freely splits infinitives but always uses the serial comma, and he dislikes sexism in language. While writing this book, we encountered the problem of sexism in language most often in the form of personal pronouns in the third person. Unfortunately, the disjunctive phrase "his or her" often needlessly clutters already complex sentences, and plural pronouns such as "they" are not always consistent with content (and we are not yet ready to match "they" or "their" with a singular noun). As a provocative response to the problem, we have alternated between male and female pronouns, for example, by referring to an associate in a law firm with the pronoun "he" and to his assigning attorney with the pronoun "she." This approach may distract readers at one time or another, perhaps because it catches readers assuming that a judge or a senior partner is male. If so, perhaps the distraction is constructive: It may help us to envision a profession so well integrated that feminine pronouns and ethnic names will sound natural and commonplace.

The text is heavily footnoted with source material and with acknowledgments to others whose ideas inspired the text. Readers may find some of the additional information in the footnotes to be illuminating or to be helpful in practice as a starting point for research. Otherwise, however, busy students can focus on the text and skip the footnotes without missing any significant points.

Charles R. Calleros and
Kimberly Y.W. Holst
January 2018

ACKNOWLEDGMENTS

My interest and enthusiasm for legal writing stem largely from the inspiration and training that I received as a court law clerk at the Office of Central Staff Attorneys for the United States Court of Appeals for the Ninth Circuit. In particular, I am grateful to United States Court of Appeals Judge Procter Hug, Jr., who sowed the seeds of my current views on flexible, policy-oriented approaches to legal writing.

Other attorneys, judges, and colleagues contributed to my first edition with their comments on early drafts. In particular, I thank the late Thomas Gordon, who was a staff attorney for the Arizona Court of Appeals, fellow legal writing instructor, and former classmate at the University of California at Davis School of Law. Mr. Gordon's keen analytic insights into the art of legal writing contributed greatly to this book. Other important contributors include the rigorous reviewers who strongly influenced the organization and content of the book, and Janet Wagner, an attorney who skillfully and artfully critiqued my writing style. Several colleagues contributed to selected portions of the book. They include Fred Cole, Amy Gittler, Mark Hielman, Susan E. Klemmer, Christopher Mason, William Monahan, Roger Perry, Frank Placenti, Thomas Quarelli, Jeffrey P. Travers, Paul Ulrich, Sherin Vitro, Judge Noel Fidel, and Professors Jane Aiken, Rebecca Berch (now Chief Justice of the Arizona Supreme Court), Paul Brand, Susan Chesler, Betsy Grey, Mark Hall, David Kader, Amy Langenfeld, Robert Misner, Cathy O'Grady, Mary Richards, Judy Stinson, Bonnie Tucker, James Weinstein, and Larry Winer.

The truly indispensable contributors to the early editions of this book, however, are the students and attorneys who accepted my instruction and used the early versions of the teaching materials from which this book is derived. I especially acknowledge the Phoenix law firm of Streich, Lang, Weeks & Cardon, now merged with Quarles & Brady, for its dedication to continuing education in legal writing during those years.

I also thank staff and student research assistants for their contributions to the seven editions, in the order of their participation over the years: Donna Blair, Gail Geer, Kay Winn, and Vera Hamer-Sonn provided word-processing assistance; Janice Fuller, Mark Burgoz, Michael Rutledge, Virginia Vasquez, Toby Schmich, Victoria Stevens, Jane Proctor, Lizzette M. Alameda, Brian M. Louisell, Lauren Elliott Stine, Robert Stultz, Jason Zasky, Ashley Stallings, Sarah White Mansfield, Nora Nuñez, and Natalya Ter-Grigoryan provided student research, cite-checking, and proofreading assistance. Ms. Ter-Grigoryan was especially conscientious and tireless in assisting me in preparing the much improved sixth edition after compositor's errors in the fifth edition had introduced errors in the files. Alyssa

Whetstine (class of 2015) provided excellent proofing, editing, and critiques for the seventh edition. Thanks to Daniel Rubinov for proofing and cite-checking for the eighth edition. I am also grateful to the law library staff at Arizona State University. Finally, I am indebted to Arizona State University College of Law, and especially to Deans Paul Bender, Richard Morgan, Patricia White, Paul Berman, and Douglas Sylvester, who fully supported my efforts to produce the eight editions of this text.

I fondly acknowledge my late mother, Emily, for her early guidance in grammar and for creating the drawings (one for the first three editions, and a new one in its place for the fourth edition, and an updated version appearing in the fifth) illustrating the discussion of restrictive and nonrestrictive pronouns.

Finally, I am pleased to welcome Kimberly Holst as a new co-author of this text and its companion text, LEGAL METHOD AND WRITING I: PREDICTIVE WRITING. I welcome the contributions that she brings to this and future editions, as she increasingly influences the shape and content of the texts.

Charles Calleros
2018

LEGAL METHOD
AND WRITING II
TRIAL AND APPELLATE ADVOCACY,
CONTRACTS, AND CORRESPONDENCE

Part I

Introduction to

Advocacy

Written advocacy is a special branch of legal method and writing that combines creative analysis, persuasive writing, and attention to local rules, special formats, and ethical considerations.

Part I provides an overview of advocacy at all stages of litigation. Parts II and III thoroughly examine and illustrate written advocacy in the context of four other kinds of pleadings or briefs: (1) complaints, answers, and motions to dismiss, (2) briefs on a motion for summary judgment, (3) briefs on a motion to exclude evidence, and (4) appellate briefs. By studying the general principles in Part I, and then some or all the documents in Parts II and III, you will develop a general grasp of the methods and purposes of brief writing, enabling you to prepare a brief for any stage of litigation.

Part IV addresses two kinds of correspondence related to litigation: advice letters to clients and demand letters to opposing parties. But it begins with a chapter on drafting contracts, which—if done well—could help the parties avoid disputes and subsequent litigation.

Chapter 1

Advocacy: Overview and Ethics

I. Overview—Procedure and General Format

A. Procedure

In a typical dispute, you will advocate your client's case in various written documents through several stages of litigation. You might engage in written advocacy in the pre-litigation phrase by writing an advice letter to your own client or a demand letter to an opposing party. If correspondence between the parties fails to resolve the dispute in its early stages, the parties can commence formal litigation by filing pleadings, typically a complaint and an answer. Before trial, you might file or respond to motions that request the judge to take certain actions, such as to make advance rulings on the admissibility of evidence or to rule on the merits of some or all the claims and defenses without a trial. During a trial with a jury, you might submit or respond to briefs that request the judge to instruct the jury on the law in a certain way or even to decide the case "as a matter of law" without the jury. At the outset of a bench trial without a jury, you might submit a trial brief that invites a judge or arbitrator to find certain facts and to apply your interpretation of the law to the facts to reach certain conclusions. Finally, if either party appeals the judgment of the trial court, you will draft one or more briefs to an appellate court, inviting the appellate court to either affirm or reverse the judgment of the court immediately below it.

Throughout these proceedings, the pleadings, motions, and appeals will follow similar briefing schedules:

1. The party seeking relief or seeking reversal of a lower court's judgment files a complaint, petition, or opening brief.

2. The opposing party responds with an answer, response, or answering brief.

3. Finally, the party who filed the petition or opening brief generally has the opportunity to file a reply brief that addresses points raised in the opposing party's answering brief or response. Under federal pleading rules, the drafter of a complaint will file an answer to any counterclaim contained in the defendant's answer;[1] otherwise, the drafter of a complaint or counterclaim will reply to the defendant's answer if the court orders a reply.[2]

B. Basic Formats for Briefs

The format of a complaint or answer, discussed in Chapter 4, differs significantly from that of a brief. Various pretrial, trial, and appellate briefs, however, have much in common. Each will include some statement of the background of the case, followed by an argument and a conclusion.

In some ways, an appellate brief may be more detailed and formal than a pretrial brief. By the time a case reaches an appellate court, the litigants have developed some record of the facts or factual allegations, and they have advanced the dispute through significant procedural steps. Accordingly, an appellate brief's description of the background of a case typically includes a formal statement of facts and a summary of the procedural history. On the other hand, when the parties litigate a pretrial motion, the facts may be sketchy and the procedural history brief. Consequently, many pretrial briefs combine the procedural history and statement of relevant facts in an "Introduction," "Background," or "Statement of Facts." As explored in Chapter 5, briefs on a motion for summary judgment are exceptional in their unusually formal pretrial presentation of facts.

An appellate brief may be more formal than a pretrial brief in other ways as well. For example, rules of procedure and local court rules typically require an appellate brief to include a table of contents, table of authorities,

---

1. Fed. R. Civ. P. 7(a)(3).
2. Fed. R. Civ. P. 7(a)(7); *see also id.* at Note on 2007 Amendment (referring both to a reply to an answer and to a reply to an answer to a counterclaim).

and formal statement of issues. These are customarily omitted from all but the most complex pretrial briefs.

These differences, however, are relatively superficial compared to the universal heart of any brief: the argument. Unlike an office memorandum, your brief will not explore the strengths and weaknesses of both sides of the dispute. Instead, you will use the brief to advocate the legal and factual analysis that best supports the claims or defenses of your client.

This perspective of a brief is reflected not only in the subtler facets of writing style but also in fundamental elements of format such as section headings. Depending on the format adopted by a writer or a law firm, a section heading in the Discussion section of an office memorandum might state a conclusion, restate the issue, or use a neutral phrase or sentence that generally describes a topic of discussion and helps your reader recall an issue stated more formally at the beginning of the memorandum. In contrast, you will uniformly use "point headings" in the argument section of a brief to state the conclusions that you want the judge to adopt. In each point heading, you will assert your conclusion in a complete sentence as a prelude to your full deductive argument on that issue.

Chapters 2 and 3 address these and other techniques of written and oral advocacy in greater depth. First, however, Section II introduces you to a few of the many ethical obligations that you assume as an advocate.

II. Good Faith, Reasonableness, and Full Disclosure

A. Assertion of Claims and Defenses

As an attorney, you owe a duty to your client to advocate her case vigorously.[3] In carrying out this duty, you will often argue for creative extension of existing law or for replacement of existing law with new rules.[4] Fundamental principles of professional responsibility, however, impose limits on your advocacy.[5] For example, Federal Rule of Civil Procedure 11 requires attorneys to certify that their written advocacy is supported by a reasonable investigation of the law and facts and is not advanced for an improper purpose:

> (b) REPRESENTATIONS TO THE COURT. By presenting to the court a pleading, written motion, or other paper—whether by signing, filing, submitting, or later advocating it—an attorney or unrepresented party

---

3. *See, e.g.*, MODEL CODE OF PROF'L RESPONSIBILITY EC 7-4 (2004); *id.* at Canon 7.

4. *See, e.g.*, Hunter v. Earthgrains Co. Bakery, 281 F.3d 144, 156 (4th Cir. 2002) (attorney was "plainly entitled (and probably obligated)" to argue that circuit precedent incorrectly applied Supreme Court precedent and should be overturned).

5. *See, e.g.*, MODEL RULES OF PROF'L CONDUCT R. (hereafter, "MODEL RULE") 3.3(a)(1) (2012) (proscribing knowingly false statements of material fact or law).

certifies that to the best of the person's knowledge, information, and belief, formed after an inquiry reasonable under the circumstances:

(1) it is not being presented for any improper purpose, such as to harass, cause unnecessary delay, or needlessly increase the cost of litigation;

(2) the claims, defenses, and other legal contentions are warranted by existing law or by a nonfrivolous argument for extending, modifying, or reversing existing law or for establishing new law;

(3) the factual contentions have evidentiary support or, if specifically so identified, will likely have evidentiary support after a reasonable opportunity for further investigation or discovery; and

(4) the denials of factual contentions are warranted on the evidence or, if specifically so identified, are reasonably based on belief or a lack of information.[6]

Rule 11 authorizes a judge to impose "an appropriate sanction on any attorney, law firm, or party that violated the rule or is responsible for the violation."[7] The sanction may include "nonmonetary directives; an order to pay a penalty into court; or, if imposed on motion and warranted for effective deterrence, an order directing payment to the movant of part or all of the reasonable attorneys' fees and other expenses directly resulting from the violation."[8]

Rule 11 also contains a "safe harbor" provision that permits a person responsible for a Rule 11 violation to escape sanctions by withdrawing the offending claim or defense within 21 days after receiving service of the motion for sanctions, or within another time set by the court.[9] As explored more fully in the following sections, however, perhaps the best guide to responsible advocacy is not the risk of sanctions but the desire shared by most advocates to maintain their reputations for candor and quality work.

B. Disclosure of Adverse Authority

As an advocate, you have no duty to argue your opponent's case or even to present a balanced analysis such as would be appropriate in an office memorandum. Nonetheless, every advocate is also an officer of the court[10] and owes a general duty of candor and fairness to the court and to other lawyers.[11] Within this framework, the American Bar Association (ABA) Model Rules of Professional Conduct specifically require every advocate to disclose significant authority adverse to the advocate's arguments:

---

6. FED. R. CIV. P. 11(b).

7. FED. R. CIV. P. 11(c)(1).

8. FED. R. CIV. P. 11(c)(4).

9. FED. R. CIV. P. 11(c)(2).

10. *E.g.*, Ex parte Garland, 71 U.S. (4 Wall.) 333, 378 (1867), *cited in* ABA Formal Opinion 146 (1935).

11. MODEL RULE 3.3 (2012) (candor to court); ABA Formal Opinion 146 (1935).

A lawyer shall not knowingly:

. . . .

(2) fail to disclose to the tribunal legal authority in the controlling jurisdiction known to the lawyer to be directly adverse to the position of the client and not disclosed by opposing counsel.[12]

As stated by Judge Posner, for example, "When there is apparently dispositive precedent, an appellant may urge its overruling or distinguishing or reserve a challenge to it for a petition for certiorari but may not simply ignore it."[13]

The scope of the duty stated in the Model Rules depends in large part on the interpretation of the phrase "directly adverse." However, the most sensible approach to disclosure is one that maintains your credibility as an advocate. If adverse authority within the forum jurisdiction is sufficiently analogous that the court would consider it in deciding a case, the judge or the judge's law clerk likely will discover the authority sometime before the end of the proceedings, even if it has escaped the notice of the opposing counsel. You can minimize the impact of such adverse authority by acknowledging it early in the proceedings, permitting you to distinguish it, discredit it, or at least frame it in a way that is less damaging to your client than the framing your opponent is likely to present.[14]

The reference to "controlling jurisdiction" in the disclosure rule appears to flatly exclude authority from outside the forum jurisdiction, even if it is squarely on point. In some circumstances, however, your desire to maintain credibility may be a better guide than a specific ethical rule. For example, if the question before the court is so novel that no authority within the forum jurisdiction addresses it, and if adverse authority from another jurisdiction would be particularly persuasive, then the court might expect you to disclose the nonbinding adverse authority and to squarely address it.

If an adverse authority does not meet these standards, you need not address it unless the other party relies on it or the court raises a question that encompasses it. In an opening brief, for example, you should not waste time by distinguishing marginally analogous adverse case law or by criticizing poorly reasoned persuasive authority on which the opposing counsel is unlikely to rely. Instead, you should concentrate on affirmatively presenting your own arguments and supporting authority, and you should attack only the most obvious adverse authority. Then, you can wait to see which authority the opposing counsel advances in the answering brief, and you can attack that adverse authority in your reply brief. Of course, if the court asks you about adverse precedent, you "should make such frank disclosure as the question seems to warrant,"[15] regardless of the scope of ethical duties or strategic considerations that might otherwise apply.

---

12. MODEL RULE 3.3(a)(2) (2012).

13. Gonzalez-Servin v. Ford Motor Co., 662 F.3d 931, 934 (7th Cir. 2011).

14. *See* Charles W. Wolfram, MODERN LEGAL ETHICS §12.8, at 682 (1986).

15. ABA Formal Opinion 280 (1949).

C. Misleading Legal Argument

The ABA Model Rules of Professional Conduct prohibit a lawyer from knowingly making "a false statement of fact or law to a tribunal."[16] However, a legal analysis will not amount to a false statement about the law unless it clearly falls outside the range of plausible interpretations of the legal authorities.

For example, defining the holding of a judicial opinion and determining its effect as precedent is an exercise that produces disagreement among able jurists. Thus, as an advocate, you often have room to take an aggressive stance in identifying facts that appear to have been material to a decision and in characterizing the holding and reasoning of the decision.

As with other ethical questions, practical considerations of effective advocacy may provide the best guide to responsible conduct. Published precedent on which you rely is readily accessible to the opposing counsel and to the court. Careless or fraudulent analyses that cross the line separating creative advocacy from misrepresentation almost certainly will be brought to the court's attention. Few things can damage your credibility and effectiveness more than a reputation for stretching legal authority beyond the limits of plausible interpretation.

Every judge has at least one story about a lawyer who ventured past the boundaries of plausible presentation and interpretation of a legal authority. The story always ends with the judge never again trusting the word of that advocate. Imagine how much more effective you will be if you develop a reputation for arguing the law and facts fairly, accurately, and persuasively.

III. Summary

In shifting from neutral analysis to advocacy, you must adopt a suitable format for your document and make the transition from an objective writing style to a persuasive one, as explored in the following chapters. Take care to satisfy ethical duties in asserting claims and defenses, in disclosing adverse authority, and in representing the content of legal authority.[17]

---

16. MODEL RULE 3.3(a)(1) (2012).

17. For much more on ethics in legal writing in various contexts, see Melissa H. Weresh, LEGAL WRITING: ETHICAL AND PROFESSIONAL CONSIDERATIONS (2d ed 2009).

Chapter 2

Developing Your
Legal Arguments

Your statements of issues, facts, and procedural history will vary greatly in style and content depending on the stage of the litigation at which you draft a legal document. Consequently, this book separately examines those elements of a pleading or a brief in Parts II and III. Many techniques of advocacy, however, apply broadly to all kinds of briefs and are appropriately introduced in Part I. Specifically, this chapter examines methods of (1) organizing arguments, (2) introducing arguments, and (3) developing the elements of a deductive argument. Chapter 3 examines techniques of persuasive writing and oral argument.

I. Engaging the Reader with an Effective Theme

Before you begin writing, try to develop a theme for your brief, a thread that runs through the fabric of the brief from the Statement of Issues to the

Conclusion. If possible, your theme should reflect some facet of the dispute that shows "that your client's position is not only legally correct but also equitably, ethically, and morally 'right.'"[1] Your best arguments are likely to be ones that not only are analytically sound but also that help you advance your underlying theme throughout your brief.

More specifically, experienced advocates often speak of developing a *theory* of the case, an analytic *framework* for the arguments, a *strategy* for trial or appeal, or a main *point, thrust, direction,* or *idea* that they want to convey to the judge. This process can help you decide which arguments to advance and which facts, case law, and policy arguments to emphasize in your brief so that a persuasive theme emerges.

In its simplest form, a theme may represent an appeal to common sense or justice that translates directly to legal and factual arguments. For example, in litigation of a products liability suit, the injured plaintiff's brief might consistently advance a theme that highlights a dangerous defect in a product. In contrast, the defendant manufacturer's brief might consistently advance a theme that emphasizes the weakness of the causal link between the product's defect and the plaintiff's injuries. Although each brief may necessarily address matters that do not directly advance the theme, each authoring attorney should endeavor to bring the brief's theme to the fore in various parts of the brief, from the issue and fact statements to the argument.

Alternatively, the theme of a brief might encourage the court to embrace a judicial approach or philosophy that would pave the way for acceptance of one or more arguments. For example, various elements of the brief might emphasize that statutory language is unambiguous and should be interpreted according to the plain meaning of its text, rather than in a strained manner that relies heavily on legislative history or statutory purpose. Another brief might advance the theme that expansion of a common law doctrine would enmesh the court in hotly debated issues of social policy that would be best addressed by a democratically elected legislature.

A theme might also consist of a mood or perspective that forms a backdrop to the arguments. One attorney, for example, used the metaphor of a lawless frontier to convey a theme in a motion for summary judgment.[2] The motion challenged an arbitration decision interpreting a collective bargaining agreement, a decision to which a reviewing court would grant substantial deference.[3] Accordingly, the author of the brief bore the burden of showing that even a deferential standard of review imposed meaningful limits on the arbitrator's interpretation and that the arbitrator had exceeded those limits as a matter of law.

Throughout the brief, the author argued those points with sound analysis of the law and facts and with traditional policy arguments. But the author of the brief wanted to create a mood as well, and the case itself invited the

---

1. Hon. Jacques L. Wiener, Jr., *Ruminations from the Bench: Brief Writing and Oral Argument in the Fifth Circuit,* 70 TUL. L. REV. 187, 190 (1995).

2. The examples in this subsection were supplied in 2000 by Christopher Mason, an attorney with the Phoenix office of the law firm of Bryan Cave LLP.

3. *See* United Paperworkers Int'l Union v. Misco, Inc., 484 U.S. 29, 36-38 (1987).

author to draw allusions to unrestrained frontier justice in the lawless Wild West: The workplace was a coal mine, and the arbitrator's last name was West. To introduce this theme, the first sentence of the argument suggested that failure to curb the arbitrator's discretion would render labor relations as chaotic and lawless as in some frontier outpost in the Wild West:

Despite the deference arbitrators are granted in reaching their decisions, one principle stands clear: the federal labor policy of promoting arbitration of industrial disputes does not create a lawless frontier where arbitrators are free to impose their own brand of "industrial justice."

The phrase "industrial justice" by itself is not pejorative, but the author linked it to an image of arbitrariness and lawlessness associated with untamed frontiers. The brief did not belabor this metaphor; however, it reminded readers of this image every time it named the arbitrator, West, and every time that it referred to West's "own brand of industrial justice." Finally, the author combined both these reminders with a new play on words at the beginning of the third subsection of the argument:

... Arbitrator West also shot holes through another provision of the [agreement], enforcing his own brand of "industrial justice."

In his response to the opposing party's cross-motion for summary judgment in the same case, this author argued that the arbitrator had refused to choose between two different plausible interpretations of the collective bargaining agreement and instead had compromised inappropriately by choosing an interpretation somewhere between the plausible meanings, arguably an interpretation that no language in the agreement supported. For this brief, the author developed a different theme, one that compared and then contrasted the arbitrator's interpretation with King Solomon's fabled solution:

Just as King Solomon threatened to do, the arbitrator in this dispute split the baby and imposed an irrational solution when a clear choice was required. Of course, once his threat produced the desired reaction, King Solomon ultimately revealed his wisdom by vacating his irrational decision. Here, the Court should likewise vacate Arbitrator West's irrational decision.

Using colorful metaphors or similes to create a theme is a matter of personal style and can never substitute for sound analysis of the law, facts, and social policies. You should never use a careless or distracting metaphor when a straightforward explanation would be clearer. A telling metaphor, however, may create an effective backdrop for the analysis, encouraging your reader to develop a gut reaction in favor of your client.

II. Organizing Your Arguments

Ordinarily, you should discuss or argue discrete issues in separate sections of your office memorandum or brief. Moreover, your section and subsection headings should show the proper relationships between your topics and subtopics. Beyond these considerations, you also must decide (1) which arguments to advance, (2) the order in which to present your arguments, and (3) the internal organization of each argument.

As you examine these matters in the following sections, reflect on the value of preparing an outline of the argument section of your brief before you begin writing it. The same techniques discussed in Volume I, Chapter 7, Section I.E for outlining the discussion section of an office memorandum will help you outline the argument section of your brief.

A. Selecting Arguments

1. Include Only Arguments That Earn a Place in Your Brief

You should be more selective in choosing arguments to advance in a brief than in choosing issues to discuss in an essay examination or an office memorandum. For example, a federal appellate judge advises you to "[f]orce yourself to omit fringe issues and far-out theories; they will only dull the thrust of your appeal and obscure the potentially winning point."[4] A professor of trial practice and advocacy emphasizes that this

> means making choices. You throw out arguments that aren't plausible. You pick between the inconsistent legal theories. You cull out the weak points. You toss out whatever gets in the way. You discard what doesn't need to be said, even if it doesn't hurt.
>
> What's left is tight. Lean. Spare. It crackles with power because it's undiluted with stuff that doesn't matter.[5]

2. Consider Your Reader's Burdens

If you can envision two or more equally reasonable theories of your client's case, such as two competing legal frameworks within which to construct your arguments, you normally should choose the one that simplifies the judge's task. If your argument is so complicated that the judge has difficulty following it, the argument will not be persuasive; moreover, the judge will anticipate difficulty explaining a decision based on your arguments. Instead, opt for the approach that is easy to follow, easy to defend as consistent with precedent, and easy to explain in a ruling or opinion. If your brief contains straightforward passages that the judge could easily borrow and adapt for her written opinion, all the better.

---

4. Wiener, *supra* note 1, at 194 (1995).

5. James W. McElhaney, *The Art of Persuasive Legal Writing: Briefs Come Alive When Every Word Sings to the Reader*, A.B.A. J., Jan. 1996, at 76.

3. Presenting Alternative Arguments

If two of your arguments are mutually exclusive, you normally should select the stronger argument and drop the weaker. However, you may choose to present both arguments if they are equally strong and are worth presenting in the alternative.

For example, imagine state law in which a prosecutor can establish the requisite state of mind for homicide in either of two ways: (1) murder, requiring proof of intent to kill, and (2) involuntary manslaughter, requiring proof of reckless disregard for human life. Manslaughter is a lesser included offense of murder, because it shares elements with murder (chiefly, causing the death of another), but the required proof of state of mind is less stringent. To argue the sufficiency of the evidence of these crimes in the alternative, you could (1) present the law and facts supporting the charge of murder, including evidence supporting a finding of intent to kill, and (2) argue in the alternative that—even if the evidence is not sufficient to support a finding of intent to kill—the defendant at least acted with recklessness and thus is guilty of manslaughter.

You should use transitions, point headings, and thesis sentences to guide the reader through the alternative arguments. For example, after presenting the argument supporting the crime of murder, your next point heading could assume an adverse outcome on the first argument and present the fallback argument:

B. Even if the evidence is not sufficient to support a finding of intent to kill Jan Dobson, the Defendant is guilty of manslaughter because the record shows without contradiction that he fired his gun at least recklessly.

Whether to argue in the alternative is a matter of judgment based on the relative merits of the arguments, your audience, and other strategic considerations. For example, imagine a defendant in a civil case, Jan Henning, who seeks to avoid liability for breach of contract, allegedly formed through an exchange of e-mails with Bob Donovan. The parties allegedly agreed to secure a license and funding to grow and distribute marijuana in a state that has legalized such activity. As Henning's attorney, you have studied the facts and the law, and you see three possible avenues for avoiding liability:

(1) Henning admits that her e-mailed response to Donovan's offer was quite positive in tone, but part of her response arguably prevented acceptance of the offer because it suggested her desire to consult a friend before she finally committed to the proposed deal. Donovan will argue that a reasonable person would interpret Henning's comment to mean that she had accepted the offer and would consult a friend for advice about performing the agreement.

(2) Although the state permits and regulates the growing and sale of marijuana, an agreement to do so might be unenforceable under state law, for violation of public policy, so long as the federal government still prohibits such actions. Donovan will argue that

state contract law will focus on legality under state law, particularly if the federal government is not actively enforcing its law in states that have legalized marijuana.

(3) Depending on whether the contract is interpreted to require Donovan to obtain a business loan for $300,000, Donovan might have materially breached the contract himself prior to Henning's performance coming due, thus releasing Henning from her obligations under state law. Donovan will argue that the contract should not be interpreted to impose that obligation on him.

All three arguments are subject to doubt and debate, but any one of them could succeed in completely defeating Donovan's claim. After assessing the arguments, you might decide to present only the second one in a motion for summary judgment, because it will turn on a purely legal question of public policy, one that is suitable for pretrial disposition; the judge might want to leave the other two issues for a jury to resolve after a full trial of the facts. On the other hand, if the e-mail communications point strongly in favor of Henning's interpretations, a judge might find the first and third arguments to have at least equal merit.

After assessing the arguments in this manner, if you decided to present all of them in the alternative, your points headings can lead the reader through the alternatives:

A. Henning did not accept Donovan's offer because she expressed her intention to consult a friend before reaching agreement.

B. Even if Henning and Donovan reached agreement, it is unenforceable under state contract law for violation of public policy, because performance of the agreement would violate the federal Controlled Substances Act.

C. Even if the parties formed an enforceable contract, Henning validly terminated the contract and her obligations under it, because Donovan materially breached his contractual obligation to secure a business loan for $300,000.

B. Determining the Order of Your Arguments

Consider beginning your argument with a paragraph that states the theme of your brief or that provides an overview or roadmap to multiple arguments that follow. Such an overview paragraph would appear at the beginning of the Argument section of your brief, even before the subsection heading for the first of several arguments.

Of course, you cannot set forth an effective roadmap without first deciding on an effective ordering of your arguments. If your brief includes a formal statement of the issues, the organization of that statement should mirror the organization of your arguments. To determine the most appropriate order of arguments, you may need to balance neutral analytic considerations against strategic considerations. Moreover, in a responsive brief, you must decide whether to adopt or depart from the organizational structure of the opposing counsel's preceding brief.

1. Leading with Your Strongest Argument

Neutral analytic considerations will lead you to argue threshold issues first and then to argue the issues that are dependent on the outcome of the threshold issues. Strategic considerations, however, may lead you to place your strongest argument first, even if that organization requires you to depart from a purely logical ordering of arguments.

The strategic considerations are based on the varying levels of emphasis associated with different parts of the argument section of the brief. Within a sentence, an idea generally will receive greater emphasis if placed at the beginning than if placed in the middle, but the place of greatest emphasis ordinarily is the end of the sentence.

The same might be true of a short brief submitted to a judge who has plenty of time to study it. The first argument in such a brief would receive the emphasis associated with any initial encounter that makes a first impression. Ideas in the middle of the brief might capture slightly less attention, but they could help lay the foundation for a forceful climax. Presumably, the climactic argument would leave a lasting impression on the judge because it is the last argument that the judge would read.

Unfortunately, briefs are seldom brief, and judges often lack time to read them carefully. Indeed, a trial judge with a full pretrial motions calendar may have time only to skim through your motions brief before oral argument. Far from occupying the place of greatest emphasis, the end of your brief may not be read with the same care that the judge devoted to the beginning of the brief. Consequently, if one of your arguments is much stronger than the others, you can exercise discretion to present it before the others even though another issue is logically prior.

In balancing neutral analytic considerations against conflicting strategic considerations, strategy is secondary to clarity. If strategic ordering creates an organization that is so illogical that it impedes the reader's understanding of the argument, the clarity of logical ordering will be more persuasive.

2. Special Considerations for Responsive Briefs

A special organizational structure is sometimes appropriate for responsive briefs. In the ordinary three-stage briefing procedure, the answering brief will respond directly to the opening brief, and the reply brief will respond to the answering brief. A responsive brief should not fail to meet the arguments of the preceding brief "head-on, issue for issue, as they are posited."[6] Nonetheless, the responsive brief can do so on its own terms, within an organizational and analytic framework that places its arguments in the best light.

---

6. Wiener, *supra* note 1, at 197.

a. Responding but Still Leading with Your Strongest Argument

When you write a responsive brief, you might choose to adopt the preceding brief's organizational structure and methodically knock down each of your opponent's arguments. On the other hand, if you can more persuasively argue your case with a different organizational structure, you should not hesitate to depart from the structure adopted by your opponent.

For example, suppose that Maya Tortilla Co. has sued Bakeway Supermarkets, alleging that Bakeway (1) formed a contract with Maya; (2) breached its obligations, at least under Maya's interpretation of the contract; (3) and is liable to Maya for $40,000 in damages. Maya has filed a pretrial motion requesting the trial court to grant it summary judgment, which is judgment as a matter of law without a full trial on the facts. Maya has supported its motion with a preliminary showing of facts and with a brief that argues each of the issues in the order presented above. Bakeway can escape summary judgment on any issue by creating a genuine dispute of material fact on that issue, a dispute that must be resolved in a full trial.

As counsel for Bakeway, you could logically begin the argument of your answering brief with Maya's issue 1 because contract formation is a threshold issue: Bakeway did not assume any contractual obligations and consequent potential liability if it did not form a contract with Maya. Moreover, the opening brief begins with issue 1, and you could simplify your task by simply adopting the organizational structure of the opening brief.

However, suppose that you can most easily avoid summary judgment against Bakeway on issue 2. Although you cannot easily refute formation of a contract, you can point to admissible evidence of contract negotiations that supports Bakeway's interpretation of the contract. Moreover, under Bakeway's interpretation of the contract, Bakeway performed rather than breached the contract. Thus, you are confident that you can create a triable issue of fact about the meaning of the contract provision that states Bakeway's obligations. In those circumstances, you could reasonably begin your argument with issue 2, even though that organization departs from a purely logical ordering and from the structure of the opening brief. If you persuade the judge in your first argument that she should deny summary judgment on issue 2, she may then be more strongly disposed to order a trial on other issues as well.

b. Delayed Analysis of Adverse Authority in a Responsive Brief

In responding to an argument in a preceding brief, you can affirmatively develop a legal theory and apply it to the facts, and then separately address authority on which the preceding brief relies. You should address each adverse authority and discredit or distinguish it, or argue that it should be overruled, or concede that it controls one issue and seek to prevail on other issues. You can use the same technique in an opening brief that anticipates a counterargument.

For example, in the following sample passage, the brief writer has affirmatively and confidently argued that Tippett denied Bennett due process under a mainstream legal theory. Only after completing that argument does he seek to persuade the judge to reject an approach based on *Parratt v. Taylor*, on which the opposing party relied in a previous motion:

II. ARGUMENT

A. Bennett Will Prove That Tippett Is Liable Under 42 U.S.C. §1983 for Violating Bennett's Civil Rights.

1. Tippett Acted Under the Color of State Law.

• • • •

2. Tippett Denied Bennett Due Process.

The Fourteenth Amendment's guarantee of due process in state proceedings is a federal . . . .

In *Catchpole*, ...

In this case, Bennett will prove that Tippett bribed Judge Bell to rule against Bennett on his motion for a preliminary injunction. . . . Therefore, Tippett violated Bennett's rights to due process.

> **Full syllogism in several paragraphs within second subargument**

Tippett argued in the reply brief to his motion to dismiss that Bennett has an adequate remedy under state tort law and that section 1983 therefore affords him no relief, citing *Parratt v. Taylor*, 451 U.S. 527 (1981). *Parratt* is distinguishable . . . .

> **Separate paragraphs distinguishing adverse authority**

In this example, *Parratt v. Taylor* does not clearly address a distinct topic; instead, it helps define the limits of due process in certain contexts. Thus, in a neutral analysis, you might consolidate your discussion of *Parratt* with your discussion of other authorities that establish the legal rule, even though you ultimately distinguish *Parratt* from your case.

In a responsive brief, however, you can invite the judge to analyze your case initially without the distraction of distinguishable adverse authority. By delaying your analysis of the adverse case law in this manner, you are free to develop the initial argument strongly and positively, without the qualifications inherent in the subsequent discussion of adverse authority.

C. Internal Organization: Deductive Arguments

Once you decide the order of your arguments, you must adopt an effective scheme of internal organization for each argument. You should exercise the flexibility and creativity to adopt any method of internal organization and advocacy that will present your client's argument most effectively. Unless you have good reason to adopt some other approach, however, you should start with the elements and organization of a deductive argument.

"IRAC," which represents the form of deductive reasoning appropriate to an objective analysis in an office memorandum, is thoroughly discussed in Volume I, Chapter 6. Moreover, Sections III and IV of Volume I, Chapter 8, examine various techniques for organizing points within a deductive argument of a memorandum or a brief. Before writing your brief, you should review those passages.

The following section in this chapter emphasizes one difference between the deductive reasoning appropriate in the discussion section of an objective office memorandum and the deductive argument appropriate to a brief: An argument in a brief leads with the advocate's desired conclusion rather than with a neutral identification of an issue. Thus, each argument in a brief should include four major elements: Conclusion, Rule, Application of the legal rule to the facts, and Conclusion. The acronym "CRAC" may help you remember these elements.

Your writing professor may alternatively use a longer acronym, such as "CRuPAC" or "CREAC" to remind you to "prove" or "explain" your asserted rules to a skeptical reader.[7] This chapter, however, will adhere to the simpler acronym CRAC, while addressing the matter of explanation or proof of rules in its discussion of in-depth development of the law.

III. Introducing Legal Arguments

Judges read an enormous volume of material, and they appreciate concise writing that quickly gets to the point. In each of your arguments, you can satisfy this judicial demand with a well-crafted point heading, sometimes supplemented with an introductory paragraph.

A. Point Headings

For each issue in the argument section of your brief, you will discuss the law and apply the law to the facts to reach a conclusion. Before you begin your full argument, however, you will introduce it in an argumentative section heading, or "point heading." In each section or subsection that addresses a discrete issue, your point heading previews the conclusion.

Depending on the style adopted by the author, a section heading in an office memorandum may neutrally identify the issue addressed in that section. The section heading of an argument in a brief, however, always advocates a position by asserting a point and inviting the judge to reach a specific conclusion. It thus sets the tone for the full argument.

---

7. Richard K. Neumann, Jr., & Kristen Konrad Robbins-Tiscione, LEGAL REASONING AND LEGAL WRITING § 12-2, at 145-47 (7th ed. 2013) (discussing rule proof and explanation and mentioning both "CREAC" and "CRuPAC"); *see* Linda H. Edwards, LEGAL WRITING: PROCESS, ANALYSIS, AND ORGANIZATION 91-96 (5th ed. 2010) (introducing and discussing "rule explanation").

If a section or subsection of your argument develops a full deductive argument, its point heading should be tailored to the facts of your case, much like the statement of an issue and holding in a student case brief. Indeed, you may view your point headings as statements of the holdings in your case that you want the court to adopt:

II. ARGUMENT

A. **O'Gorman is not liable for medical costs associated with Wallace's heart failure, because O'Gorman's conduct did not proximately cause that injury.**

. . . .

B. **O'Gorman is not liable for punitive damages because he did not act with the requisite malicious intent or recklessness.**

Because these point headings refer to the parties and incorporate important facts, they convey a clear, concrete point, even when read in isolation. The bold letters and the indentation help the point headings stand out on the page, providing conspicuous road signs for the reader.[8]

In some cases, you might develop only one element of a deductive argument, such as an abstract legal principle, within a section or subsection. In such cases, of course, each point heading should be limited to stating a conclusion on the point developed in the section or subsection:

II. ARGUMENT

A. **O'Gorman is not liable for punitive damages because he lacked the requisite scienter.**

   1. **The jury may be permitted to award punitive damages only when the evidence is sufficient to permit a jury finding of malicious intent or recklessness.**

. . . .

   2. **The evidence at trial will show that O'Gorman acted in a careful manner and certainly not with recklessness or malicious intent.**

The advantages of point headings are obvious in multiple-issue briefs, in which you must divide the argument into sections and subsections. Within the argument section of the brief, the point headings pop up periodically as road signs that signal an entrance to a new street or highway of your argument. Additionally, at least in an appellate brief, you will set forth your point headings together in the table of contents near the beginning of the brief, providing a quick summary of all your points and presenting a useful road map for the judge's journey through your brief.

---

8. For more tips on designing documents for legibility, *see* Ruth Anne Robbins, *Painting with Print: Incorporating Concepts of Typographic and Layout Design into the Text of Legal Writing Documents*, 2 J. ALWD 108 (Fall 2004).

Even in a single-issue brief, however, you should begin your argument with a point heading. It will simply stand alone in the argument section without any number or letter denoting division of the argument into sections:

III. ARGUMENT

The alleged agreement is unenforceable because it was not signed by the party against whom enforcement is sought.

The UCC statute of frauds requires .…

B. Paragraphs

Immediately after the point heading, but before discussing the legal authority, you might use an introductory sentence or paragraph to illuminate the issue and to expand on the point heading, or to place it within a larger context:

A. **The alleged agreement is unenforceable under the UCC Statute of Frauds because it is not evidenced in a signed writing, as required for goods priced at more than $500.**

Sun Printing Co. denies that it ever agreed to the contract alleged by Scott Paper Supply. This lawsuit presents precisely the kind of groundless contract claim that statutes of frauds are designed to bar by requiring a signed written contract as a requisite to enforcement.

The Uniform Commercial Code statute of frauds generally bars .…

Such an introductory paragraph can be particularly helpful in a responsive brief. Rather than abstractly addressing the issues, an answering or reply brief should respond directly to each of the preceding brief's arguments.

Nonetheless, the response normally should begin by stating its counter-argument affirmatively rather than by restating the opponent's argument. The introductory paragraph following a point heading can set up your full response by adding more detail to the point heading, thus explaining generally why the opposing argument lacks merit, usually saving citation to authority for the more detailed discussion of law that follows:

A. **Scott Paper Supply's timely confirmation of the agreement satisfied the UCC statute of frauds, because Sun Printing Co. failed to object to it.**

The confirmation signed by Scott Paper Supply satisfied the statutory requirements of a signed writing. The UCC deems Sun Printing Co. to have implicitly adopted that confirmation, as though it had signed it, when Sun Printing Co. failed to object to the confirmation.

The UCC provides that .…

In rare cases, you may begin with a summary of your opponent's argument if that serves as an effective means of revealing the weaknesses in that argument and placing your own argument in a favorable light. When using this technique, you must immediately and convincingly refute your opponent's argument in the same breath with which you present his argument.

This technique works best, of course, if the opponent's argument sounds extreme even when presented on its own terms. If so, you can "set up" your opponent's argument for an easy response. Specifically, you should try to restate your opponent's argument fairly and accurately but in a way that fully reveals its weaknesses.

For example, suppose that your opponent's opening brief on appeal argues that the trial judge erred in denying injunctive relief, but it acknowledges the trial judge's broad discretion in such matters only in a vague passage buried in the middle of a lengthy section. In your answering brief, you will take greater pains to emphasize the discretionary nature of such relief. You might begin that emphasis not only in your point heading but also in an opening paragraph that summarizes your opponent's argument in a way that immediately reveals its weakness or the challenges it faces:

A. The trial court properly exercised its discretion to deny the extraordinary remedy of injunctive relief.

Redrock Co. bears the heavy burden of showing that Judge Norris abused her discretion by denying Redrock's demand for an injunction against further construction on the Big River Project. In fact, the record establishes a balance of equities that tip sharply against injunctive relief. Judge Norris's careful decision reflects a routine and proper exercise of discretion.

Injunctive relief is ....

IV. Developing the Deductive Argument

A. Arguing the Law

Volume I of this text has provided you with the legal method and the techniques of organization and writing with which you can construct an argument about the content of applicable law on a specific issue or subissue. An outline of these principles will illustrate the range of considerations that may influence your strategic decisions when arguing the law within the argument portion of your brief.

1. Hierarchy of Authority

First, you must be sensitive to the hierarchy of authority. For example, suppose that (1) your client is not liable under state common law standards for actions that he took as an employer, but (2) a federal statute will impose liability if it applies to your client's business. If applicable, the statutory law will supersede the common law. Therefore, you must analyze the statute and determine whether you can argue either that it is unconstitutional or that it does not apply to your case. This statutory analysis might include arguments concerning the statutory language, the legislative history, the policy under-lying the statute, or the limitations imposed by constitutional provisions.

For illustration, consider the first issue addressed in the final sample office memorandum in Volume I, Chapter 7. It raises a question about the interpretation of a recently enacted, fictitious statute that created a form of liability beyond that recognized under the state's common law. Moreover, the statute is sufficiently new that no published judicial decision has yet interpreted the statutory term that is currently in dispute. One can imagine how the office memorandum's balanced analysis could be transformed into an argument on behalf of the defendant hospital:

A. Recently enacted New Maine legislation does not apply to a hospital's administration of general anesthesia.

A recently enacted statute of New Maine imposes strict liability on commercial enterprises for injuries caused by the use of "any toxic material." 12 N. Me. Rev. Stat. Ann. §242 (Supp. 2013) (effective Jan. 1, 2014). Although the New Maine courts have not yet had an opportunity to interpret section 242 in a published opinion, the text and purpose of the statute establish that the anesthetic administered to Souza is not a "toxic material." This interpretation of the statute advances sound legal policies that support widespread availability of affordable medical care administered with due care.

The common meaning of the word "toxic" is "poisonous." *E.g.*, The Random House Dictionary of the English Language 1500 (unabridged) (1970). "Toxic" thus applies most naturally to substances that are universally harmful to humans, such as cyanide, DDT, or sulfuric acid. It strains the common meaning of "toxic" to apply it to an anesthetic that medical professionals use daily in surgeries that preserve the lives or improve the health of countless patients. A generally safe anesthetic is not transformed into a toxic substance simply because it may provoke an unusual reaction in a patient with a rare disorder; otherwise, wholesome cow's milk would be classified as poisonous or toxic simply because a small percentage of people may have a serious allergy to it.

Legislative history also supports a restrictive interpretation of the statutory term "any toxic material." The report of the New Maine Senate Committee ....

Finally, general state policy supports an interpretation that excludes medically prescribed substances from the reach of the statute. To encourage the availability of affordable medical services throughout the state, the legislature and judiciary of New Maine have recognized a policy of limiting the liability of physicians. For example, under the New Maine "Good Samaritan" statute ....

In this case, the prescribed anesthetic, ethane, is a frequently prescribed substance that produces beneficial results with only minor side effects in all but the most unusual cases. Souza's tragic reaction to ethane during her surgery is a product of her rare disorder, rather than any "toxic" characteristics of the ethane ....

2. Strength of Case Law as Precedent

Second, in analyzing case law, regardless of whether it interprets a statute or applies common law, you must appreciate the relative strength of different kinds of authorities. Case law from a higher court within the forum jurisdiction is potentially controlling on the facts of your case, and you must argue for a broader or narrower interpretation of its holding, depending on whether it supports or undermines your position. Case law from other jurisdictions may have persuasive value, but only in the absence of controlling law within the jurisdiction.

For example, in the following passage of an argument set in a fictitious jurisdiction and governed by common law, the counsel for Beatty, a lender, encourages the court to synthesize mandatory precedent in a favorable manner and to brush aside adverse persuasive authority from another jurisdiction:

Principles derived from a synthesis of the Calzona cases establish that Beatty's promise is not illusory. The consideration requirement therefore is satisfied, and Weeks's promise is enforceable.	**Introduction to argument**
Even if a promise leaves open the possibility that the promisor will escape obligation, the promise is not illusory if the promisor does not have complete control over the events on which the promisor's obligation is conditioned. *Bonnie v. DeLaney*, 158 Calz. 212, 645 P.2d 887 (1982). In *Bonnie*, an agreement for the sale of a house provided that the buyer could cancel the agreement if the buyer "cannot qualify for a 30-year mortgage loan for 90% of the sales price" with any of several banks listed in the agreement. *Id.* at 213, 645 P.2d at 888. In enforcing the agreement against the seller, the court emphasized that the word "cannot" referred to the buyer's ability to obtain a loan rather than to his desire. Because his ability to obtain a loan was partly controlled by events and decisions outside his control, the promises in the sale agreement were nonillusory and binding. *See id.* at 214-15, 645 P.2d at 889-90.	**In-depth analysis of favorable case law**

In-depth analysis of adverse case law

The *Bonnie* court distinguished its earlier decision, *Atco Corp. v. Johnson*, 155 Calz. 1211, 627 P.2d 781 (1980). In *Atco Corp.*, the manager of an automobile repair shop promised to forbear "until I want the money" from asserting a claim against the owner of an automobile for $900 in repairs. In exchange, a friend of the owner promised to act as guarantor of the owner's obligation. *Id.* at 1212, 627 P.2d at 782. The word "want" stated no legal commitment because it permitted the manager at his own discretion to refuse to perform any forbearance at all. Because the manager did not incur even a conditional obligation, the guarantor's promise was gratuitous and unenforceable. *Id.* at 1213-14, 627 P.2d at 783-84.

Synthesis that emphasizes favorable case law

Together, these cases show that any limitation on the promisor's freedom will validate his promise. A promise is illusory only if it leaves the promisor complete control over his actions.

Application to facts

Under these controlling principles, the parties in this case each assumed valid obligations ....

Thus, *Atco* is distinguishable from our case, and *Bonnie* is controlling.

Argument against application of nonbinding authority

Weeks attempts to salvage his flawed analogy to *Atco* by interpreting it in light of authority from New Maine. The New Maine cases, however, are not binding on this court and are inconsistent with the reasoning of the controlling authority in *Bonnie*. ...

In this example, counsel for Beatty placed her affirmative arguments in positions of priority before distinguishing or discrediting authority supporting counterarguments. She summarized her argument in the first paragraph.

In the second and third paragraphs, she synthesized local case law by reconciling two decisions with apparently contrasting holdings, starting with the supporting precedent. In the fourth paragraph, she concluded her synthesis with a form of inductive reasoning in which she derived a legal rule by generalizing from the two cases, emphasizing the supporting case law. In the fifth paragraph, as illustrated more fully in Section B below, counsel for Beatty applied this rule to the facts of her case, taking care to analogize the favorable precedent and to distinguish the adverse precedent. In the final paragraph, she protected this analysis by explaining why case law from another jurisdiction should not be used to interpret the local case law in a different manner.

The persuasive influence of authority from a lower court or from a court in another jurisdiction may be stronger in the absence of any applicable authority from the forum state. If persuasive authority undermines your client's position, you can try to distinguish it from the facts of your case or to discredit its reasoning as unworthy of adoption as the rule of law in the forum jurisdiction. Conversely, if persuasive authority supports your position, you should argue that its reasoning is sound and is consistent with the policy of the forum jurisdiction.

For example, in the following passage, in which fictitious case law has interpreted a fictitious federal statute in imaginary courts, an advocate attempts to persuade a court in the state of New Maine to adopt the reasoning of Calzona case law and to reject precedent from the jurisdictions of Floridia and the U.S. Court of Appeals for the Fifteenth Circuit:

> The federal Food Quality Act (FQA) pre-empts more stringent state legislation seeking to ensure the quality and purity of food produced or sold in interstate commerce. *State v. Biggs*, 123 Calz. 56, 567 P.2d 765 (2009). In *Biggs*, state officials sought to enjoin the marketing and sale of fruits and vegetables advertised as "organic." The officials invoked a Calzona statute that set criteria for food labeled or advertised to be organic. *Id.* at 57, 567 P.2d at 766. The Calzona Supreme Court held that the FQA's provisions regarding organic produce were intended to be exclusive and to eliminate unreasonable restrictions on commerce. *Id.* at 58-60, 567 P.2d at 767-69. It therefore held that the FQA barred the state from prohibiting such regulation. *Id.* at 61, 567 P.2d at 770.
>
> In reaching its decision, the California Supreme Court exhaustively analyzed the legislative history of the FQA. It noted that . . . .

In-depth analysis of favorable case law

> One other state court and one federal court had previously rejected the preemption argument adopted in *Biggs*, but each of them overlooked the critical legislative history that *Biggs* so carefully analyzed. *Arzani v. Matlock*, 332 So. 2d 234 (Fldia. 2008); *Michigan v. Smedley*, 439 F.3d 166 (15th Cir. 2006).
>
> For example, in *Arzani*, the court summarily held that . . . .

Critical analysis of adverse case law

The advocate obviously hopes that the preceding passage will persuade the court to adopt the reasoning of *Biggs*. In the fact analysis, the advocate can argue further that *Biggs* is analogous to the facts of her case and that the rule of law it represents thus applies to those facts.

3. Depth of Analysis

In presenting your legal arguments and authority, you must exercise firm control over depth of analysis, as introduced in Volume I, Chapter 6, and discussed more thoroughly in Section II.A.2 of Volume I, Chapter 9. If Volume I is among your course materials, you should review those passages, which examine three different levels or depths of analysis:

1. light analysis to present fundamental and undisputed propositions with direct statements of law and citation to authority,
2. direct statements of law and citation to authority with parenthetic explanations for a slightly deeper level of analysis, and
3. in-depth analysis of statutes or case law to explore policy and reasoning or to explain a rule by showing how precedent has applied the rule to facts in previous cases.

For example, the following introduction to an argument uses technique 2 above to quickly establish an undisputed point about federal law before addressing state law claims in greater depth:

Because Comcon has always employed fewer than fifteen employees [Hart SofF ¶1], Rembar has no claim against Hart under federal employment discrimination law. *See* 42 U.S.C. § 2000e(b) (2006) (defining employers covered by Title VII of the Civil Rights Act of 1964).

A good brief typically will employ the full range of depths of analysis. If a dispute reaches a court without a negotiated settlement, the issues are presumably substantial and reasonably contested by both parties. Consequently, neither party will be able to prevail on crucial issues with conclusory statements of the law and application to the facts. Instead, the brief likely will advance in-depth arguments of the law, the facts, or both for all but general background points.

Nonetheless, general legal background may set the context for your more specific legal analyses. Rather than jump too quickly to the details of a complex argument, you should first provide your reader with necessary foundational points, which often can be summarized quickly and succinctly.

In the following argument, for example, the author sets forth basic standards in "light analysis" in a synthesis paragraph, before explaining an element of the legal rule by engaging in in-depth analysis of case law:

Hart is not liable for intentional infliction of emotional distress unless his conduct was so "extreme and outrageous" that it fell "within that quite narrow range" of conduct "at the very extreme edge of the spectrum." *Watts v. Golden*

Age Nursing Home, 127 Ariz. 255, 258, 619 P.2d 1032, 1035 (1980). Moreover, "it is extremely rare to find conduct in the employment context that will rise to the level of outrageousness necessary to provide a basis for recovery for the tort of intentional infliction of emotional distress." *Mintz v. Bell Atl. Sys. Leasing Int'l, Inc.*, 183 Ariz. 550, 554, 905 P.2d 559, 563 (Ct. App. 1995) (quoting *Cox v. Keystone Carbon Co.*, 861 F.2d 390, 395 (3d Cir. 1988)).

In *Mintz*, an employee was hospitalized after suffering a nervous breakdown as the alleged result of gender discrimination in the workplace. The employer terminated her disability benefits, ordered her to return to work, and then — while the employee was again hospitalized after returning to work for one day — notified her of a reassignment of her duties by a letter delivered to the hospital. *Id.* at 552, 905 P.2d at 561. The Arizona Court of Appeals affirmed a finding that, as a matter of law, this alleged conduct was not extreme and outrageous, even assuming the employer had failed to promote the employee because of gender discrimination and assuming the employer knew that the employee was unusually susceptible to emotional distress. *Id.* at 553-54, 905 P.2d at 562-63.

In light of cases such as *Mintz*, a federal district court has characterized Arizona's standard for extreme and outrageous conduct as one requiring "extraordinary" conduct. *Tempesta v. Motorola, Inc.*, 92 F. Supp. 2d 973, 987 (D. Ariz. 1999). Applying *Mintz*, the *Tempesta* court granted summary judgment for the defendant employer on the employee's claim of intentional infliction of emotional distress, even after assuming the truth of the employee's allegations that he had suffered harassment and wrongful termination because of his sex. *Id.* at 986-87.

It is even clearer in this case that Hart did not engage in extreme and outrageous conduct....

---

4. Elements or Factors in Legal Rules

Legal rules come in a variety of types. Some statutory or common law rules require proof of several mandatory elements. Failure to prove any one of the elements prevents satisfaction of the legal rule.

Other legal rules identify factors that a court should consider in determining whether the facts satisfy a general standard. The list of factors may not be exclusive, and the standard may be met without proof of every factor. Some legal rules, including many constitutional tests, contemplate the balancing of two or more competing factors or values.

The nature of a legal rule will influence your presentation and analysis of the rule. For example, the following argument introduces three mandatory elements of a tort and then presents separate arguments on each element.

Each argument in a subsection then presents more detailed legal requirements for the element discussed in that subsection:

C. The undisputed facts show that Hart is not liable for intentional inflic-tion of emotional distress.

The Arizona Supreme Court has adopted the Restatement test for intentional
infliction of emotional distress, requiring proof of three elements: (1) extreme
and outrageous conduct, (2) engaged in with intent to cause distress or with
reckless disregard of the near certainty that distress will result, (3) causing severe
emotional distress. *Watts v. Golden Age Nursing Home*, 127 Ariz. 255, 258, 619 P.2d
1032, 1035 (1980) (citing to the Restatement (Second) of Torts § 46 (1965)). Rembar
cannot genuinely dispute that the facts fail to satisfy these elements.

1. Hart did not engage in extreme and outrageous conduct.

Conduct is not "extreme and outrageous" unless it is falls "within that quite
narrow range" of conduct "at the very extreme edge of the spectrum." *Watts*, 127
Ariz. at 258, 619 P.2d at 1035. Moreover, "it is extremely rare to find conduct in
the employment context that will rise to the level of outrageousness necessary
to provide a basis for recovery for the tort of intentional infliction of emotional
distress." *Mintz v. Bell Atl. Sys. Leasing Int'l, Inc.*, 183 Ariz. 550, 554, 905 P.2d 559,
563 (Ct. App. 1995) (quoting *Cox v. Keystone Carbon Co.*, 861 F.2d 390, 395 (3d Cir.
1988)).

In *Mintz*, an employee was hospitalized after suffering a nervous breakdown
as the alleged result of gender discrimination in the workplace....

In light of cases such as *Mintz*, a federal district court has characterized Arizona's standard for extreme and outrageous conduct as one requiring "extraordinary" conduct. *Tempesta v. Motorola, Inc.*, 92 F. Supp. 2d 973, 987 (D. Ariz. 1999).
Applying *Mintz*, the *Tempesta* court granted ....

In this case, the record on summary judgment will show that ....

2. Hart did not act with intent or reckless disregard.

. . . .

3. Rembar did not suffer severe emotional distress.

The following argument, in contrast, addresses material breach of contract, which permits the non-breaching party to cancel the contract. The
concept of material breach is a standard for which several factors serve as
guidelines. The argument rejects an assertion that every factor in the guidelines must be satisfied, and it argues that the preponderance of factors in
favor of material breach outweigh a single factor supporting a finding of
minor breach:

2. Tarasenko did not materially breach the contract.

In this jurisdiction, materiality of breach is not governed by a "single touch-
stone." Instead, the Michigan Supreme Court has drawn guidance from the six
"influential" factors of section 275 of the Restatement (First) of Contracts:

In determining the materiality of a failure fully to perform a promise the following circumstances are influential:

> (a) The extent to which the injured party will obtain the substantial benefit which he could have reasonably anticipated;
>
> (b) The extent to which the injured party may be adequately compensated in damages for lack of complete performance;
>
> (c) The extent to which the party failing to perform has already partly performed or made preparations for performance;
>
> (d) The greater or less hardship on the party failing to perform in terminating the contract;
>
> (e) The willful, negligent or innocent behavior of the party failing to perform;
>
> (f) The greater or less uncertainty that the party failing to perform will perform the remainder of the contract.

Walker & Co. v. Harrison, 347 Mich. 630, 635, 81 N.W.2d 352, 355 (1957) (quoting the Restatement (First) of Contracts § 275 (1932)).

In 1981, the second Restatement updated the relevant factors, providing a slightly modified guide to material breach, based on five "circumstances" that "are significant." Restatement (Second) of Contracts § 241 (1982). For example, the second Restatement refers to "standards of good faith and fair dealing" in place of the first Restatement's reference to "willful, negligent or innocent behavior." *Id.* at § 241(e). But the precise formulation of the Restatement's guidance is not significant. The Restatements characterize their factors only as "circumstances" that are "influential" or "significant." Moreover, the Court in *Walker* analyzed the facts of its case in a common sense fashion, without specifically relating facts of the case to every factor in the Restatement section that it had quoted. *Walker & Co.*, 347 Mich. at 636, 81 N.W.2d at 356 (adopting trial court's factual analysis and conclusion of no material breach).

Accordingly, Tarasenko misapplies the law in this state when she argues that her breach could not be material because her failure to fully perform was not the product of bad intentions or lack of care. Contrary to the premise of Tarasenko's argument, bad faith or other culpability is not a required element of material breach; instead, it is only one of "many factors" that are relevant. *Id.* at 635, 81 N.W.2d at 355 ("Many factors are involved."). This single factor in Tarasenko's favor is easily outweighed by the other relevant circumstances, which together strongly support a finding of material breach.

First, Jenkins received almost none of the benefit that he had expected . . . .

Second, ...

5. Presenting and Framing Your Authority

Finally, you must lead your reader through each of your arguments and support your assertions of law with supporting authority. Three techniques are explored in Volume I, Chapter 10, Sections II and III. You should

1. express your syntheses of authorities or other thesis statements in topic sentences or paragraphs;
2. unless the citations are independently significant, focus attention on your ideas and relegate citations to subordinate citation sentences; and
3. introduce quotations with substantive overviews that invite the judge to adopt your interpretation of the quoted material.

When you present case law, recognize that the scope of nearly every precedent's holding is subject to interpretation and thus to reasonable dispute. Consequently, within reasonable bounds, you have the opportunity to frame the holding of a precedent relatively narrowly or broadly, as dictated by the outcome that favors your client.

For example, one advocate might argue that (1) the holding of a precedent should extend no further than the compelling facts in that case, and (2) the applicable law should apply differently to the facts of the current case, (3) leading to a different result. The opposing advocate can respond that the reasoning of the precedent suggests that the authoring court would apply the legal rule in the precedent broadly, to a wide array of factual contexts— including that of the current case—and would reach the same result in the current case.

A case discussed in Volume I, Chapter 5, provides a good illustration. Imagine a dispute about whether the Fourth Amendment requires a warrant to search a fully mobile motor home, in which the defendant was residing permanently, while the motor home was parked in public parking lot. Supreme Court precedent #1 held that police need only probable cause, and not a warrant, to search a car, because of the car's mobility and reduced expectations of privacy. Supreme Court precedent #2 held that police generally must secure a warrant to enter and search an apartment, because of the exceptional expectations of privacy in one's home. In a motion to suppress evidence found in the motor home, the defense counsel would argue that the reasoning of precedent #2 extends broadly to any permanent home, including a motor home, because the resident would have great expectations of privacy and would keep his most personal effects in that space. Counsel for the State would argue instead for a narrow interpretation of the reach of precedent #2, limiting it to fixed homes, and excluding motor homes that can be driven on public streets and thereby be subject to numerous administrative regulations, which reduce expectations of privacy. State's counsel would also attempt to frame the holding and reasoning of precedent #1 broadly, arguing that its holding should apply to any vehicle that can move rapidly to a place of hiding or across state lines.

Opposing advocates normally can offer opposing interpretations of case law whether the precedent develops a common law rule or interprets a statutory or constitutional provision. Further, if the issue turns on the interpretation of a newly enacted statute, one that has not yet been judicially interpreted and applied, advocates typically enjoy particularly rich opportunities to advance opposing interpretations of the breadth of the statutory mandate. A statute typically states a rule in relatively general language so that it can apply to a broad array of future cases fitting within a defined category. If the facts of a case lie close to the statutory line, this feature of legislation frequently leaves ample room for debate about whether specific facts fall inside or outside the boundary defined in general terms by the statutory rule.

As explored in Chapter 1, Section II, your interpretation and framing of the breadth of an authority will be persuasive only if reasonable. If you stretch statutory language or the holding of a case beyond any plausible interpretation, you will lose credibility and might violate ethical rules.

B. Analyzing the Facts

As discussed in greater detail in this volume in Chapter 8 in the context of appellate briefs, the opening statement of facts in a brief is most effective if it does not prematurely argue the law or the application of the law to the facts. In contrast, when you analyze the relevant facts in the argument section of a brief, you should explicitly reach a conclusion by relating the facts to the previously discussed legal rules. You may accomplish this by (1) directly applying the law to the facts or (2) using a form of inductive reasoning to analogize or distinguish precedent by comparing the facts and reasoning of the precedent to your own case.

To illustrate the first technique, suppose that you have established in your discussion of the law that a state police officer can be liable for punitive damages for recklessly depriving a citizen of her right to be free from arrest without probable cause. In the fact analysis of your argument, you could directly apply that rule of law to the facts by showing how the defendant police officer acted recklessly. In the following sample passage, the notations within brackets refer to pages of the trial court reporter's transcript on which critical testimony of witnesses is found.

Substantial evidence in the record supports the jury's finding that Officer Mullins acted with at least reckless disregard for Wong's clearly established Fourth Amendment rights. Mullins's actions show that even he did not believe that Wong fit the dispatcher's description of the robbery suspect. According to his own testimony, when he initially spotted Wong moments after receiving the robbery report, he passed by her and continued looking for the suspect. [RT at 324.] Only after failing to find a suspect who fit the dispatcher's description did he relocate Wong and summarily arrest her. [RT at 326.]

The jury could infer from these facts that Officer Mullins felt compelled to arrest somebody for the robbery and that he recklessly gambled that Wong might have been involved simply because of her general proximity to the robbery. This is precisely the kind of reckless disregard for constitutional rights that an award of punitive damages is designed to deter.

Alternatively, your discussion of the law may include in-depth case analysis and synthesis of arguably controlling, analogous, or distinguishable authority. If so, you may want to use the second technique of inductive reasoning to compare those cases directly to your dispute in your fact analysis:

Analogizing favorable case law on the facts	*Bonnie* is closely analogous to our case and thus supports the conclusion that Beatty's promise was not illusory. In both *Bonnie* and our case, the promised performance was conditioned on events not entirely within the control of the promisor. In *Bonnie*, the buyer could escape his obligations only if market conditions rendered him *unable* to obtain a satisfactory mortgage loan. Similarly, in our case, Beatty could terminate his obligation to refrain from collecting on the debt only if economic conditions affected his income and expenses so as to create a need for the money.
Distinguishing adverse case law on the facts	Conversely, *Atco Corp.* is distinguishable from our case. The promisor in that case retained the freedom to escape all contractual obligations if, at his own discretion, he *wanted* to. In contrast, the Guarantee Agreement in this case did not permit Beatty to demand his money whenever he *wanted* it. Instead, ...

C. Conclusions

Immediately after your fact analysis in each argument of your brief, you should briefly repeat the conclusion that you previewed in the point heading for that section or subsection:

Scott Paper Supply timely objected to Sun Printing Co.'s written confirmation of the alleged agreement. Therefore, the confirmation does not satisfy the requirements of the statute of frauds.

Additionally, every brief should end with a formal conclusion section. Many attorneys squander this opportunity to summarize their analyses. The following boilerplate is typical:

III. CONCLUSION

For the foregoing reasons, Appellant respectfully requests this Court to reverse the judgment of the superior court.

Although this style is conventional, a more substantive conclusion ordinarily is more satisfying, particularly if the brief presents more than one argument.

A substantive conclusion need not take up much space. If your arguments are simple, your conclusion need only briefly and generally repeat the request for relief and the supporting grounds, as in this closing to a brief in support of a motion to exclude evidence before trial:

III. CONCLUSION

Under Rule 403, Powell is entitled to pretrial exclusion of all evidence of his membership in the Black Panther Party. The danger of confusion and the prejudicial effect of the evidence substantially outweigh its probative value, and the prejudice can be avoided only through exclusion of the evidence before trial.

In a more complex case, the conclusion might briefly summarize multiple arguments:

III. CONCLUSION

Yazzi's statement to the police officer is inadmissible on three grounds. First, it is not relevant to any issue in this suit. Second, even if it were relevant, it would be excludable because its prejudicial value substantially outweighs its probative value. Finally, it is inadmissible hearsay not falling within the exception for statements for purposes of medical treatment. This evidence should be excluded before trial to avoid exposing it to the jury and causing irremediable prejudice.

V. Summary

To effectively advocate your client's case in a written document,

1. organize your legal arguments in logical order, subject to considerations of strategy if clarity can be retained;
2. introduce each of your arguments with an effective point heading and, if helpful, an introductory paragraph; and
3. present your analysis of the law, apply the law to the facts, and state the conclusion that you want the court to reach.

The next chapter examines persuasive writing style, as well as oral argument.

Chapter 3

Expressing Your Advocacy: Persuasive Writing Style and Oral Argument

Persuasive brief writing begins with your developing a theme and selecting arguments, as discussed in Chapter 2. Additionally, depending on the nature of the brief and the procedural posture of the case, the brief frequently should include a fact statement that tells your client's story in a compelling fashion, which is discussed in Chapter 8. This chapter addresses persuasive style in presenting legal arguments.

I. Persuasive Writing Style

Supervising attorneys often complain that law students or recent graduates from law school do not use sufficiently strong language to write persuasively. Admittedly, advocacy calls for a writing style that departs from the more nearly neutral style appropriate for an office memorandum. Unfortunately, however, many supervising attorneys equate persuasive writing style with hyperbole, and they advise writers to pepper every sentence of a brief with exaggerated modifiers. Such a style may grab a judge's attention, but it does not often persuade. Judges recognize overstatement and tend to take everything in such a brief with an extra pinch of salt. Even worse, a writing style that is too obvious in its advocacy tends to divert the judge's attention from the substance of the argument and to focus it on the style itself.

The most persuasive writing style may be one that the judge hardly notices. It uses an engaging writing style that keeps the judge's attention riveted on the substance of the arguments, and it presents those arguments so reasonably and clearly as to give her the impression that the brief merely confirms her own independent conclusions. The most important element of such writing is good substantive analysis; a few extra hours of research and reflection may lead to an argument that is easily written in a persuasive manner. Beyond that, persuasive legal writing is distinguished by (1) strong, but not exaggerated, language and (2) effective emphasis through sentence structure, specificity, and vivid, concrete language.

A. Persuasive Language

1. The Adversarial Approach

To clearly communicate your legal analysis to a supervising attorney in an office memorandum, you must candidly reveal uncertainties in the law and weaknesses in your client's case. In contrast, a brief in the same litigation generally should not explore the weaknesses of a client's case except as necessary to satisfy ethical duties or maintain credibility. The adversary system ensures that opposing counsel will challenge your arguments.

Thus, in an office memorandum, you might candidly admit the weakness of the support for a client's argument, as with the following fictitious analysis of a client's preemption argument:

Only one state court has held that the federal Food Quality Act preempts more stringent state regulation. *State v. Biggs*, 123 Calz. 56, 567 P.2d 765 (2009). Two other courts have interpreted the Act to permit more stringent state controls that are consistent with its policy. *Arzani v. Matlock*, 332 So. 2d 234 (Fla. 2008); *Michigan v. Smedley*, 439 F.3d 166 (15th Cir. 2006). To support our argument that federal law preempts the New Maine regulation of organic food labeling, we should emphasize the thorough reasoning of *Biggs* and try to discredit or distinguish *Arzani* and *Smedley*.

In *Biggs*, ...

In contrast, in a brief to the court in the same case, you must state your client's argument more positively, while acknowledging and attempting to distinguish or discredit the contrary authority:

The federal Food Quality Act preempts more stringent state regulations. *State v. Biggs*, 123 Calz. 56, 567 P.2d 765 (2009). In *Biggs*, state officials sought to prohibit ....

Two courts had previously rejected the preemption argument adopted in *Biggs*, but each of them overlooked the critical legislative history so carefully analyzed in *Biggs*. *See Arzani v. Matlock*, ...; *Michigan v. Smedley*, ... For example, in *Arzani* ....

The proposition for which *Biggs* is cited in the second example illustrates the power of the simple, unqualified statement:

The federal Food Quality Act preempts more stringent state regulation.

You should avoid unnecessary qualifiers that weaken arguments, such as the following introduction to the argument of your client, Mason:

Mason contends that the federal Food Quality Act preempts more stringent state regulation.

Because the argument section of your brief obviously comprises a series of legal contentions, specific introductions to that effect are superfluous. You may set up a response to your opponent's propositions by referring to them as "arguments" or "contentions," but such a characterization of your own conclusions or statements of law tends to weaken them.

2. Clichés That Weaken or Offend

Ironically, modifiers that are designed to reinforce a proposition some-times sap the strength from an otherwise powerful statement. For example, comments such as "it is abundantly clear that" and "obviously" have little effect on the judge except to make him wonder whether the words were added to shore up a shaky proposition that in fact is subject to great debate. Along with other forms of exaggeration, clichés such as these tend to make the advocacy in the writing too obvious and distracting. A judge will accept your conclusions more readily if you offer persuasive arguments than if you invoke stock phrases that describe your arguments as persuasive.

The line between strong advocacy and overstatement is most delicate when referring directly to a matter within the court's discretionary power. For example, the word "should" in the following argument reflects lack of confidence in the argument:

This court should exclude evidence of Jenkins's subjective intentions regarding the lease.

On the other hand, a stronger verb suggests a presumptuous challenge to the power of the court:

This court must exclude evidence of Jenkins's subjective intentions regarding the lease.

On reading such an argument, the judge might be subconsciously inclined to demonstrate that she does indeed have the discretionary power to admit the evidence, the exercise of which would not likely be overturned on appeal. Restating the proposition in passive voice tends to soften and depersonalize the challenge:

Evidence of Jenkins's subjective intentions regarding the lease must be excluded.

Nonetheless, the challenge to the judge's power remains implicit in this construction. Perhaps the best statement is one that focuses directly on the character of the evidence rather than on the power of the judge:

Evidence of Jenkins's subjective intentions regarding the lease is inadmissible.

This proposition is strong and unqualified, yet it avoids expressing or directly implying a personal challenge to the judge.

3. Personal Attacks

Avoid personal attacks on opposing counsel. Although you may become exasperated with apparently unreasonable or offensive conduct by your opponent, judges do not appreciate being caught in a crossfire of personal insults. Unless misconduct by a party or his attorney is properly the subject of a motion, judges are far more interested in your response to the opposing counsel's arguments than in your personal opinion of your opponent's intelligence, research skills, or personality. Thus, you may safely characterize the opposing counsel's argument as internally inconsistent, but you should not comment that he is unable to write a coherent brief. Similarly, if your statement of the procedural history unemotionally records events that reflect the opposing counsel's bad faith, the judge will undoubtedly draw negative conclusions about his advocacy without any further comment from you.

A court's published reaction to a derogatory characterization of opposing counsel's argument is illuminating:

There are good reasons not to call an opponent's argument "ridiculous" .... The reasons include civility; the near-certainty that overstatement will only push the reader away (especially when, as here, the hyperbole begins on page one of the brief); and that, even where the record supports an extreme modifier, "the better practice is usually to lay out the facts and let the court reach its own conclusions." *Big Dipper Entm't, L.L.C. v. City of Warren*, 641 F.3d 715, 719 (6th Cir. 2011).[1]

B. Sentence Structure

To preserve your credibility and ethical standards, you often must candidly acknowledge law that is adverse to your client's case and that you can neither discredit nor distinguish. You can minimize the resulting damage by using techniques of persuasive writing style to de-emphasize the adverse law and to focus attention on more helpful points.

One such technique consists of placing helpful information in the main clause and relegating adverse information to a dependent subordinate clause, a clause that cannot stand by itself as a complete sentence. For example, as counsel for the plaintiff in a contract action, you can de-emphasize the general rule against damages for emotional distress by disposing of it in an opening subordinate clause:

Although damages for emotional distress are not often awarded for breach of contract, Jones is entitled to such an award because of the exceptional nature of his case: The central purpose of his contract with Runyon Pet Cemetery was to alleviate his grief over the loss of his dog. *See generally* ....

You maintain credibility with this passage by facing, rather than evading, the general rule. Moreover, by placing the general rule in a subordinate clause, you invite the reader to give it only brief pause, as you might invite a guest at a restaurant to dine lightly on appetizers in anticipation of the main course.

Location of information within a sentence also affects emphasis. Generally, the end of a sentence conveys the greatest emphasis, the beginning of a sentence conveys secondary emphasis, and a parenthetic phrase or clause at a natural breaking point in the middle of the sentence conveys the least emphasis. For example, if you represent the defendant in the example above, you can emphasize the general rule by placing it at the end of the sentence:

In demanding an award of damages for emotional distress, Jones runs afoul of the general rule that such damages are not awarded for breach of contract.

---

1. Bennett v. State Farm Mut. Auto. Ins. Co., 731 F.3d 584, 584-85 (6th Cir. 2013).

Generally, you will emphasize the general rule least by placing it in a parenthetic clause at a natural breaking point in the middle of the sentence:

Jones is entitled to an award of damages for emotional distress in this exceptional case, even though such awards are rare in contract actions, because the central purpose of his contract with Runyon Pet Cemetery was to alleviate his grief over the loss of his dog.

This passage may be the best of the three for the plaintiff because it places favorable information in the positions of greatest emphasis.

Of course, if you are willing to sacrifice other style objectives, you can create unusual emphasis in the middle of the sentence with an abrupt, dramatic, or unnatural interruption of the sentence:

Jones unreasonably demands — while admitting that such damages generally are not awarded in contract actions — an award of damages for emotional distress.

C. Introducing Block Quotations

You can use a substantive introduction to a block quotation as effective preliminary advocacy. Your introduction will emphasize the point of the quotation by presenting it in summary form.

Moreover, quotations from contracts, statutes, or case law often are reasonably subject to varying interpretations, and a substantive introduction can encourage the reader to interpret the quoted passage in a favorable manner. For example, the following passage from an employment contract lists several grounds for discharging an employee, but it doesn't expressly state whether the list is exclusive:

XI. Ajax Co. reserves the right to discharge any employee who

1. fails to perform satisfactorily,
2. commits gross insubordination, or
3. commits a criminal act on the work site.

Assuming an employee hired under this contract is employed for an indefinite term, the traditional common law at-will rule would permit the employer to discharge the employee for any reason if the contractual list of grounds for discharge is not intended to be exclusive. On the other hand, if the contract provision quoted above is interpreted to include an implicit promise by the employer to refrain from discharging an employee except for the listed reasons, then the contract would override the otherwise applicable common law rule.

When quoting this passage in the argument section of the brief for either the employer or a discharged employee, you will achieve the least impact with a stock introduction such as:

Section XI of the Employment Contract provides, in relevant part, as follows:

Instead, as counsel for the discharged employee, you should use an argumentative introductory sentence to characterize the provision as a restriction on the employer's freedom to terminate the employment:

The Employment Contract expressly identifies only three grounds for discharge, all relating to poor performance or serious misconduct:

XI. Ajax Co. reserves the right to discharge any employee who

1. fails to perform satisfactorily,
2. commits gross insubordination, or
3. commits a criminal act on the work site.

Employment Contract § XI.

The parties intended this list to be the exclusive, because . . . .

Conversely, as counsel for the employer, you can use an argumentative introduction to characterize the provision as an affirmation of the employer's common law freedom to terminate:

No provision of the contract expressly limits Ajax Co.'s common law right to discharge any employee at Ajax's will. Indeed, the only provision addressing termination selects three particularly strong grounds for illustration and emphasis:

XI. Ajax Co. reserves the right to discharge any employee who

1. fails to perform satisfactorily,
2. commits gross insubordination, or
3. commits a criminal act on the work site.

Employment Contract § XI.

Nothing in the contract suggests that these listed grounds are exclusive. Instead, ...

You can always begin arguing for a favorable interpretation after neutrally presenting the quoted passage. However, the reader is more likely to adopt your proposed interpretation if a substantive introduction prepares him for the interpretation before he reads the quoted passage.

Exercise 3-1

Foreclosure Falsities

In October 2010, in the wake of class action lawsuits and official investigations, some United States lending institutions suspended their home foreclosures nationwide to review their foreclosure procedures. Litigation challenging a home foreclosure in Maine revealed that GMAC, servicing a home loan for the Federal National Mortgage Association, had routinely engaged in a practice that the media soon dubbed "robo-signing": a "limited signing officer" would prepare hundreds of foreclosures each day, signing affidavits attesting that the requisites for foreclosure had been met even though the officer had not reviewed the relevant documents to confirm the assertions in the affidavits.

After discovering this practice in a deposition, a volunteer attorney for the homebuyer, Thomas Cox, persuaded the trial court in Maine to set aside its earlier partial summary judgment in favor of GMAC and to order GMAC to pay expenses associated with the deposition. Mr. Cox's brief included the following application of law to facts in his argument that the signing official (named in this exercise only as "S.O.") submitted his affidavit in bad faith, a legal prerequisite for an order of sanctions against GMAC:

> When [S.O.] says in an affidavit that he has personal knowledge of the facts stated in his affidavits, he doesn't. When he says that he has custody and control of the loan documents, he doesn't. When he says that he is attaching "a true and accurate" copy of a note or a mortgage, he has no idea if that is so, because he does not look at the exhibits. When he makes any other statement of fact, he has no idea if it is true. When the notary says that [S.O.] appeared before him or her, he didn't, and when the notary says that [S.O.] was sworn, he wasn't. The practice of GMAC Mortgage, LLC in submitting foreclosure affidavits such as this, knowing that they will be relied upon by a judge to enter an order taking away a family's home, must be seen as a quintessential definition of a summary judgment affidavit "presented in bad faith."[2]

1. Impact of the Facts

If you were the judge in this case, how would the preceding fact analysis affect your view of the case? If the case presented close legal issues or ones that permitted exercise of your discretion as the trial judge, would you be inclined to rule in favor of the homebuyer if any reasonable interpretation or application of the law permitted that result?

---

2. The facts for this exercise are taken from court documents in Fed. Nat'l Mortg. Ass'n v. Bradbury, No. BR-OE-09-65 (9th Dist. Ct., ME), and from David Streitfeld, *From This House, a National Foreclosure Freeze*, N.Y. TIMES, Oct. 15, 2010, at A1. The quoted paragraph from Mr. Cox's brief omits a footnote that appeared in the brief after the third sentence of the paragraph. The author thanks Richard Neumann for bringing this example of persuasive writing to the attention of the legal writing community.

2. Analyzing the Presentation

Analyze the author's writing style. Explain how the style of presentation helps to maximize the persuasive effect of these compelling facts. Be specific in your description.

3. Persuasive Presentation in Other Styles

Can you rewrite the fact analysis in an alternative style of presentation, while still matching or exceeding the persuasive effect of the original? Describe the techniques of persuasive writing that you employ in your version.

II. Oral Argument to the Court

In many appeals and pretrial or trial motions, you will argue your client's case orally to the court after submitting your written brief. In most cases, your written brief will influence a judge more strongly than your oral argument. Indeed, before oral argument, most judges read both parties' briefs and come to a tentative decision on the merits.

Nonetheless, oral argument is not yet a meaningless formality in our courts. It provides you with a final opportunity to emphasize critical points, respond to judges' questions, change the mind of a judge who had tentatively decided to rule in favor of the opposing party, or strongly influence a judge who has not formed a tentative opinion.

A. General Format

The typical oral argument follows a pattern similar to that of filing written briefs: The advocate seeking relief or reversal of a judgment in a lower court argues first, the opposing advocate responds, and the first advocate has an opportunity for rebuttal. In some courts, the advocate arguing first must tell the court before she begins her argument whether she wishes to divide her time between opening argument and rebuttal.

Rebuttal is a powerful weapon. It provides the advocate who opens the oral argument with an opportunity to respond directly to the oral argument of the opponent. It also permits the advocate with the opening argument to have both the first and last word on the issues. Therefore, if you give the opening oral argument, you should always preserve the opportunity for rebuttal. Of course, if you are responding to the opening argument, and if the court permits you to give a brief surrebuttal to the opponent's rebuttal, you should reserve time for a possible retort to the rebuttal.

B. Formality and Demeanor

Appropriate courtroom attire is mandatory for any oral argument. For both men and women, this generally consists of a conservative, dark-colored suit. Beyond that, the level of formality of the proceedings will vary among courts.

For pretrial and trial motions, some state trial court judges hold oral arguments in their chambers rather than in the courtroom. After friendly, informal introductions, all are seated. As the judge listens from behind his desk, you and the opposing counsel will deliver your arguments while seated in office chairs. Similarly, oral argument while seated at tables is common in arbitration proceedings and some agency hearings.

Other trial judges and virtually all appellate panels of judges, however, conduct oral arguments with greater formality. In those courts, you deliver your oral argument from a lectern in the courtroom, or in some arguments in trial court, while standing at the counsel table.

If you are uncertain about the customs in a court or the expectations of a judge, you can observe another attorney's oral argument before the judge, speak with a colleague who has practiced before the judge, or seek advice from the staff of the clerk's office or from the judge's personal law clerk. To consult with them, you can contact them by telephone or simply arrive early on the day of the argument.

Your demeanor in oral argument should be as formal as your attire. You should be confident and relaxed, but respectful of the judge, always addressing him or her as "Your Honor." If you disagree with a judge during the argument, you need not be disagreeable. For example, if the judge asks you whether your formulation of a legal rule will have certain adverse policy ramifications, you should answer the question confidently but without arrogantly suggesting that the question is silly.

Thus, you should *not* respond to a judge's question or assertion with a challenge to the judge's analytic skills, such as the following:

No, Your Honor, you are incorrect on that point.

Instead, you should answer the question without casting doubt on the questioner:

No, Your Honor, the Court can avoid those potential problems of line-drawing by stating its holding in this appeal narrowly. Appellant suggests the following formulation: ....

In some cases, you may even want to validate the question as you answer it:

Yes, Your Honor. That question has occupied the attention of many courts and scholars. To explain Appellant's interpretation, I must review the rationale for the exclusionary rule.

C. Content of the Argument

1. Introducing Yourself and Your Argument

In a formal courtroom argument, you should begin your presentation by introducing yourself and your representative capacity:

May it please the court, I am Terry Malloy. I represent Bakeway Stores, the appellant on this appeal and the defendant in the trial court.

The opening phrase, "May it please the court," oddly suggests that you hope that your name literally pleases the court. However, it also signals respect to the court and a willingness to allow the judges to set the agenda for the dialogue through their questions and comments. Moreover, if a judge expects this traditional salutation, your departing from it may place the judge in an unreceptive mood. Accordingly, you probably should introduce yourself with this traditional phrase unless you are confident that the judge or judges hearing your argument are comfortable with a more natural greeting, such as "Good morning, Your Honor. I am ...."

After the personal introduction, you can capture a judge's attention with a brief characterization of the motion or appeal. If the facts are compelling, you can describe the general nature of the case in a sentence or two that conveys the theme of your argument, as explored in Chapter 2. For example, suppose that a state is prosecuting an 18-year-old student for felony possession of illegal drugs on the premises of his high school. The attorney for the defendant student has filed a motion in the trial court to exclude evidence obtained in an allegedly illegal detention and search. He might introduce his oral argument at the suppression hearing with the following characterization of the case:

Your Honor, this motion concerns the reasonableness of a search by armed police officers who — acting solely on information about previous drug sales by a former student — rushed into a high school hallway with a barking police dog, ordered all fifteen high school students in the hallway to fall to their knees with hands behind their heads, and searched them, one-by-one. As the Supreme Court held in *Redding* ....

Of course, the prosecutor might respond with a very different characterization of the case:

Your Honor, the seizure of the crack cocaine in this case was the product of a thorough investigation in an ongoing effort by police and school administrators to protect all students from trafficking in illegal drugs at Richland High School.

2. Body of the Argument

a. General Strategy

Many courts impose a time limit on each oral argument. Although some courts of last resort may allow up to 60 minutes for each side in a complex case, 15 to 30 minutes is more typical, and arguments on simple pretrial motions may be limited to an even shorter time. In most motions or appeals, you will not have time to address all the issues in the depth in which you explored them in your brief. Consequently, you should carefully study the arguments presented in both parties' briefs to determine the most effective strategy for oral argument.

Your strategy will differ depending on the circumstances of each case. In one appeal, for example, you might rely on multiple arguments that are both complex and interdependent. You might fear that, even with a well-organized brief to guide them, the judges may not fully appreciate how the arguments fit together to form the larger picture. Accordingly, you could decide to present an oral outline of all the arguments and their relationships, leaving the detail of each to your brief.

More often, you can identify an argument in your brief that you wish to emphasize. Perhaps it addresses a critically important threshold issue or is your strongest theory. In other cases, you might select an argument for oral presentation because it is the weakest link in your argumentative chain and needs extra support.

Whatever strategy you choose, you should communicate your intentions immediately after the introduction to your argument. For example, at a hearing to suppress evidence obtained in an allegedly illegal search, the prosecutor might try to justify the search on several grounds. Although she will introduce evidence at the hearing supporting each of the grounds and will advocate each ground in her brief, she might use her oral argument to focus on the determinative issue of consent to search. If so, she should reveal her plans to the court:

This hearing presents three major issues, all of which the briefs examine in detail. I will be happy to answer questions on any of the issues. However, I would like to focus my presentation on the issue of consent to search. If the facts show that the defendant consented to the detention and the search, this court need not address difficult legal issues such as those related to expectations of privacy on a high school campus.

---

b. Using the Facts

Many judges will advise oral advocates before argument that the judges are familiar with the facts of the case and that the advocates should proceed with their legal analyses. Even absent such an instruction, you ordinarily should not begin your argument with a lengthy recitation of the facts beyond a general characterization of the nature of the case. You might depart from this advice if the facts are particularly compelling and your legal arguments are not. In most cases, however, you will make better use of your limited time by arguing the law and applying the law to the facts without a separate introductory recitation of facts.

Whenever you rely on facts in an oral argument, be certain of the source of the facts. Be prepared to cite to the portion of the record that establishes the facts.

c. Responding to Questions

Questions from the bench constitute the most uncertain variable in oral argument. They ensure that oral advocacy in most cases is not a series of speeches but a dialogue, primarily between each advocate and the judges, and secondarily between the advocates as they respond to one another. Oral argument also permits judges on a panel to establish a coy dialogue between the judges, as they attempt to persuade each other with comments and questions ostensibly directed to the advocates.

You should genuinely welcome the opportunity to respond to questions. A judge's questions may reveal areas in which she has doubts, permitting you to directly influence her thinking on those points.

Occasionally, a judge will press you for a concession on your weakest of several alternative arguments. Your waiving the argument might be the most effective way to turn the judge's attention to your stronger arguments. However, you should not too quickly waive a major argument that you had earlier determined was sufficiently meritorious to warrant discussion in your brief. If you are arguing before a panel of judges, the other panel members may not share the doubts of the questioning judge; yet, if you expressly waive the controversial point during oral argument, none of the judges will take up that argument. Thus, even though it appears that you must waive the argument to preserve your credibility, you should first try to shift to a more productive topic of discussion after making a minor concession:

Your Honor, as explored in detail in the Appellee's Brief, Todd maintains that he has standing to establish unreasonable use of force based on the totality of the circumstances, including evidence showing how the entire police operation affected all the students. However, Todd's principal argument on appeal is that the police violated the Fourth Amendment by detaining and searching Todd without even reasonable suspicion that any illegal activity was taking place.

Except when trying to avoid a waiver of an argument, you should not give the appearance of evading questions from the bench. Instead, you should confront and answer the questions directly. To answer judges' questions effectively, you must come to the argument thoroughly prepared. In particular, you should be ready to

- discuss the facts, holding, and reasoning of any case that you seek to distinguish or on which you rely;
- cite to the record to identify the source of facts on which you rely; and
- discuss the policy implications of alternative holdings among which the court must choose.

An excellent method of preparing for the oral argument is to hold practice sessions with colleagues acting as judges. Your colleagues can provide constructive criticism and can help you anticipate the questions likely to be asked by the judges in the actual oral argument.

Even with excellent preparation, you may not always anticipate every question that a judge will ask you. If you cannot formulate a satisfactory answer to a truly unexpected and excessively challenging question, you probably will do better to acknowledge the difficulty of the question and to offer to address it in your rebuttal or in a supplementary brief than to simply bluff or brush the question aside.

Because you cannot always predict the number of questions from the bench, you must build maximum flexibility into your argument. You should be prepared to do either of the following or anything in between:

- present your arguments without interruption until your time elapses or you otherwise finish your argument; or
- present a brief introduction, respond without break to a series of questions that takes up all your allotted time, and request that the court permit you to end with a prepared conclusion no longer than a few sentences.

3. The Conclusion

You should end your argument on a compelling note, perhaps with a summary of your strongest points. A carefully planned conclusion will be particularly helpful if persistent questioning from the bench prevents you from covering all the points that you had planned to address in your oral argument. Faced with the impending expiration of your allotted time, you can fall back on the conclusion as a quick means of stating your points, if only in summary fashion.

D. Nervousness and Verbal Stumbling

All but the most experienced oral advocates feel some anxiety at the prospect of facing an inquisitive panel of judges in a public setting. If you feel such anxiety, you may be concerned that your nervousness will interfere with your speech patterns, causing your voice to shake or causing you to stumble over your words or to pause to collect your thoughts. You need not worry excessively about such problems for two reasons.

First, so long as the judge can understand you, the substance of your arguments and of your responses to questions will be more important than your charisma and stage presence. Some debate competitions may exalt form over substance: You may earn points if you can glibly respond to a judge's questions without pause, or lose points if you occasionally stumble over a difficult word. In actual oral arguments, however, a judge will be more concerned with establishing a genuine dialogue with you. She will not be uncomfortable with a few moments of silence from you; indeed, most judges will expect you to pause to think deeply before answering a difficult question. Moreover, if you speak sufficiently slowly and clearly to make yourself understood, most judges will forgive you for the occasional verbal stumbling that nervousness may produce.

Second, you can minimize distracting imperfections in your delivery caused by nervousness. Perhaps the best way to bring such nervousness under control is to approach your oral argument with the confidence that comes from thorough preparation. If you have carefully prepared your analysis, mastered the facts and the record, anticipated questions, and rehearsed your argument before colleagues playing the role of inquisitive judges, you can confidently assume that you will bring an expertise to the courtroom that the judge will appreciate.

Just prior to the argument, consider spending a few minutes taking slow, deep breaths, while you clear your mind of doubts and distracting thoughts. Try to focus your thoughts on viewing the oral argument positively, as an opportunity for a constructive dialogue with the judge.

To deal with remaining nervousness at the beginning of your argument, you should prepare a carefully worded introduction that you can commit to memory, so that you will not find yourself groping for words at the outset. Then, after you have warmed up your speaking voice, you can speak more flexibly from a rough outline of your main argument before closing with a carefully planned conclusion. Remember, your oral argument is more akin to a formal conversation with the court than a formal speech. Active engagement in the conversation coupled with solid preparation beforehand are key to a successful oral argument.

III. Summary

Effective advocacy requires sound analysis, sensible organization, and effective writing style. In addition to the matters examined in Chapter 2, you should adopt a persuasive writing style and carefully prepare an oral argument that strategically supplements your brief.

The following chapters examine further techniques of persuasive writing in the context of various legal documents.

Part II

Pretrial Advocacy—

Pleadings and Motions

You might file different kinds of pleadings and briefs to a court from the inception of a lawsuit to its final disposition in a court of last resort. This part of the book explores a few kinds of pretrial pleadings and briefs with the aim of preparing you to initiate or respond to any form of written advocacy. Part III will examine appellate brief-writing.

The following three chapters introduce you to three kinds of pretrial written advocacy: pleadings (and surviving a motion to dismiss a pleading), motions for summary judgment, and pretrial motions to exclude evidence. When combined with the discussion of appellate briefs in Part III, Part II should provide you with the skills and confidence you need to perform any task of written advocacy.

Chapter 4

Pleadings and
Motions to Dismiss

I. The Complaint

"A civil action is commenced by filing a complaint with the court."[1] Because a complaint is such a fundamental and significant document, law schools are increasingly offering students opportunities to draft complaints in legal writing or clinical courses. Still, when faced with the task of preparing a complaint, you may be tempted to turn to canned language in formbooks.

Forms may provide general guidance in some cases. In fact, many jurisdictions have officially authorized pleading forms for certain kinds of suits. Nonetheless, you will more quickly and thoroughly master pleading skills if you understand the components of a complaint well enough to draft one "from scratch." Your primary tools in such a task are the results of your

---

1. Fed. R. Civ. P. 3.

investigation of facts and your knowledge of the applicable law. Beyond that, rules of procedure and local court rules provide the necessary guidance.

A. Overview: Format and Content

Local court rules on pleading often specify a standard caption that identifies the case and the nature of the document. For example, the Rules of Practice for the United States District Court for the District of Arizona specify the line spacing and precise location in the caption on the first page of a document for, among other things, the following information: (1) the name, address, e-mail address, state bar attorney number, telephone and fax number of the representing attorney, and the party represented; (2) the title of the court; (3) the names of the parties in a "title of the action"; (4) the docket number (or a space for it if the clerk has not yet assigned one); and (5) a designation of the nature of the document.[2]

More substantively, Federal Rule of Civil Procedure 8(a) requires a complaint to contain three elements:

(1) a short and plain statement of the grounds for the court's jurisdiction . . . ;

(2) a short and plain statement of the claim showing that the pleader is entitled to relief; and

(3) a demand for the relief sought, which may include relief in the alternative or different types of relief.

Each of these elements warrants further examination.

B. Jurisdictional Statement

The jurisdictional statement is particularly important in a complaint filed in federal court, because the subject matter jurisdiction of federal courts is limited to that authorized by Article III of the United States Constitution and by federal statutes.[3] Therefore, in the initial paragraphs of a complaint in federal court, you should allege facts establishing subject matter jurisdiction based on a federal question,[4] diversity of citizenship,[5] or a special statutory grant of jurisdiction.[6] Although the jurisdictional statement is sufficient if it alleges facts that support the court's exercise of jurisdiction,[7] federal pleaders customarily cite to the specific statutes that grant jurisdiction:

---

2. D. ARIZ. LRCIV. 7.1(a); *see also* FED. R. CIV. P. app. at Forms 1, 2 (caption and signature block, including e-mail address of attorney).

3. *See, e.g.,* Mayor v. Cooper, 73 U.S. (6 Wall.) 247, 252 (1868).

4. *See* 28 U.S.C. §1331 (2012).

5. *Id.* §1332.

6. *See, e.g.,* 42 U.S.C. §2000e-5(f)(3) (2012) (granting jurisdiction of actions brought under Title VII of the Civil Rights Act of 1964).

7. Aguirre v. Auto. Teamsters, 633 F.2d 168, 174 (9th Cir. 1980).

1. This claim arises under Title VII of the Civil Rights Act of 1964; therefore, this court has subject matter jurisdiction under 42 U.S.C. §2000e-5(f)(3) and 28 U.S.C. §1331.[8]

Pleading subject matter jurisdiction is less important in state court than in federal court, because most state trial courts are courts of general jurisdiction. When state pleaders address subject matter jurisdiction at all, it is often with simple introductory allegations that the amount in controversy exceeds the amount reserved for state courts of limited jurisdiction. This is often coupled with a citation to the state constitutional or statutory provision that authorizes the court's exercise of general trial jurisdiction.

Nonetheless, many state rules of civil procedure have adopted all the elements of the governing federal rule of civil procedure, thus requiring some statement of "jurisdiction" in state court complaints. Because a special allegation of subject matter jurisdiction is less clearly necessary in a state court complaint, state pleaders often begin their complaints with allegations of *personal* jurisdiction over the defendants. Such statements typically introduce the parties and allege in conclusory fashion that the defendant has engaged in conduct in the state out of which the claim arises or has otherwise established the requisite contacts with the state.

Some federal complaints also include allegations establishing that the court has personal jurisdiction over the defendant, even though the appendix of forms to the federal rules, published until 2015, included no such allegations in their samples.[9] Assuming that lack of personal jurisdiction is treated as an affirmative defense for pleading purposes, a complaint will not be insufficient for failure to affirmatively plead personal jurisdiction over the defendant.

C. Claim for Relief

Federal Rule of Civil Procedure 8(a)(2) omits any reference to "facts" in its requirement of a statement of the claim for relief. Nonetheless, "Rule 8(a)(2) envisages the statement of circumstances, occurrences, and events in support of the claim presented."[10] Most people would use the word "fact" to describe allegations of that nature. Similarly, this book will use "fact" in this context while attempting to avoid the historical confusion surrounding the term.

---

8. *See also* FED. R. CIV. P. app. at Form 7 (2012) (form allegations for federal question jurisdiction, published until 2015, included both requisite fact allegations and citation to federal statute granting jurisdiction), *abrogated* FED. R. CIV. P. 84 (2015).

9. *See id.*

10. Advisory Committee on Rules for Civil Procedure, *Report of Proposed Amendments to the Rules of Civil Procedure for the United States District Courts* 18-19 (1955), *reprinted in* Richard H. Field, Benjamin Kaplan & Kevin M. Clermont, CIVIL PROCEDURE: MATERIALS FOR A BASIC COURSE 1151 (10th ed. 2010).

Thus, in the main body of the complaint, you will allege facts and conclusions of liability that establish entitlement to relief. This may require preliminary legal research as well as a reasonable investigation of the facts, to help satisfy your ethical obligations under Rule 11.[11] Your knowledge of the law will enable you to identify legally significant facts, and your knowledge of the case will help you to determine what facts you can allege reasonably and in good faith.

To draft your claim for relief effectively, you must determine

1. the extent, if any, to which you should supplement fact allegations with references to the law;
2. the specific content of the fact allegations; and
3. the appropriate level of specificity of the allegations.

1. Allegations of Fact and Citations to Law

Your complaint normally should allege facts and ultimate conclusions establishing a claim for relief; you need not cite to supporting legal authority.[12] Thus, you need allege only two of the three elements of the syllogism of deductive reasoning:

[Major premise:	Rule of Law]
Minor premise:	Allegations of Fact
Conclusion:	Allegation of Liability or Other Ultimate Conclusion

A complaint with the minimum necessary elements will explicitly set forth the minor premise and the conclusion, and it will leave the major premise implicit.

For a simple example, a form complaint formerly appended to the Federal Rules of Civil Procedure stated a claim on a promissory note, alleging the subsidiary facts that the defendant has failed to pay money owed to the plaintiff on the note:

> 2. On <u>date,</u> the defendant executed and delivered a note promising to pay the plaintiff on <u>date</u> the sum of $_____ with interest at the rate of ___ percent. A copy of the note [is attached as Exhibit A] [is summarized as follows: _____.]
> 3. The defendant has not paid the amount owed.[13]

---

11. See Chapter 1, Section II.B (discussing ethical duties in filing documents with the court).

12. *E.g.,* Skinner v. Switzer, 562 U.S. 521, 530 (2011) ("a complaint need not pin plaintiff's claim for relief to a precise legal theory" or "provide an exposition of his legal argument"); Doss v. South Cent. Bell Tel. Co., 834 F.2d 421, 424-25 (5th Cir. 1987) (improper to dismiss complaint that pleaded improper legal theory if the allegations state a claim on any other legal theory).

13. FED. R. CIV. P. app. at Form 10, alternative allegation (a) (2012), *abrogated* Fed. R. Civ. P. 84 (2015). The forms appended to the federal rules were abrogated in 2015 with the explanation that they had fulfilled their purpose and were no longer necessary. *Infra* note 29.

These sample allegations do not explicitly state the major premise that a promise to pay money expressed in a written promissory note is enforceable under the common law of contracts or under some other legal authority. Whether the alleged facts state a claim for relief under applicable legal authority can be addressed in subsequent proceedings, such as on a motion to dismiss.[14]

Thus, in practice, citation to specific legal authority is much less common in the claim for relief than in the jurisdictional statement. The only references to legal authority commonly found in claims for relief are descriptive headings that introduce counts with general legal theories of relief, such as "Negligence," "Wrongful Discharge," "Employment Discrimination," or "Breach of Contract."

Nonetheless, a pleader will sometimes cite to authority in the claim for relief for a strategic purpose. For example, in cases in which the plaintiff seeks a settlement at the outset of litigation, his attorney may briefly cite to authority in the complaint to demonstrate to the defendant that the claim is substantial and that further litigation is unlikely to reduce the risk of liability. In most cases, however, the attorney could achieve the same result with a demand letter that explains the merits of the claim. Such a letter could either precede or accompany the complaint.

In other cases, an attorney may cite to legal authority in the body of the complaint because the claim is admittedly novel and thus would not be readily recognized as meritorious on the basis of the factual allegations alone. The author of the complaint may hope that the citations will help the judge understand the advocate's legal theory and keep an open mind pending further proceedings.

When the allegations are unusually complex or the underlying legal theories novel or complex, some attorneys recommend a middle ground: Limit your allegations to factual matters but explain the nature of the claims and allegations in a short "Introduction" or "Overview" that precedes the specific factual allegations. In one or two paragraphs, you can help the reader see the whole forest before entering the confusing stands of trees by (1) briefly identifying any novel legal theories on which your claims depend, or (2) summarizing how numerous complicated transactions or other facts relate to one another, or both.[15]

2. Substance of Allegations

One writer has recommended that a claim for relief state the journalist's "five Ws": who, what, where, when, and why.[16]

Who—In some complaints, you will introduce the parties in the jurisdictional allegations. Otherwise, your statement of the claim for relief should

---

14. *See* FED. R. CIV. P. 12(b)(6).

15. The authors thank Peter Friedman for sharing this idea.

16. Delmar Karlen, PROCEDURE BEFORE TRIAL IN A NUTSHELL 41-42 (1972).

identify them and their relationship to one another. It should also identify any other significant actors.

What, Where, When—The statement of the claim should describe the events that give rise to the claim. You should take care to allege all facts or conclusions needed to support the request for relief. For example, you should support a request for specific performance with an allegation that the legal remedy of money damages is inadequate.

Why—You should allege any state of mind that is material to the claim or to the availability of special relief. For example, a request for punitive damages in a common law tort claim must be supported by an allegation of malice, willful misconduct, or at least recklessness, depending on the jurisdiction.

You need not allege all matters that may ultimately be in dispute; you need allege only the legal elements of your client's claim for relief, with sufficient factual allegations to make the claim plausible. The defendant must plead affirmative defenses in the answer,[17] and the complaint need not anticipate them. The federal rules list 18 affirmative defenses;[18] statutes and case law may help you define the burdens of pleading on other matters. In case of doubt, you should plead a matter as part of the claim for relief.

For example, suppose that the jurisdiction in which the complaint is filed recognizes a cause of action for intentional infliction of emotional distress on proof of four elements: (1) The defendant engaged in extreme and outrageous conduct (2) with the intent to cause severe emotional distress or with reckless disregard for the possibility of those consequences, and (3) the conduct caused the plaintiff to suffer (4) severe emotional distress.[19] After introductory allegations establishing personal jurisdiction and identifying Jansen as the plaintiff and Bostich as one of the defendants, the count for this claim should allege facts supporting each of the four elements of the prima facie case:

COUNT I

Infliction of Emotional Distress

Relationship of parties

3. Jansen worked on an assembly line at the Zydeco Radio factory under the direct supervision of Bostich. As Jansen's supervisor, Bostich had the authority to impose production quotas on Jansen and to impose discipline, including termination, for failure to meet quotas.

---

17. FED. R. CIV. P. 8(c)(1). Rule 8(c)(1) formerly listed 19 affirmative defenses, FED. R. CIV. P. 8(c)(1) (2007), but the reference to "discharge in bankruptcy" was eliminated in 2010 to avoid confusion with a statute that addressed the effect of discharge, 11 U.S.C. §524(a) (2012).

18. *Id.*

19. *See, e.g.*, Watts v. Golden Age Nursing Home, 619 P.2d 1032, 1035 (Ariz. 1980) (citing RESTATEMENT (SECOND) OF TORTS §46).

4. From April 1 to June 10, 2014, Bostich engaged in the extreme and outrageous conduct of imposing impossible production quotas on Jansen and causing Jansen to believe that his job security depended on his meeting the quotas.[20]	**Conduct**
5. Bostich maliciously engaged in this conduct for the purpose of causing Jansen to suffer severe emotional distress. Alternatively, Bostich recklessly disregarded the likelihood that Jansen would suffer such distress.[21]	**State of mind**
6. On June 10, 2014, as a direct result of Bostich's conduct, Jansen suffered a complete nervous breakdown requiring bed rest for three weeks and extensive medical care.	**Causation and severe distress**
7. Jansen continues to suffer insomnia, headaches, inability to concentrate at work, general nervousness, and other emotional distress as a result of Bostich's conduct. In an effort to address these symptoms, Jansen has frequently consulted a general physician and a psychological counselor, incurring substantial medical expenses.	**Injuries**

In contrast, even if the allegations raise some question of whether the statute of limitations has expired, the complaint need not affirmatively allege that the statute of limitations has not expired or has been tolled. Instead, expiration of the statute of limitations is an affirmative defense that the defendant has the burden of pleading.[22]

3. Specificity of Fact Allegations

The early, rigid common law forms of action largely disappeared in this country in the nineteenth century with widespread enactment of versions of the Field Code, named for David Dudley Field, which required complaints to set forth a "statement of the facts constituting the cause of action, in ordinary and concise language."[23] In the twentieth century, the federal system

---

20. Whether the allegations of paragraphs 3 and 4 establish "extreme and outrageous conduct" will depend on the law of that jurisdiction and could be litigated on a motion to dismiss for failure to state a claim. *See, e.g.,* FED. R. CIV. P. 12(b)(6).

21. This allegation of scienter should suffice not only to satisfy the second element of the tort but to support a request for punitive damages as well.

22. FED. R. CIV. P. 8(c).

23. *See* Richard L. Marcus, *The Puzzling Persistence of Pleading Practice*, 76 TEX. L. REV. 1749, 1753 & n.28 (1998) (discussing and quoting the Field Code).

and most states replaced their versions of the Field Code with rules permitting pleadings that give the court and the opposing party more general notice of most claims and defenses.[24] Federal Rule of Civil Procedure 8(a)(2) requires the main portion of a complaint to include only a "short and plain statement of the claim showing that the pleader is entitled to relief." For the most part, revelation of specific factual and evidentiary details is left to the discovery and disclosure process, motions for summary judgment, and the pretrial conference.[25] These standards, however, are complicated by a recently implied "plausibility" requirement for federal complaints, discussed in Subsection b below.

a. Notice Pleading—Minimum Requirements

Of course, a bare allegation of liability or legal conclusions without any supporting factual context would be insufficient even under the traditional relaxed "notice pleading" standards of the federal rules: Although Rule 8(a)(2) "does not require 'detailed factual allegations,'" none of the following would meet its requirements: (1) "'labels and conclusions,'"(2) "'a formulaic recitation of the elements of a cause of action,'" (3) "'naked assertion[s]' devoid of 'further factual enhancement,'"[26] or (4) "conclusory statements without reference to its factual context."[27]

The appropriate level of detail or generality of the factual context can be illustrated by a continuum that represents varying degrees of specificity in fact allegations. The continuum begins with allegations of legal conclusions based on underlying facts. It gains steadily in specificity until it presents specific evidence from which factual inferences can be drawn and on which factual conclusions can be based:

LEGAL CONCLUSION	FACTUAL CONCLUSION	SPECIFIC EVIDENCE
Negligence	D exceeded the speed limit, breaching duty of care	eyewitness estimate of speed and analysis of skid marks

As an example of extreme specificity, a complaint could state a claim for negligent operation of an automobile by alleging each bit of evidence with which the plaintiff hopes to prove negligence at trial:

3.... Jill Graham and Ben Cooper were standing at the corner of 7th Avenue and Washington Street in Smallville at noon and observed the defendant driving his automobile west on Washington Street past 7th Avenue and toward 8th

---

24. *See id.* at 753-54.

25. *See* FED. R. CIV. P. 16, 26-37, 56.

26. Ashcroft v. Iqbal, 556 U.S. 662, 678 (2009) (quoting Bell Atl. Corp. v. Twombly, 550 U.S. 544, 555, 557 (2007)).

27. *Id.* at 686.

Avenue. Each of them observed that the defendant was traveling at a substantially greater speed than all other cars proceeding normally in the same direction, passing them easily. An expert who examined skid marks at the accident scene estimated that the defendant's automobile was traveling at 40-50 miles per hour when it entered the intersection of Washington Street and 8th Avenue....

Nearer to the other extreme, the complaint could allege the ultimate legal conclusion of negligence, coupled with a brief description of factual context:

2. On January 1, 2014, at the intersection of Washington Street and 8th Avenue in Smallville, defendant negligently drove a motor vehicle into the plaintiff, striking her in the crosswalk.

3. As a result, the plaintiff was physically injured, lost wages ....

This second example is adapted from a sample form appended to the Federal Rules of Civil Procedure until 2015.[28] This example illustrated the apparent acceptability of surprisingly terse allegations on simple matters under federal notice pleading. It provides the defendant with general notice of the event that allegedly created legal liability, and the legal classification of the alleged wrongdoing (negligence), but little more.

b. Plausibility and Other Departures from Minimal Notice Pleading

The federal forms, however, were abrogated in 2015 with the explanation that they had fulfilled their purpose and were no longer necessary.[29] In practice, very few complaints had stated the claim for relief in the exceedingly spare manner illustrated by the federal forms. The reasons for this are varied. Some states have retained rules that require greater specificity for complaints in state court than are traditionally required by the federal standards for notice pleading. Even under the federal rules, moreover, some kinds of matters must be alleged with greater specificity than is ordinarily required. Finally, as a matter of strategy and style, many advocates prefer to allege claims in greater detail than the minimum degree required by the applicable rules.

In states that retain the more fact-oriented pleading requirements of the Field Code, the appropriate level of specificity probably would lie somewhere in the middle of the continuum. For example, the complaint might allege that the defendant operated the car negligently by exceeding the

---

28. FED. R. CIV. P. app. at Form 11 ¶¶2, 3 (abrogated 2015); *see also* Swierkiewicz v. Sorema, 534 U.S. 506, 508 (2002) (under federal general notice pleading standards, a complaint need not "contain specific facts establishing a prima facie case of discrimination").

29. FED. R. CIV. P. 84 & Committee Notes on Rules—2015 Amendment (eff. Dec. 1, 2015).

speed limit, but it need not contain allegations of the specific evidence of speeding, such as the analysis of skid marks.[30]

Even the federal rules occasionally depart from the minimal demands of notice pleading. Rule 9(b), for example, provides that allegations of "fraud or mistake" must state the circumstances with particularity.[31]

Moreover, the federal rules governing pleading and motions to dismiss are subject to interpretation, and courts in some jurisdictions have developed a reputation for demanding greater specificity than might seem to be required by the plain language of the rules.[32] In 2007 and 2009, the United States Supreme Court placed its stamp of approval on this trend by requiring allegations in federal complaints to "state a claim to relief that is plausible on its face."[33] This new "plausibility" standard does not require allegations that establish the "probability" of liability,[34] nor does it transfer the more rigid particularity requirement of Rule 9(b) to Rule 8(a)(2).[35] On a motion to dismiss under Rule 12(b)(6), however, the plausibility requirement does direct a federal judge to use "experience and common sense" to determine whether the factual allegations permit a plausible inference of wrongdoing, rather than the "mere possibility" of wrongdoing.[36] For example, if the allegations of fact, assumed to be true, more readily permit an inference of innocent behavior than of wrongdoing, the complaint might be insufficient to resist dismissal under the plausibility standard.[37]

The plausibility requirement should not add significantly to the pleading burdens in a large percentage of cases. For one thing, states that have adopted notice pleading standards are not bound to adopt the plausibility requirement as an interpretation of their state versions of Rules 8(a)(2) and 12(b)(6).[38] Moreover, even when it does apply, the plausibility requirement

---

30. *See generally* Field et al., *supra* note 10, at 1148-49, 1152 (discussing Garcia v. Hilton Hotels Int'l, Inc., 97 F. Supp. 5 (D.P.R. 1951) and stating that a code pleader should not "plead his evidence").

31. FED. R. CIV. P. 9(b); *see also* Ziemba v. Cascade Int'l, Inc., 256 F.3d 1194, 1202 (11th Cir. 2001) (explaining purposes of Rule 9(b) but noting that it is not intended to abrogate the concept of notice pleading).

32. *See, e.g.*, Marcus, *supra* note 23, at 1774 ("courts sometimes construct dubious new pleading barriers," such as when they "apparently still strain to justify the application of [Rule 9(b)'s particularity requirements] outside their natural sphere"); Patricia M. Wald, *Summary Judgment at Sixty*, 76 TEX. L. REV. 1897, 1941-42 (1998) (partly "fueled by the overloaded dockets of the last two decades," courts are increasingly using summary judgment to weed out marginal cases, and "appear to be requiring plaintiffs to plead facts with ever greater detail in order to survive motions to dismiss").

33. Ashcroft v. Iqbal, 556 U.S. 662, 678 (2009) (quoting Bell Atl. Corp. v. Twombly, 550 U.S. 544, 570 (2007)). *Iqbal* and *Twombly* effectively overrule Conley v. Gibson, 355 U.S. 41 (1957).

34. *Iqbal*, 556 U.S. at 678 (quoting *Twombly*, 550 U.S. at 556).

35. *Id*. at 686-87.

36. *Id*. at 678 (quoting or citing *Twombly*, 550 U.S. at 556, 557-58).

37. *Id*. at 678-80. The court will not assume the truth of allegations that amount to legal conclusions. *Id*. at 679-80.

38. *E.g.*, Walsh v. U.S. Bank, N.A., 851 N.W.2d 598 (2014) (rejecting plausibility requirement for the State of Minnesota rules of procedure); McCurry v. Chevy Chase Bank, FSB, 169 Wash. 2d 96, 233 P.3d 861 (2010) (same for State of Washington's rules of procedure).

should be easily satisfied in complaints that allege simple matters such as negligent operation of an automobile or breach of contract through delayed and substandard construction. The new standard will more likely be a factor in claims perceived to be more speculative, such as those relying on general or circumstantial allegations to support an inference that independent entities acted in concert pursuant to a conspiracy or that a remote party directed the allegedly wrongful acts of others.[39]

c. Strategic Considerations

Once you have identified the minimum standards of specificity for allegations under applicable rules, you must determine whether to allege facts in substantially greater detail than is required. This determination may turn on your personal style and on strategic considerations peculiar to the case at hand.

Some attorneys will prefer to allege little more than is minimally required by the rules in each case. They might argue that unnecessarily complete and specific allegations could prematurely commit the plaintiff to a particular factual theory of the case, perhaps requiring amendment of the complaint after discovery is underway.

Some commentators, however, have argued for relatively complete and compelling narratives in complaints, to advance effective advocacy at the earliest stages of litigation.[40] For example, if a claim rests on clear and compelling facts that paint a vivid picture of injustice, strategic considerations may argue in favor of telling the client's story in greater detail than is required by applicable rules of procedure.[41] Alternatively, if a claim arises from complex events, detailed allegations may help the reader understand the relationships between multiple parties and numerous transactions.

In summary, once pleading rules have been satisfied, any additional specificity in your allegations is partly a matter of style and strategy. So long as you take care to allege facts supporting every element of your prima facie case, you can tailor the specificity of your allegations to your personal style and strategic needs. Even so, you should start with general allegations and add specificity only if you have good reason to do so. If excessively detailed allegations unnecessarily transform your pleading into a cumbersome tool

---

39. *E.g.,* Ashcroft v. Iqbal, 556 U.S. 662 (2009) (conclusory allegations that U.S. Attorney General condoned or shared the alleged discriminatory intent of lower-level F.B.I. agents); Bell Atl. Corp. v. Twombly, 550 U.S. 544 (2007) (allegations of parallel activity of firms was more consistent with innocent behavior than with a conspiracy in violation of antitrust laws); Moss v. U.S. Secret Serv., 572 F.3d 962 (9th Cir. 2009) (conclusory allegations that protestors were removed pursuant to a policy of the Secret Service to suppress anti-Bush message).

40. *E.g.,* Anne E. Ralph, *Not the Same Old Story: Using Narrative Theory to Understand and Overcome the Plausibility Pleading Standard,* 26 Yale J.L. & Human. 1 (2014); Elizabeth Fajans & Mary R. Falk, *Untold Stories: Restoring Narrative to Pleading Practice,* 15 Legal Writing: J. Legal Writing Inst. 3 (2009).

41. *See e.g.,* Elizabeth Fajans, Mary R. Falk & Helene S. Shapo, Writing for Law Practice 37 (2004) (advocating for "artful pleading" rather than bare notice pleading, especially in cases with compelling stories, such as civil rights claims).

for its intended audiences, you may face a court that is receptive to a motion to strike your pleading.[42]

D. Request for Relief

Your complaint should end with a simple statement of the relief sought by your client. The main request for relief typically is for an injunction, an award of money damages, or both. Consult local rules to determine whether you must request a specific dollar amount for some kinds of damages and an unspecified amount for others.

Additionally, you should request an award of reasonable costs and attorneys' fees if your client has a legal basis for such an award. Finally, you can retain flexibility by closing the request for relief with a catch-all request for "other appropriate relief":

Jansen therefore requests judgment granting the following relief:

1. an award of compensatory damages in an amount to be set at trial;

2. an award of punitive damages in an amount to be set at trial;

3. an award of reasonable costs and attorneys' fees; and

4. such other relief as the court deems appropriate.

E. Style and Organization

1. Writing Style

Some of lawyers' stuffiest jargon can be found in antiquated pleadings:

Comes now the plaintiff before this honorable court and, through his attorneys, Jenkins, Brown, and Little, alleges, pleads, and avers as follows:

....

3. That the defendant did employ said plaintiff as a designer of clothes ...;

4. That on July 6, 1927, said defendant did ...;

Wherefore, the plaintiff prays that this honorable court grant judgment ....

---

42. *See* Anserve Ins. Serv., Inc. v. Albrecht, 960 P.2d 1159, 1161 (Ariz. 1998) (en banc) ("Early on, the trial judge should have granted the motion to strike" a 269-page complaint.); McHenry v. Renne, 84 F.3d 1172, 1180 (9th Cir. 1996) (affirming dismissal with prejudice of a complaint that was "written more as a press release, prolix in evidentiary detail, yet without simplicity, conciseness and clarity").

The federal rules reject jargon in favor of plain English: "Each allegation must be simple, concise, and direct. No technical form is required."[43] When stated in plain English, the allegations in the preceding example are unquestionably simpler and more concise:

Plaintiff alleges:

    ....

3. The defendant employed the plaintiff as a designer of clothes....

4. On July 6, 1927, the defendant ....

Plaintiff requests the following relief: ....

---

2. Organization

To facilitate analysis of the claims by the court and the parties, set forth the allegations of your complaint in consecutively numbered paragraphs. Separation of different claims for relief into separate counts may be permissible or required, depending on the circumstances.

If you have joined separate claims for relief based on different transactions or occurrences, federal rules require you to state the claims in separate counts "[i]f doing so would promote clarity."[44] Otherwise, presentation of allegations in separate counts appears to be discretionary.

Even if your client's claims arise out of a single transaction, separate counts should be helpful if you rely on distinct legal theories that are based on different fact allegations. For example, a consumer injured by a faulty electrical appliance may have a cause of action against the retailer on two legal theories: products liability in tort and breach of a contractual warranty. If you divide the allegations into separate counts, you can identify which fact allegations are material to each theory of relief. If some facts are common to both theories, one count can incorporate some of the allegations of the other:

COUNT I
Tort—Products Liability

4. On January 1, 2011, Green purchased a microwave oven from Retailer.

5. The microwave oven had an unreasonably dangerous defect....

    ....

---

43. FED. R. CIV. P. 8(d)(1). The Federal Rules of Civil Procedure were stylistically revised in 2007 to state the rules more concisely and in plain English. Therefore, much of the case law will refer to rules in their prior form, in slightly different language and organization of subsections.

44. FED. R. CIV. P. 10(b).

COUNT II
Contract — Breach of Warranty

8. Green realleges the allegations in paragraphs 4-7.

9. Babcock Appliance Center warranted the microwave oven to be free of defects....

You must also exercise discretion to determine whether to follow each count with a separate request for relief or to consolidate them in a single request after presenting all counts. As with separation of theories into counts, separation of requests for relief to accompany different counts normally will be helpful if the available remedies vary with each count. For example, if punitive damages are available only on the products liability count and if attorneys' fees are available only on the count for breach of warranty, separate requests for relief after each count may facilitate subsequent analysis of the claims. On the other hand, if the requests for relief on different counts are identical, consolidation in a single request obviously avoids pointless repetition.

II. The Answer

To avoid judgment against him by default, the defendant must respond to a complaint by filing an answer or other appropriate response.[45] The defendant may move to dismiss the complaint on its face before filing an answer.[46] The answer must admit or deny each allegation of the complaint.[47] In addition, the answer may set forth any affirmative defenses,[48] assert counterclaims against the plaintiff,[49] or both. If the answer asserts a counterclaim, the original plaintiff must file an answer to the counterclaim to avoid default judgment on the counterclaim.[50]

A. Admissions and Denials

If a defendant contests liability, he is prepared to deny in good faith some of the material allegations of the complaint. On the other hand, nearly every complaint will contain some allegations that the defendant admits. Therefore, the typical answer will not generally deny all allegations of the complaint; instead, it will address each paragraph of the complaint and iden-

---

45. *See* FED. R. CIV. P. 12(a).
46. *See* Fed. R. Civ. P. 12(b).
47. FED. R. CIV. P. 8(b)(1)(B).
48. *See* FED. R. CIV. P. 8(b)(1)(A), (c)(1).
49. *See* FED. R. CIV. P. 7(a), 8(a), (c)(2).
50. *See* FED. R. CIV. P. 7(a).

tify areas of dispute.[51] For example, an answer to the complaint partially set forth earlier in this chapter might admit and deny allegations in the following manner:

ADMISSIONS AND DENIALS

1. Defendant Bostich admits the allegations in paragraphs 1-3 of Plaintiff Jansen's complaint.

2. Bostich denies the allegations in paragraph 4 of the complaint that he set impossible goals for Jansen and that he intimidated Jansen in his work. Bostich admits that he warned Jansen of the possibility of termination for failing to meet goals.

3. Bostich denies the allegations in paragraph 5 of the complaint.

4. Bostich has no information on which to form a belief in the truth of the allegations in paragraph 6 of the complaint, and he therefore denies them.

If the complaint is more than a few paragraphs long, it may help to match up the paragraphs of the complaint and answer, rather than admitting several paragraphs of allegations in the first paragraph of the answer:

---

1. Defendant Bostich admits the allegations in paragraph 1 of Plaintiff Jansen's complaint.

2. Defendant Bostich admits the allegations in paragraph 2 of the complaint.

3. Defendant Bostich admits the allegations in paragraph 3 of the complaint.

4. Bostich denies the allegations in paragraph 4 of the complaint that ....

One attorney even recommends that each paragraph of the answer restate or summarize the corresponding allegation of the complaint before admitting or denying it. The judge might be disposed to refer repeatedly to such a self-contained answer, rather than refer to the complaint, which would not include the defendant's denials.[52]

Conversely, you can consolidate your admissions and denials to the maximum degree if you prefer the most concise possible answer:[53]

---

1. Defendant Bostich admits the allegations in paragraphs 1-3 of Plaintiff Jansen's complaint.

2. Bostich admits that he warned Jansen of the possibility of termination for failing to meet goals.

3. Bostich denies all other allegations.

---

51. *See generally* FED. R. CIV. P. 8(b) (form of denials).

52. Benjamin R. Norris, *Writing Pleadings,* ARIZ. ATT'Y, Dec. 2000, at 37.

53. *See* FED. R. CIV. P. 8(b)(3).

B. Affirmative Defenses

In a separate section of your answer, you should allege facts and conclusions supporting any affirmative defenses that your client, the defendant, may reasonably assert.[54] Even if the allegations of the complaint are true and are legally sufficient to state a claim for relief, a meritorious affirmative defense to the prima facie case will justify judgment for the defendant.

For example, in the litigation between Jansen and Bostich, suppose that the statute of limitations for tort actions in the jurisdiction is one year, that Jansen filed his complaint on June 9, 2018, and that Bostich last communicated a supervisory ultimatum to Jansen on June 6, 2017. Bostich might be prepared to argue that the statute of limitations has expired on the ground that Jansen's cause of action accrued at the latest on June 6, 2017, the date of Bostich's last act, rather than on June 10, 2017, the date of Jansen's nervous breakdown. If so, Bostich could assert this in fairly conclusory fashion as an affirmative defense:

AFFIRMATIVE DEFENSE

5. Bostich last exercised any supervisory control over Jansen on June 6, 2010. Therefore, Jansen's cause of action accrued more than one year before the filing of his complaint, and the statute of limitations bars his action.

C. Counterclaims

The defendant named in a complaint might wish to assert an independent claim for relief against the plaintiff. If so, the roles of the parties are reversed for purposes of the counterclaim, and the principles of pleading discussed in Section I above apply to the counterclaim.

For example, in the litigation between Jansen and Bostich, additional facts might support a claim against Jansen for battery:

COUNTERCLAIM
Battery

6. On the evening of July 16, 2010, Jansen struck Bostich over the head with a baseball bat as Bostich left the Zydeco Radio factory.

7. Jansen acted maliciously and for the specific purpose of causing serious injury to Bostich.

---

54. *See* Fed. R. Civ. P. 8(b)(1)(A), (c).

8. As a result of Jansen's malicious attack, Bostich lost consciousness, required treatment in a hospital emergency room, and suffered debilitating pain for 24 hours.

Therefore, Bostich requests the following relief: ....

III. Motion to Dismiss

A. Standards and Procedure

As discussed above, Federal Rule of Civil Procedure 8(a)(2) requires that a complaint in federal court include "a short and plain statement of the claim showing that the pleader is entitled to relief." Under Rule 12(b)(6), a defendant may move to dismiss all or part of a complaint "for failure to state a claim upon which relief can be granted."

On a motion to dismiss, the defendant is essentially taking the following position: *If this case proceeds, I will deny some of the factual allegations of the complaint, and I am confident that the plaintiff will not be able to prove those allegations at trial. But we do not need to proceed to trial or even to discovery. Even if the allegations in the complaint were true, they would not amount to a claim under applicable law. In this motion and the response to it, the plaintiff and I will present our arguments about the content of the applicable law. Then, after applying the law to the facts of the complaint, the court should rule that the plaintiff's alleged facts, even if true, would not satisfy the legal requirements of any claim for relief.*

For trials in state court, many states have adopted the language of the federal rules in their state rules of civil procedure. Nonetheless, state courts are free to interpret their state rules differently than the Supreme Court has interpreted the federal rules, even if both sets of rules are worded identically. For example, as discussed earlier in this chapter, the Supreme Court has interpreted Federal Rule of Civil Procedure 8(a)(2) to require the stated claim to be factually "plausible." State courts, however, are free to follow the plain text of section 8(a)(2) of their state rules, without adding a requirement of plausibility.[55]

In a state that has adopted the language of the pleading federal rules but has *not* interpreted it to include a plausibility requirement, the complaint must plead facts that meet the relatively undemanding "notice pleading" requirements discussed in Section I.C.3.a above. As a matter of procedure, a court in such a state will do the following on a motion to dismiss:

- analyze the law without deferring to allegations of the complaint that amount to legal propositions;
- assume the truth of all factual allegations in the complaint, drawing inferences in favor of the nonmoving party;

---

55. *Supra* note 38.

- limit its analysis to the allegations in the complaint, without considering other allegations or evidence; and

- dismiss only if the plaintiff can prove no set of facts entitling the plaintiff to recover.[56]

In federal court, or in a state court that adopts the equivalent of the federal plausibility requirement, a motion to dismiss the complaint benefits from that additional burden on the complaining party, as described in Section I.C.3.b above. The court will still assume the truth of the allegations in the complaint. However, the court must use its experience and judgment to determine whether the complaint's factual conclusions are *plausible* and not merely *possible*. To deem a claim plausible, the court might require more specific intermediary factual allegations to support a factual conclusion that appears far-fetched to the court, such as the factual conclusion that a high official ordered or condoned the actions of a lower-level official.

B. Format

1. The Motion

As with any motion, you should state your request for dismissal on a free-standing page, as illustrated in Exercise 4-2 below, with a caption title such as "Motion to Dismiss Complaint." You should state your request for dismissal in a simple, plain sentence that cites to Rule 12(b)(6) or its equivalent in the jurisdiction. This request can simply state the legal conclusion that the allegations in the complaint (or in one or more counts of the complaint) do not state a claim for which relief can be granted. If you can explain that conclusion more specifically without adding undue length to your request, you can tailor that standard to the issue in your case:

Defendant, Hi-Tech Filter Co., moves this Court to dismiss the complaint for failure to state a claim. *See* [Fed. or state] R. Civ. P. 12(B)(6). The complaint fails to allege actions that amount to breach of contract under the plain meaning of the language of the contract.

The plaintiff can respond to the motion with a similar cover page, which might be entitled "Opposition to Motion to Dismiss." It will not advance any motion but will simply request that the court deny the motion to dismiss, while adding a succinct summary of its ground for denial:

---

56. Rooney v. Ohio State Highway Patrol, ___ N.E.3d ___ ¶¶ 13-14, 2017-Ohio-1123 ¶¶ 13-14 (Ohio Ct. App. 2017); Greenwood v. Taft, Stettinius & Hollister, 105 Ohio App. 3d 295, 297, 663 N.E.2d 1030, 1031 (Ohio Ct. App. 1995).

Plaintiff, Crystal Pools, Inc., requests that this Court deny Defendant's Motion to Dismiss. The complaint states a valid claim for breach of contract: It alleges with specificity that Defendant delivered goods that materially deviated from contract specifications, as section V of the contract should be interpreted with the aid of admissible extrinsic evidence.

2. The Supporting Brief

Appended to your motion will be a legal brief supporting your request. Typically entitled "Memorandum of Law," it will typically include three sections:

I. Facts [or "Introduction," or "Background," or "Statement of the Case"]

II. Argument

III. Conclusion

Section I of your brief can concisely summarize the nature of the dispute, the critical allegations of the complaint, and any relevant procedural developments in the case.

Section II should follow the style, ethical considerations, and organizational structures explored in Part I of this book. In the final section of your brief, concisely conclude by restating your request and the grounds for it, much like your summary in the motion itself.

IV. Summary

When drafting pleadings, follow the format prescribed by applicable rules. For example, federal rules require the drafter of a complaint to allege

1. jurisdiction,
2. a claim for relief, and
3. a demand for judgment.

In an answer, you

1. must admit or deny the allegations of the complaint, and
2. may also assert affirmative defenses or a counterclaim.

Generally, pleadings should allege ultimate conclusions and supporting facts but not legal standards. Although the claim for relief must allege all elements of the prima facie case, most allegations may be general and need not develop specific, evidentiary facts. In federal court and some state courts, however, a court might require additional and relatively specific factual allegations on some claims, to satisfy a test of plausibility. Whatever the applicable pleadings standards, the sufficiency of a complaint can be challenged in a motion to dismiss the complaint for failure to state a claim for relief.

Exercise 4-1

Compare and critically evaluate the following three versions of a complaint in the same wrongful discharge action. Which level of specificity of allegations do you prefer? What other differences in style do the complaints reflect? Which styles do you prefer? Note that the line spacing of the sample complaints in this book do not conform with the line-spacing requirements of most local rules.

For further practice with pleadings, complete Assignments 1 through 3 in the Appendix.

IN THE SUPERIOR COURT
MARICOPA COUNTY, ARIZONA

GEORGE BRYANT,

            Plaintiff,

     v.

MARIE JARDON, d.b.a.
Chez Marie,

            Defendant.

No._____

COMPLAINT

Plaintiff alleges:

COUNT 1

I

Plaintiff George Bryant is a resident of Phoenix, Arizona. Defendant Marie Jardon owns and operates Chez Marie, a restaurant located in Phoenix, Arizona.

II

Bryant worked for Jardon as a waiter at Chez Marie from August 16, 2016 to September 28, 2017.

III

At the time of his discharge on September 28, 2017, Bryant had an employment contract with Chez Marie that imposed substantive and procedural restrictions upon Jardon's right to terminate Bryant's employment.

IV

Acting through her agent, Mario Prieto, Jardon discharged Bryant on September 28, 2017, in breach of her employment contract with Bryant.

V

As a result of Jardon's breach of contract, Bryant has suffered lost wages and other incidental and consequential losses.

COUNT 2

VI

Bryant realleges and incorporates paragraphs I-V above.

VII

Acting through her agent, Jardon maliciously and unlawfully discharged Bryant for reasons that violate public policy, causing Bryant lost wages and other injuries.

Bryant therefore requests judgment granting the following relief:

1.   an order reinstating Bryant to his position as waiter at Chez Marie;

2.   an award of compensatory and punitive damages;

3.   an award of costs and attorneys' fees; and

4.   other appropriate relief.

Dated _____

by _____,

Thomas Sanchez

Simpson, Sanchez & Summers

303 North Central Avenue

Phoenix, Arizona 85002

(602) 229-1111

Bar No. 28371

Attorney for the plaintiff

ARIZONA SUPERIOR COURT
MARICOPA COUNTY

GEORGE BRYANT,

        Plaintiff, | No._____

    v.

MARIE JARDON, d.b.a.   COMPLAINT

Chez Marie,

        Defendant.

Plaintiff alleges:

I

BREACH OF PROMISE

1. Plaintiff George Bryant is a resident of Phoenix, Arizona. Defendant Marie Jardon owns and operates Chez Marie, a restaurant located in Phoenix, Arizona.

2. Bryant worked for Jardon as a waiter at Chez Marie from August 16, 2016 to September 28, 2017. Mario Prieto acted as the maître d' and supervisor of waiters at Chez Marie during Bryant's employment at Chez Marie. In all the events alleged below, Prieto acted on behalf of Jardon.

3. At the time of his discharge on September 28, 2017, Bryant had an employment contract with Chez Marie that included the terms of an "Employee Handbook."

4. The Employee Handbook contains promises of job security, including promises that (i) Jardon will not discharge any waiter except for inadequate performance and (ii) any waiter recommended for discharge has the right to meet with Jardon and Prieto to persuade them that the waiter should not be discharged. The Handbook also provides that Jardon will make the final determination in the event of disagreement between Prieto and Jardon on a discharge matter.

5. At all times during his employment at Chez Marie, Bryant performed his job in a manner that met the highest standards at Chez Marie. Despite the adequacy of Bryant's performance, Prieto discharged Bryant on September 28, 2017. Although Bryant immediately requested a meeting with Prieto and Jardon to discuss the discharge, both Prieto and Jardon refused to convene such a meeting.

6. As a result of Jardon's breach of promises in the Handbook, Bryant has suffered lost wages and other incidental and consequential losses.

7. Jardon's breach of promises in the Handbook constitutes a breach of her employment contract with Bryant. Moreover, Bryant foreseeably relied on promises in the Handbook, and Jardon's breach has created an injustice that can be avoided only by enforcing the promises.

II

WRONGFUL DISCHARGE

8. Bryant realleges and incorporates paragraphs 1-7 above.

9. In discharging Bryant, Prieto was motivated by malice, by an invidiously discriminatory animus, and by concerns unrelated to the successful operation of Chez Marie. Jardon's termination of Bryant's employment therefore violated public policy.

III

REQUEST FOR RELIEF

10. Bryant requests:

    i. an order reinstating Bryant to his position as waiter at Chez Marie;

   ii. an award of compensatory damages in an amount to be set at trial;

  iii. an award of punitive damages in an amount to be set at trial;

  iv. an award of costs and attorneys' fees; and

   v. such other relief as the court deems appropriate.

Dated _____

by _____,
Thomas Sanchez

. . . .

IN THE SUPERIOR COURT OF THE STATE OF ARIZONA
IN AND FOR THE COUNTY OF MARICOPA

GEORGE BRYANT,	
Plaintiff,	No._____
v.	
MARIE JARDON, d.b.a. Chez Marie, and	COMPLAINT
MARIO PRIETO,	(JURY TRIAL REQUESTED)
Defendants.	

Plaintiff George Bryant, by and through his attorneys, Simpson, Sanchez and Summers, alleges the following:

1. This is an action for injunctive relief and for compensatory damages exceeding $50,000. This court has original jurisdiction pursuant to the Arizona Constitution, Article 6, § 14(3).

2. Plaintiff is a resident of Phoenix, Arizona. Defendant Marie Jardon owns and operates Chez Marie, a restaurant located in Phoenix, Arizona. Defendant Mario Prieto acted as the maître d' and supervisor of waiters at Chez Marie during Bryant's employment at Chez Marie. All material events alleged below took place in Maricopa County.

I

FIRST CLAIM FOR RELIEF
(Breach of Contract)

3. Plaintiff worked for Defendants as a waiter at Chez Marie from August 16, 2016 to September 28, 2017. In all the events alleged below, Defendant Prieto acted on his own behalf as well as on behalf of Defendant Jardon.

4. On January 1, 2016, Defendants modified Plaintiff's employment contract to include promises of job security contained in the terms of an "Employee Handbook" and in oral assurances.

5. Among other things, the Employee Handbook contains the following promises of job security: (i) Defendants will not discharge any waiter except for inadequate performance and (ii) any waiter recommended for discharge has the right to meet with Defendants to persuade them that the waiter should not be discharged. The Handbook also provides that Defendant Jardon will make the final determination in the event of disagreement between Defendants on a discharge

matter. (Copy of text of excerpts of Handbook is attached and incorporated by this reference.)

6. At all times during his employment at Chez Marie, Plaintiff performed his job in a manner that met the highest standards at Chez Marie. Despite the adequacy of Plaintiff's performance, Defendants discharged Plaintiff on September 28, 2017. Although Plaintiff immediately requested a meeting with Defendants to discuss the discharge, Defendants refused to convene such a meeting.

7. As a result of Defendant's breach of contract, Plaintiff has suffered lost wages and other incidental and consequential losses.

THEREFORE, Plaintiff demands judgment granting the following relief:

   i. an order reinstating Plaintiff to his former position at Chez Marie;

   ii. an award of compensatory damages for all consequential and incidental losses;

   iii. an award of costs and attorneys' fees; and

   iv. such other relief as the court deems appropriate.

II
SECOND CLAIM FOR RELIEF
(Promissory Estoppel)

8. Plaintiff realleges paragraphs 1-7 above and incorporates them by this reference.

9. On January 1, 2016, Defendants gave Plaintiff promises of job security by making oral assurances and by distributing the Employee Handbook. Plaintiff relied to his detriment on those promises by performing extraordinary services and by forbearing from taking other job opportunities. That reliance was reasonably foreseeable by Defendants.

10. Defendants' termination of Bryant's employment on September 28, 2017 constituted a breach of their promises of job security and has created an injustice that can be avoided only by enforcing the promises.

THEREFORE, Plaintiff demands judgment granting the following relief:

   i. an order reinstating Plaintiff to his former position at Chez Marie;

   ii. an award of compensatory damages for all consequential and incidental losses;

   iii. an award of costs and attorneys' fees; and

   iv. such other relief as the court deems appropriate.

III

THIRD CLAIM FOR RELIEF

(Wrongful Discharge)

11. Plaintiff realleges paragraphs 1-10 above and incorporates them by this reference.

12. Defendants maliciously discharged Plaintiff because of his sexual orientation and because Plaintiff's exemplary performance made Defendant Prieto jealous. Those reasons for discharge reflect bad faith and violate the public policy of state laws.

THEREFORE, Plaintiff demands judgment granting the following relief:

   i. an order reinstating Plaintiff to his position as waiter at Chez Marie;

   ii. an award of compensatory damages in an amount to be set at trial;

   iii. an award of punitive damages in an amount to be set at trial;

   iv. an award of costs and attorneys' fees; and

   v. such other relief as the court deems appropriate.

Dated _____

by _____,

Thomas Sanchez

. . . .

Exercise 4-2

Motion to Dismiss—Use the instructions below to draft a brief supporting or opposing a motion to dismiss a complaint.

Study Count I of the sample complaint in the Appendix, Assignment 1, which alleges breach of a promise to marry. For purposes of this exercise, disregard Count II of the complaint, and assume that Count I, in paragraphs I through XIII, constitutes the entire complaint. Research the law in your state, or in a state designated by your professor, to determine whether state law provides a claim for relief for such a breach, whether the designated state's law instead abandons or restricts such a claim, or whether the state's law has not yet addressed this question. As attorney for the defendant, James Clyde, determine whether you have good legal grounds to file a motion to dismiss the complaint for failure to state a claim, or at least to dismiss some of the complaint's requests for certain kinds of relief.

If you conclude that you can file a motion to dismiss in good faith, consider whether filing the motion represents a good expenditure of your client's resources. You might ask whether the motion has a good chance of succeeding, assuming the truth of the allegations in the complaint.

If you conclude that filing a motion to dismiss represents sound strategy, prepare a motion using the following template, and with any further formatting required by your professor:

CALZONA SUPERIOR COURT
WARMS SPRINGS COUNTY

Georgia Anne TUCKER,
        Plaintiff,
 	
v.
 	
James CLYDE,
                Defendant.
	No. CIV-9X-79
	
	MOTION TO DISMISS
	
	(Oral argument requested)

Defendant, James Clyde, moves this Court to . . . . [In plain language, state the disposition you request. If you can do so in a simple clause or sentence, add a brief preview or summary of the general legal ground on which you base your request.]

> [Signature of student representing Clyde]
> [Name of student signing motion]
> [Fictitious address of law firm]
> Attorney for Defendant, James Clyde
> [Date]

You should accompany the motion with a supporting brief. Unless your professor provides different instructions, you may use the following template for your brief:

**MEMORANDUM OF LAW
IN SUPPORT OF MOTION TO DISMISS**

   I. Facts [or "Introduction," or "Background," or "Statement of the Case"]

   II. Argument

   III. Conclusion

   Signature block and date (as in the motion)

If the law in your designated state permits good faith argument on both sides of this issue, and if you are assigned to oppose the motion, begin with a cover page that identifies the court, the parties, and the signing attorney in the same manner as in the motion. However, replace "Motion to Dismiss" with "Opposition to Defendant Clyde's Motion to Dismiss," and identify "Plaintiff, Georgia Anne Tucker" as the represented party. Below that, without stating a motion of your own, you can simply state the plaintiff's intent to oppose the motion, perhaps with a very brief reference to the nature of your argument. You can then begin your brief with the same heading as the Memorandum of Law above, except with the phrase "IN OPPOSITION TO" in place of "IN SUPPORT OF."

Chapter 5

Motion for Summary
Judgment

I. Procedural Context

A pretrial motion for summary judgment is a popular means of determining whether the court should dispose of all or part of a dispute before the parties proceed to trial. In most cases, you will have little difficulty alleging facts that state a claim for relief; therefore, your complaints will seldom be susceptible to attack for failure to state a claim. On the other hand, even if you allege a claim or defense in good faith, you may fail to gather substantial admissible evidence supporting the claim or defense. In such cases, the opposing party's motion for summary judgment exposes the absence of a triable issue of fact. It compels you to choose between making at least a preliminary showing of the evidence supporting your allegations or suffering adverse judgment before trial. In other cases, both parties concede the absence of any dispute of fact, stipulate to the facts, and use the motion for summary judgment to argue unsettled questions about the law and its application to the stipulated facts.

Summary judgment litigation often takes place only after each party has thoroughly investigated the case through the discovery and disclosure process.[1] Indeed, the trial judge may delay resolution of a motion for summary judgment if further discovery is needed to permit the nonmoving party to support its opposition. Nonetheless, if you successfully move for summary judgment, you will avoid the greater burdens of a full trial.

On the other hand, if the trial court denies your motion for summary judgment, your unsuccessful motion may hamper your ability to settle the case before trial. If the opposing counsel initially expected to settle the case, he may have only minimally prepared the case prior to summary judgment litigation. Your motion for summary judgment, however, will have forced your opponent to organize his facts and legal arguments. If the motion fails, he likely will be much more demanding in settlement negotiations for three reasons. First, the denial of the motion will strengthen his belief in the potential merits of his client's claims or defenses. Second, he will be more nearly prepared for trial after researching the law and gathering the facts to oppose your motion for summary judgment. Finally, his client will have invested significant resources in opposing the motion, expenditures that his client will likely incorporate into the client's new settlement position.[2] Consequently, you should not move for summary judgment unless you have a reasonable chance of success.

Summary judgment litigation provides you with a stimulating vehicle for developing brief-writing skills. You must remain constantly sensitive not only to the merits of the underlying claims or defenses but also to the standards for summary judgment. Moreover, the local rules of many courts prescribe a special format for summary judgment briefs, providing you a valuable opportunity to examine the role of procedural rules in written advocacy.

II. Standards for Summary Judgment

The federal rules authorize a court to grant summary judgment if the parties do not genuinely dispute any material facts and if the moving party is entitled to judgment as a matter of law.[3]

---

1. The federal procedures for discovery and disclosure are set forth in FEDERAL RULES OF CIVIL PROCEDURE 26-37.

2. *See, e.g.,* Raymond L. Ocampo, Jr., *Moving Violations,* CAL. LAW., Aug. 1984, at 47, 48.

3. *See* FED. R. CIV. P. 56(a). The citations and quotations in this chapter are based on amendments to Rule 56 effective December 1, 2010. Some of the new language and organization of subsections in Rule 56 depart from references to the rule in much of the case law, but judicial interpretations of prior statements of the rule should be compatible with the substance of the new rule. *See* Joseph Kimble, *Lessons in Drafting from the New Federal Rules of Civil Procedure*, 12 SCRIBES J. LEGAL WRITING 25 (2008-2009) (discussing project of redrafting federal rules for style only). Beyond the scope of this discussion are state standards for summary disposition that deviate from the federal rules. Many states follow the federal standards closely. *See, e.g.,* Orme Sch. v. Reeves, 802 P.2d 1000 (Ariz. 1990) (en banc) (interpreting Ariz. R. Civ. P. 56); *cf.* Aguilar v. Atl. Richfield Co., 24 P.3d 493, 512-14 (Cal.

To illustrate the materiality requirement, let's imagine that the record on summary judgment establishes without dispute that a seller repudiated a binding sales contract with the buyer, compelling the buyer to purchase the goods from another supplier at a higher price. If the buyer moved for summary judgment on her contract claim against the seller, the repudiating seller could not successfully respond to the motion by establishing even a genuine dispute of fact about whether he had changed his mind and retracted his repudiation after the buyer had purchased the substitute goods. Under the governing Uniform Commercial Code, once the buyer had relied on the seller's repudiation by making a substitute purchase, the repudiation was final,[4] and the seller's attempted retraction would have no bearing on his liability. Thus, any dispute of fact about whether the seller in fact had attempted a late retraction would be immaterial to the buyer's contract claim and could not preclude summary judgment for the buyer on that claim.

The court does not resolve genuine factual disputes on summary judgment. Nonetheless, to evaluate the genuineness of a purported factual dispute, the court may undertake a limited evaluation of the strength of the facts presented by the nonmoving party. A factual issue is not genuine if the nonmoving party's factual support is so trivial that "the record taken as a whole could not lead a rational trier of fact to find for the non-moving party."[5] In short, the nonmoving party "must do more than simply show ... some metaphysical doubt as to the material facts."[6]

When moving for summary judgment, you may request summary judgment on one or more claims or defenses, or even on part of a claim or defense.[7] Alternatively, you may request a ruling that identifies some uncontested material facts without granting any final judgment.[8]

As the moving party, you have the initial burden of showing that the pretrial record supports judgment in your favor. If you move for summary judgment on the strength of a claim or defense on which you would have the burden of proof at trial, you must support your motion for summary judgment with admissible evidence tending to prove all the elements of the claim or defense.[9] You could make such a showing with deposition testimony, answers to interrogatories, admissions, or other information and documents obtained during discovery or disclosure, or with affidavits prepared specifically for the motion.[10]

2001) (amended California summary judgment rules are similar, though not identical to, federal standards).

4. *See* U.C.C. §2-611(1) (2011).

5. Matsushita Elec. Indus. Co. v. Zenith Radio Corp., 475 U.S. 574, 587 (1986).

6. *Id.* at 586.

7. FED. R. CIV. P. 56(a).

8. *See* FED. R. CIV. P. 56(g) (permitting court to find the absence of material fact on an issue not resolved on summary judgment).

9. *See* Celotex Corp. v. Catrett, 477 U.S. 317, 331 (1986) (Brennan, J., dissenting); FED. R. CIV. P. 56(c)(1)(b), (c)(2) (allowing showing or objection that supporting evidence would not be admissible at trial).

10. *See generally* FED. R. CIV. P. 56(c)(1)(A), (c)(4).

As an alternative basis for summary judgment, you may demonstrate that the opposing party lacks factual support for an element of her claim or defense. If so, you need not affirmatively produce evidence tending to negate that element. Instead, you may satisfy your initial burden simply by reviewing the existing record and demonstrating that it contains no admissible evidence supporting the critical element.[11]

Once you have satisfactorily supported your motion, the opposing party can avoid summary judgment by establishing a genuine issue of material fact for trial. She may not rely on the allegations or denials in her own pleading but must point to the moving party's admissions or to facts in affidavits, deposition testimony, or other documentary evidence or fruits of discovery, unless she can show that the requisite information is not available to her.[12]

If the materials establish grounds for summary judgment, the federal rules state that the court "shall grant summary judgment,"[13] but some courts and commentators believe that the court nonetheless retains discretion to deny summary judgment and refer the matter to trial.[14]

III. Format for Summary Judgment Briefs—Overview

Rules of procedure, local court rules, and custom suggest that materials supporting a motion for summary judgment should include the following:

1. a motion requesting action by the court;
2. a statement of material facts;
3. affidavits, or other materials not already in the record, that support the fact statement and the motion; and
4. a supporting brief, sometimes referred to in court rules as a "memorandum of law" or, in less modern terms, a "memorandum of points and authorities."

The requirements for the response are similar except that the nonmoving party need not file a formal motion opposing the motion for summary judgment. Under typical local court rules, the nonmoving party's first page would resemble the motion but would identify itself as an "Opposition" or

---

11. *See* Celotex Corp. v. Catrett, 477 U.S. 317, 322-24 (1986) (majority opinion); *id.* at 329-31 (Brennan, J., dissenting); FED. R. CIV. P. 56(c)(1)(b), (c)(2).

12. *See* FED. R. CIV. P. 56(c)-(e); *see also* Southern Rambler Sales, Inc. v. Am. Motors Corp., 375 F.2d 932, 937 (5th Cir. 1967) ("Rule 56 [is] saying in effect, 'Meet these affidavit facts or judicially die.'").

13. FED. R. CIV. P. 56(a).

14. *See* Orme Sch. v. Reeves, 802 P.2d 1000, 1008 n.11 (Ariz. 1990) (en banc) (referring to the discretion to deny summary judgment as the "traditional rule"). Indeed, for a few years, the language of Rule 56 was amended to state that summary judgment "should be rendered" when the requirements were satisfied, FED. R. CIV. P. 56(c)(2) (2007), until the traditional term "shall" was restored in 2010.

"Response" to the motion, and could briefly introduce the supporting brief and other materials. The moving party's reply, if any, might consist of a brief that replies to the nonmoving parties' legal arguments and a fact statement that responds to additional facts asserted by the nonmoving party.

Some local rules describe parts of the required format in surprising detail. For example, local rules for some United States District Courts specify the information required on designated lines of the caption of the title page of each document filed in support of the motion.[15] The most interesting of the local rules addressing summary judgment, however, are those specifying formats for the statements of facts.

IV. Statements of Facts

Before the advent of local rules governing motions for summary judgment, briefs and supporting materials often failed to pinpoint areas of factual dispute. Often, counsel for the moving party summarized the materials supporting the motion in a general narrative fact statement, and counsel for the nonmoving party summarized supporting materials in a general counterstatement of the facts. Worse yet, in some cases, one or both advocates omitted any consolidated statement of the facts and simply referred to the record in fact analyses dispersed throughout the argument section of the brief.

To help trial judges identify the potential areas of factual dispute, many courts have enacted local rules specifying a methodical point/counterpoint format for the statements of facts in motions for summary judgment. For example, a local rule for the United States District Court for the District of Nebraska requires the moving party to state the facts in numbered paragraphs, similar to allegations in a complaint, while citing to the original source of each fact:

> The statement of facts should consist of _short_ numbered paragraphs, each containing pinpoint references to affidavits, pleadings, discovery responses, deposition testimony (by page and line), or other materials that support the material facts stated in the paragraph.[16]

Unlike allegations in a complaint, this fact statement must include citations to supporting materials: "As to each fact, the statement shall refer to the specific portion of the record where the fact may be found."[17] If you represent the moving party, you could reasonably entitle this section "[Moving Party's] Statement of Material Facts." Alternatively, to reflect the moving party's hopes, you could add "Undisputed" before "Material Facts,"

---

15. _See, e.g.,_ D. Ariz. LRCiv. 7.1(a).

16. D. Neb. Civ. R. 56.1(a)(2); _see also_ Malec v. Sanford, 191 F.R.D. 581, 583 (N.D. Ill. 2000) (quoting and interpreting Local Rule 56.1(a) for the United States District Court for the Northern District of Illinois, setting forth a similar format for the moving party's statement of material facts).

17. Ariz. R. Civ. P. 56(c)(3).

although in all but unusual cases, such a title sounds a tad presumptuous before the nonmoving party has an opportunity to respond and identify areas of factual dispute.

Interpreting another court's local rules, one judge has stated that (1) a statement of material facts supporting a motion for summary judgment should "contain only factual allegations . . . limited to facts pertinent to the outcome of the issues identified in the summary judgment motion," and (2) "the numbered paragraphs should be short," containing "only one or two individual allegations, thereby allowing easy response."[18]

The Arizona rules instruct the nonmoving party to respond to the moving party's statement of material facts by identifying areas of factual dispute in much the same way that an answer sets forth denials of allegations in a complaint:

> Any party opposing a motion for summary judgment shall file a statement in the form prescribed by this Rule, specifying those paragraphs in the moving party's statement of facts which are disputed, and also setting forth those facts which establish a genuine issue of material fact or otherwise preclude summary judgment in favor of the moving party.[19]

If you represent the nonmoving party, you might reasonably entitle this section "Response to [Moving Party's] Statement of Material Facts," or "[Nonmoving Party's] Statement of Material Facts," or even "[Nonmoving Party's] Statement of Undisputed and Disputed Material Facts" because you obviously hope that the court will rule that your documents establish a dispute with respect to at least some of the material facts.

Fact statements following this format provide the court with a clear guide to the parties' positions on summary judgment, because the nonmoving party must methodically respond to each factual assertion of the moving party, point by point, organized by numbered paragraphs.

This point/counterpoint format is not popular with all attorneys and in all fields of litigation, so your assigning attorney may prefer a less regimented format when permitted by local rules. Because the point/counterpoint format for fact statements is required by the local rules of many courts, however, and because it provides a systematic guide for the novice litigant, this chapter will adopt it for its instruction and examples.

For illustration, the following represents excerpts from the plaintiff's statement of facts on his motion for summary judgment in a suit alleging race discrimination in violation of federal law:

---

18. *Malec*, 191 F.R.D. at 583.

19. Ariz. R. Civ. P. 56(c)(3). *See also Malec*, 191 F.R.D. at 583-84 (quoting and interpreting N.D. Ill. R. 56.1(b), setting forth a similar format for the opposing party's statement of undisputed and disputed facts). The Arizona rules also permit the nonmoving party to join with the moving party in stipulating to facts not in dispute. Ariz. R. Civ. P. 56(c)(3).

1. Defendant, Irma Barnes, owns and operates "Irma's Diner," a restaurant and bar located in Mesa, Arizona. Barnes employs more than 15 employees in this business. (Exh. D, Barnes Dep. at 3-4.)

2. Plaintiff, Michael Powell, is African American. He worked as the night manager of the bar at Irma's Diner from January 1, 2018 to June 17, 2018. (Exh. B, Personnel Record for Michael Powell.) . . . .

3. . . . .

4. On June 17, 2018, Barnes confronted Powell about Powell's selection of a rhythm and blues band as musical entertainment for the bar. After using several racial slurs in the ensuing discussion, she fired Powell solely because of his race. (Exh. A, Powell Aff. ¶ 8.) . . . .

Barnes's response to the motion for summary judgment should specifically identify which portions of Powell's statement of facts she disputes. To highlight areas of dispute with maximum clarity, you can respond to each of the moving party's paragraphs with a corresponding, identically numbered paragraph:

1. Barnes does not dispute paragraph 1 of Powell's Statement of Facts.

2. Barnes does not dispute paragraph 2 of Powell's Statement of Facts.

3. Barnes does not dispute paragraph 3 of Powell's Statement of Facts.

4. Barnes does not dispute the assertions in paragraph 4 that Barnes fired Powell on June 17, 2018, after confronting Powell about his selection of musical entertainment. Barnes disputes that she used racial slurs or that race played any factor in her termination of Powell's employment. . . .

In addition, Barnes should identify the specific facts that reflect a genuine factual dispute on the material issue of Barnes's racial animus. Unless these facts appear in Powell's fact statement, Barnes normally would state them as "Additional Facts" in a separate section that follows her identification of areas of dispute:

STATEMENT OF UNDISPUTED AND DISPUTED FACTS

1. Barnes does not dispute . . . .

. . . .

4. Barnes does not dispute the assertions . . . musical entertainment. Barnes disputes . . . Powell's employment.

. . . .

ADDITIONAL FACTS

1. Barnes never used racial slurs in Powell's presence, and she fired Powell solely because he displayed insubordination in the face of direct instructions by

Powell to replace the band Barnes had hired. (Plaintiff's Exh. D, Barnes Dep. at 24-25.)

Court rules should then permit the moving party to respond to the nonmoving party's statement of additional facts.[20]

Most court rules requiring separate fact statements for summary judgment can be interpreted to permit you to attach the statement of facts under the same title sheet that states the motion and covers the supporting brief, or that presents the opposition and supporting brief, so long as you set forth the statement of facts separately from the brief itself. Nonetheless, most attorneys prefer to file the formal statement of facts under a caption as a separate document.

V. Supporting Evidentiary Materials

You must support each assertion in your statement of facts with admitted alleged facts from the opposing party's pleading or with facts reflected in affidavits, materials generated through discovery and disclosure, or other evidence. Federal Rule of Civil Procedure 56 specifically provides that the affidavits must "be made on personal knowledge" and "set out facts that would be admissible in evidence."[21] Therefore, even though your opponent may overlook this matter,[22] your summary judgment materials should preliminarily establish the admissibility of (1) documents included in the summary judgment materials[23] or (2) the expected trial testimony represented in the materials, such as in affidavits or deposition testimony.[24]

For example, the following excerpt from an affidavit asserts the admissibility of other documents under the "business records" exception to the "hearsay rule" of evidence:[25]

---

20. *See Malec*, 191 F.R.D. at 584 (citing to N.D. ILL. R. 56.1(a)(3) (final unnumbered paragraph)).

21. FED. R. CIV. P. 56(c)(4); *see* Vandeventer v. Wabash Nat'l Corp., 867 F. Supp. 790, 798 (N.D. Ind. 1994) (rejecting and expressing displeasure with affidavit that was prepared by attorney and that did not reflect personal knowledge of party who signed affidavit).

22. *See, e.g.*, Catrett v. Johns-Manville Sales Corp., 826 F.2d 33, 37 (D.C. Cir. 1987) (regardless of whether letter qualified as a business records exception to the hearsay rule, trial court properly considered it on summary judgment because other party failed to object to its use).

23. *See* Andrews v. R.W. Hays Co., 998 P.2d 774 (2000) (court disregarded hearsay statements in affidavit because neither the affidavit nor other materials established exception to hearsay rule); *cf.* Olympic Ins. Co. v. H.D. Harrison, Inc., 418 F.2d 669, 670 (5th Cir. 1969) (document produced in ordinary course of business was sufficiently reliable to form basis for summary judgment).

24. *See Malec*, 191 F.R.D. at 585. ("[A]lthough the evidence supporting a factual contention need not be admissible itself, it must represent admissible evidence. For example, a deposition transcript is not usually admissible at trial but (obviously) may be used in support of summary judgment; ....").

25. *See* FED. R. EVID. 803(6).

5. The Payroll Action forms in Exhibits B and C are true copies of records that I prepared and kept in the course of my regularly conducted business activity, which includes maintaining such employment records as a uniform practice. Those forms include information within my own knowledge and information that my supervisor transmitted to me on matters within his knowledge.

Some attorneys separately file supporting affidavits and other evidence. If those materials are not voluminous, however, you can more conveniently and appropriately attach them to the formal statement of facts.

VI. The Motion

As with every document that you separately file with the trial court, you should begin your motion with a caption identifying the case and the nature of the document. In the motion itself, you should simply and clearly state your request for action and should briefly introduce the grounds supporting the request.

Unfortunately, many lawyers have developed a tradition of loading motions with abstract boilerplate that says almost nothing about the motion or the dispute:

Defendant, Sun Printing Co., by and through its undersigned attorneys, Jenkins, Powell, and Smith, P.C., hereby moves, pursuant to the Arizona Rules of Civil Procedure, Rule 56, for an order granting summary judgment against Plaintiff, Scott Paper Supply, on the grounds that there exists no genuine issue of material fact and that Defendant is entitled to summary judgment as a matter of law. This motion is supported by the attached memorandum of law, the Statement of Material Facts separately filed with this Court, and the documents and exhibits filed with this Court.

A judge learns almost nothing from such boilerplate. She does not need a superfluous reference to the legal representation; your identity as legal counsel is revealed in your signature at the end of the motion, and as well at the top of the cover page under the format prescribed by some local rules. In addition, the judge is well aware of the basic abstract standards for summary judgment;[26] repeating those standards in the motion adds nothing to her knowledge about your case.

---

26. *See* Noel Fidel, *Some Do's and Don'ts of Motion Writing*, Ariz. B.J., Aug. 1983, at 8, 9 (advising legal writers to omit "canned" recitations of basic summary judgment standards).

The judge will read your motion with greater interest if you clearly and concisely state what relief your client wants and why he is entitled to it. You should convey new information to the court by tailoring the abstract standards to the facts:

Pursuant to Arizona Rule of Civil Procedure 56, the defendant, Sun Printing Co. ("Sun"), moves for summary judgment against the plaintiff, Scott Paper Supply ("Scott"). Sun is entitled to judgment under the UCC Statute of Frauds because Scott cannot genuinely dispute that the agreement alleged by Scott was for paper priced at more than $500 and was never reduced to writing.

This motion is supported by the attached memorandum of law, by the separately filed Statement of Undisputed Facts and accompanying exhibits, and by the record in this case.

By conveying the theme of the full argument, such a motion whets the judge's appetite for the supporting memorandum of law. An even crisper motion could present a more concise summary of the argument:

Defendant, Sun Printing Co., moves for summary judgment against Plaintiff, Scott Paper Supply. *See* Ariz. R. Civ. P. 56. Sun Printing Co. is entitled to judgment because the oral agreement alleged by Scott Paper Supply is unenforceable under the UCC Statute of Frauds as a matter of law. This motion is supported by ....

As terse as this passage may sound, it contains more useful information than the longer string of boilerplate in the first example.

When opposing a motion, you need not state a formal countermotion in the title page of your opposition materials. You may follow the caption immediately with your responsive brief. At the most, you might include a cover page with a brief statement of opposition parallel to the motion:

Plaintiff, Scott Paper Supply ("Scott"), opposes Defendant's motion for summary judgment. Defendant, Sun Printing Co. ("Sun"), is not entitled to judgment as a matter of law, because Scott's supporting materials show that Sun adopted Scott's written and signed confirmation of the agreement, thus satisfying the UCC Statute of Frauds under Ariz. Rev. Stat. Ann. §47-2201(B) (20176). This opposition is supported by the attached memorandum of law, by the ....

VII. The Brief

Your brief, or Memorandum of Law, is your tool of persuasion. With it, you argue for a favorable interpretation of the law and analysis of the facts. A motions brief typically includes three sections:

1. an introduction,
2. an argument, and
3. a conclusion.

In a complex case, you should consider adding a formal statement of the issues at the beginning of your brief. Such a statement of issues would not be typical in a brief supporting or opposing a motion, but it could be helpful in unusual circumstances.

A. The Introduction

The first section of your supporting brief should summarize the facts, with the brief opposing summary judgment sometimes emphasizing material disputes of facts. In either party's brief, you might reasonably title this section "Introduction" or "Summary of Facts." In this introductory section, you can summarize the facts in a more concise and less formal manner than is possible in the separate, formal statement.

For each statement of a fact in this introduction, you should cite to a source—either to (1) the underlying evidentiary sources already in the record or added to the record in your summary judgment materials, or (2) paragraphs in your separately filed statement of facts, which in turn will cite to underlying evidentiary sources. Some courts prefer, or even require, the brief to cite only to paragraphs in the separately filed statement of facts.[27] When court rules or other judicial pronouncements do not specify a preference or requirement, you can exercise discretion to cite either to the original source or to your separately filed fact statement. If, for example, each of the fact statements in the Introduction is supported by a single underlying evidentiary source, such as an affidavit or deposition testimony, citation to that original source could be concise, informative, and helpful to the reader. On the other hand, if each of many fact statements is supported by several underlying sources, or if the citations to some underlying sources are quite lengthy, direct reference to those sources could impede the flow of the Introduction, and your reader will probably prefer more concise citations to the numbered paragraphs in your separately filed statement of facts.

In addition, you may use an introductory section to present a summary of your argument or a combination of facts, procedural history, and a summary of your argument. For example, you might begin your Introduction with a paragraph-long overview of your arguments or the issues in

---

27. *See, e.g., Malec*, 191 F.R.D. at 586.

the case, to provide a context for a summary of the facts in chronological order. Other passages of this book advise against premature legal argument in a statement of facts in other kinds of briefs, such as an appellate brief. However, this admonition applies with less force in the introduction to your summary judgment brief, because you will separately file a formal statement of facts for summary judgment.

Accordingly, the Introduction may be a suitable place to advance any theme that you have developed for your brief. Alternatively, you can express your theme or brief overview of your arguments in the first paragraph of your Argument section.

B. The Argument

Chapter 2 discusses techniques of constructing legal arguments. Indeed, some of the examples in Chapter 2 are taken from sample summary judgment briefs. This section addresses techniques of persuasion peculiar to summary judgment briefs.

Argument on purely legal questions can be crucial in some summary judgment litigation. If the court determines that material facts are not in dispute, or if the parties have stipulated to the absence of factual dispute, the court will decide whether a moving party is entitled to judgment as a matter of law.

Typically, however, the parties will also argue about the presence or absence of a genuine dispute of fact. In such a case, once you have established the law on an issue or subissue, you should thoroughly analyze the facts. As discussed in greater detail in the immediately preceding section, when you argue the facts, remember to cite to your formal, separately filed statement of facts or to the original evidentiary sources that are already in the record or are included in your supporting materials. The samples in this chapter suggest several ways to cite to either kind of source; unless local rules specify a format, any reasonable citation form is acceptable.

Also, remember to incorporate the standards for summary judgment into your argument. For example, if you are moving for summary judgment, you should not argue that the preponderance of the evidence shows that Sun Printing Co. objected to the contents of the confirmation within ten days after receipt. Such an argument gives the impression that you are inappropriately asking the judge to resolve a factual issue without a trial. Instead, your brief should refer to the "undisputed evidence" and the inferences that can be drawn from it, thus properly asserting the absence of a factual dispute.

Conversely, if you are opposing summary judgment, your brief should remind the judge periodically that nothing more than a genuine and material question of fact is needed to defeat summary judgment. In making this point, you should not simply reiterate the abstract standard; rather, you should identify issues of fact that make summary judgment inappropriate:

Scott Paper Supply's letter confirming the purchase agreement is dated September 1 (Exh. 2), and Scott's Distribution Manager personally mailed it that day (Exh. 3, Connor Aff. ¶3). Scott Paper Supply never received any objection to the terms of the confirmation. (*Id.* ¶4.) Moreover, Sun Printing Co. concedes that it has no record of making any such objection. (Exh. 4, Sun's Ans. to Scott's First Set of Inter., No. 23.)

Opposition facts

In direct opposition to Sun Printing Co.'s assertions, this evidence shows that Sun Printing Co. received the confirmation and failed to object to it. At the very least, this evidence raises a genuine dispute of fact that must be resolved at trial.

Dispute of fact

C. The Conclusion

You should end each section of the argument of your brief with a conclusion about the topic of that section, similar to the conclusion stated in the point heading that introduces the argument. Together, the point heading and the conclusion provide maximum emphasis in their positions as the first and last statements the judge reads within a section. Finally, as illustrated in Chapter 2, the entire brief should end with a section entitled "Conclusion" that encompasses all the arguments of the brief.

VIII. Summary

To prepare a motion for summary judgment,

1. draft a motion that requests summary judgment and briefly introduces the judge to the grounds for your motion;

2. prepare evidentiary materials that will support your statement of facts, if they are not already in the record;

3. draft a separate statement of facts that cites to the supporting materials; and

4. draft a supporting brief that

   a. summarizes the facts and procedural history,

   b. argues the law and facts relating to the issues, with attention to the standards for summary judgment, and

   c. states your conclusions.

When opposing a motion for summary judgment, you should prepare a brief and a separate statement of facts with supporting materials. To oppose a motion or to reply to an opposition brief, you need not file a separate motion. Instead, you should submit a brief that responds to the arguments presented in the preceding brief.

Study the following sample and think about the law and facts that you would need to respond successfully to it. For further practice with summary judgment, perform Assignments 4 and 5 in the Appendix. Along with Assignment 3 in the Appendix, Assignment 5 presents evidence with which the plaintiff in the sample below can oppose the motion for summary judgment, partly by contesting the moving party's factual assertions.

Sample

ARIZONA SUPERIOR COURT

MARICOPA COUNTY

CHARLOTTE REMBAR, Plaintiff, v. ALEXANDER HART d.b.a. COMCON, Defendant.	No. C732431 Defendant Hart's Motion for Summary Judgment (Judge Wisdom)

Defendant Alexander Hart d.b.a. Comcon moves for summary judgment on all claims in this action. Under Arizona Rule of Civil Procedure 56, Hart is entitled to judgment as a matter of law because the undisputed facts show that Hart did not promise Rembar job security and did not discharge Rembar for an unlawful reason or in a wrongful manner.

This motion is supported by the attached Memorandum of Law, the separately filed Statement of Material Facts, and the entire record before the Court.

August 5, 2018

_____

Lisa Hall
Kendricks, Hall, & Oats, P.C.
3310 Alma School Rd., Suite 200
Mesa, Arizona 85283
(480) 839-0365
Bar No. 0076089

MEMORANDUM OF LAW IN SUPPORT OF
MOTION FOR SUMMARY JUDGMENT

I. INTRODUCTION

As documented and set forth more fully in Defendant Hart's Statement of Material Facts ("Hart SofF"), Alexander Hart employed Charlotte Rembar as a computer systems consultant for Hart's sole proprietorship, Comcon. (Hart SofF ¶ 2.) Although Hart distributed an employment manual to Rembar, their employment contract permitted either party to terminate the contract at will. (Hart SofF ¶¶ 2-5.)

On November 1, 2017, Hart discharged Rembar because of her "negative attitude." (Hart Sof F ¶¶ 7-8.) During her employment, Rembar often flirted with Hart, and Hart sometimes returned the flirtations; however, Hart and Rembar did not have a romantic relationship, and Hart never made any unwelcome advances toward Rembar. (Hart SofF ¶ 6.)

Rembar has asserted four claims for relief in her complaint: (1) breach of an alleged promise of job security, (2) sex discrimination in violation of the Arizona Civil Rights Act ("the ACRA"), (3) wrongful discharge in violation of public policy, and (4) intentional infliction of emotional distress. Because the record shows that Hart employed Rembar at will and that Hart discharged Rembar for a legitimate business reason and in a proper manner, Hart is entitled to judgment as a matter of law on all these claims.

II. ARGUMENT

A. Hart did not breach his employment contract with Rembar by discharging Rembar for her negative attitude.

"The employment relationship is severable at the pleasure of either the employee or the employer unless both the employee and the employer have signed a written contract to the contrary. . . ." Ariz. Rev. Stat. Ann. § 23-1501(2) (2016). In some circumstances, an employee manual can become part of the employment contract, and promises of job security in the manual can restrict the employer's freedom to terminate the contract. *See id.* Nonetheless, even assuming for purposes of summary judgment that Hart and Rembar's employment contract included the terms of the Comcon Policy Manual, Hart did not breach those terms for two reasons. First, neither the Policy Manual nor any other term of the contract imposed any restriction on Hart's freedom to terminate Rembar's employment. Second, even if the contract permitted Hart to fire Rembar only for unsatisfactory performance, her negative attitude created such grounds for discharge.

1. The Employment Contract Remained Terminable at Will.

Even assuming the Comcon Policy Manual was incorporated into the employment contract, the manual did not change the at-will nature of the contract because it did not contain requisite "provisions of job security." *Leikvold v. Valley View Cmty. Hosp.*, 141 Ariz. 544, 547, 688 P.2d 170, 173 (1984) (quoting *Pine River State Bank v. Mettille*, 333 N.W.2d 622, 628 (Minn. 1983)). Because the terms of the contract "are clear and unambiguous, the construction of the contract is a question of law for the court" and thus is appropriate for summary judgment. *Id.* at 548, 688 P.2d at 174.

Comcon hired Rembar for an indefinite term of employment, rather than for a fixed term. (Hart SofF ¶ 2.) The terms of Comcon's Policy Manual unambiguously left Hart free to terminate his contract with Rembar at his will. No provision of the Policy Manual purports to restrict the grounds for discharge of an employee. (Hart SofF ¶ 3.) Instead, the only provisions relating to termination affirmatively reserve Hart's right to discharge employees. (Hart SofF ¶¶ 4-5.) Because Rembar had worked at Comcon for more than 60 days, she was classified as a nonprobationary employee at the time of her discharge. (Hart SofF ¶¶ 2, 4-5.) Under the heading "Nonprobationary Employment," the Policy Manual especially emphasizes a particular ground for discharge: "Comcon reserves the right to terminate the employment of any employee who is not performing satisfactorily." (Hart SofF ¶ 5.) However, it does not state or even suggest that unsatisfactory performance is the exclusive ground for discharge. Absent such a stated restriction, Hart remains free under the general rule to terminate the contract for any reason or for no reason at all.

Hart's employment contract with Rembar was terminable at will.

2. Hart Validly Fired Rembar for Unsatisfactory Performance.

Even if the Policy Manual had identified unsatisfactory performance as the sole ground for discharging nonprobationary employees, Hart would not have breached such a provision.

Hart discharged Rembar because of her "negative attitude." (Hart SofF ¶¶ 7-8.) Because Rembar's position required her to work closely with clients, a pleasant personality and a positive attitude were indispensable qualities for satisfactory job performance. (Hart SofF ¶ 7.) Therefore, even assuming that the employment contract provided for limited job security, Hart did not breach the contract because the undisputed facts show that he discharged Rembar for unsatisfactory performance.

B. Hart did not engage in unlawful sex discrimination.

Because Comcon has always employed fewer than fifteen employees (Hart SofF ¶ 1), Rembar has no claim against Hart under federal employment discrimination law. *See* 42 U.S.C. § 2000e(b) (2012) (defining employers covered by Title VII of the Civil Rights Act of 1964). Comcon is a covered employer under the Arizona Civil Rights Act ("ACRA"), Ariz. Rev. Stat. Ann. § 41-1461(2) (2017); however, he did not violate its provisions.

The ACRA makes it an "unlawful employment practice for an employer: 1. To . . . discharge any individual or otherwise to discriminate against any individual with respect to his compensation, terms, conditions or privileges of employment because of such individual's . . . sex . . . ." Ariz. Rev. Stat. Ann. § 41-1463.B (2017). Rembar alleges that Hart discriminated against her by subjecting her to unwelcome sexual advances and discharging her in retaliation for her refusal to submit to the alleged advances. The record, however, contradicts these allegations.

Rembar's own frequent flirtations with Hart showed that she welcomed Hart's harmless flirtations and attentions. Hart never made advances that were not welcomed by Rembar, and he never conditioned benefits of employment on Rembar's acquiescing to his flirtations. (Hart SofF ¶ 6.) Most important, Rembar's discharge had nothing to do with any flirtations between Hart and Rembar; Hart discharged Rembar solely because of her unsatisfactory job performance. (Hart SofF ¶¶ 7-8.)

As a matter of law, Hart did not engage in sexually discriminatory conduct in violation of the ACRA.

C. Hart is not liable in tort for wrongfully discharging Rembar, because the Arizona Civil Rights Act provides the exclusive remedy for such alleged misconduct.

Before its statutory modification, the common law tort of wrongful discharge imposed liability for a violation of an important public policy reflected in the state's constitution, its statutes, or, in limited circumstances, its judicial decisions. *See Wagenseller v. Scottsdale Mem'l Hosp.*, 147 Ariz. 370, 378-79, 710 P.2d 1025, 1033-34 (1985). Rembar's complaint demands tort damages for common law wrongful discharge in violation of the public policies reflected in the ACRA, a tort claim previously recognized in this state. *See Broomfield v. Lundell*, 159 Ariz. 349, 767 P.2d 697 (Ct. App. 1988). Her claim fails as a matter of law, however, both on the facts in this record and through statutory preemption.

First, as stated in arguments A and B above, Hart did not engage in sexual harassment or any other sexually discriminatory employment practice that would violate the policies of the ACRA. Second, even if Rembar can genuinely dispute those facts, her wrongful discharge claim is now governed by the Arizona Employment Protection Act ("AEPA"), Ariz. Rev. Stat. Ann. §23-1501 (2016).

The AEPA provides that an employer may be liable for discharging an employee "in violation of a statute of this state." Ariz. Rev. Stat. Ann. § 23-1501(3)(b) (2016). If the violated statute provides its own civil remedies, however, those remedies are exclusive; indeed, the AEPA lists the ACRA as its first example of a source of such exclusive remedies:

> [T]he remedies provided to an employee for a violation of the statute are the exclusive remedies for the violation of the statute or the public policy set forth in or arising out of the statute, including the following:
> (i) The civil rights act prescribed in title 41, chapter 9.

Id.; *see also* Ariz. Rev. Stat. Ann. § 41-1481 (2017) (setting forth enforcement procedures and remedies for violations of the ACRA). Because Rembar bases her wrongful discharge claim on alleged violations of the ACRA, her remedy is limited to the relief available in the ACRA. *See Cronin v. Sheldon*, 195 Ariz. 531, 991 P.2d 231 (1999) (finding that the AEPA constitutionally preempted the tort remedy recognized in *Broomfield*).

Accordingly, regardless of whether Rembar can establish a factual dispute about the reasons for her discharge, Hart is entitled to summary judgment on Rembar's tort claim of wrongful discharge.

D. Hart did not engage in extreme and outrageous conduct and therefore is not liable for infliction of emotional distress.

The AEPA would not preempt a claim of intentional infliction of emotional distress for an unlawfully discriminatory discharge. *Cronin*, 195 Ariz.

at 541, 991 P.2d at 241 (dictum). However, Hart is not liable for intentional infliction of emotional distress unless his conduct was so "extreme and outrageous" that it fell "within that quite narrow range" of conduct "at the very extreme edge of the spectrum." *Watts v. Golden Age Nursing Home*, 127 Ariz. 255, 258, 619 P.2d 1032, 1035 (1980). As discussed above, Hart discharged Rembar for legitimate business reasons. (Hart SofF ¶¶ 7-8.) Moreover, Hart communicated his decision in a normal professional manner. (Hart SofF ¶ 8.) Because of its economic consequences, termination of employment is often an extremely distressing event for the discharged employee. However, discharge for business reasons is an economic fact of life and hardly amounts to a basis for tort liability.

Moreover, even if Rembar could establish a dispute of fact regarding the reason for her discharge, the dispute would not be material. "[I]t is extremely rare to find conduct in the employment context that will rise to the level of outrageousness necessary to provide a basis for recovery for the tort of intentional infliction of emotional distress." *Mintz v. Bell Atl. Sys. Leasing Int'l, Inc.*, 183 Ariz. 550, 554, 905 P.2d 559, 563 (Ct. App. 1995) (quoting *Cox v. Keystone Carbon Co.*, 861 F.2d 390, 395 (3d Cir. 1988)).

In *Mintz*, an employee was hospitalized after suffering a nervous breakdown as the alleged result of gender discrimination in the workplace. The employer terminated her disability benefits, ordered her to return to work, and then—while the employee was again hospitalized after returning to work for one day—notified her of a reassignment of her duties by a letter delivered to the hospital. *Id.* at 552, 905 P.2d at 561. The Arizona Court of Appeals affirmed a finding that, as a matter of law, this alleged conduct was not extreme and outrageous, even assuming the employer had failed to promote the employee because of gender discrimination and assuming the employer knew that the employee was unusually susceptible to emotional distress. *Id.* at 553-54, 905 P.2d at 562-63.

Based on cases such as *Mintz*, a federal district court has characterized Arizona's standard for extreme and outrageous conduct as one requiring "extraordinary" conduct. *Tempesta v. Motorola, Inc.*, 92 F. Supp. 2d 973, 987 (D. Ariz. 1999). Applying *Mintz*, the *Tempesta* court granted summary judgment for the defendant employer on the employee's claim of intentional infliction of emotional distress, even after assuming the truth of the employee's allegations that he had suffered harassment and wrongful termination because of his sex. *Id.* at 986-87.

It is even clearer in this case that Hart did not engage in extreme and outrageous conduct. Even if Rembar's allegations of mild sexual advances and retaliatory discharge were supported by the record, that conduct would not satisfy the demanding test of egregiousness applied in Arizona courts. As a matter of law, Hart is not liable for intentional infliction of emotional distress.

III. CONCLUSION

Rembar cannot genuinely dispute Hart's showing on the facts that Hart promised Rembar no job security, Hart discharged Rembar for poor performance, and Hart did not engage in sexual harassment. Therefore, Hart is entitled to summary judgment on all claims.

August 5, 2018

_____

Lisa Hall for
Kendricks, Hall, & Oats, P.C.
3310 Alma School Rd., Suite 200
Mesa, Arizona 85283

COPY OF THE FOREGOING MAILED
August 5, 2018 to:
Roberts and Cray
101 E. Washington St., Suite 600
Phoenix, Arizona 85001

ARIZONA SUPERIOR COURT
MARICOPA COUNTY

CHARLOTTE REMBAR, Plaintiff, v. ALEXANDER HART d.b.a. COMCON, Defendant.	No. C732431 Defendant Hart's Statement of Material Facts and Exhibits Supporting Motion for Summary Judgment (Judge Wisdom)

For purposes of summary judgment only, Defendant Alexander Hart d.b.a. Comcon presents the following material facts:

1. Alexander Hart is the sole owner and manager of Comcon, a firm that provides expert consulting on computer systems to businesses in the Phoenix metropolitan area. From January to November 2017, Comcon employed eight employees other than Hart himself; Comcon has never employed a greater number of employees before or since. [Hart Aff. ¶ 1 (Exh. D).]

2. Effective January 1, 2017, Hart hired Charlotte Rembar for the position of Comcon consultant at a salary of $5,000/month. [Dec. 30, 2016 Payroll Action (Exh. B).] The only written record of Rembar's contract with Comcon is the Payroll Action form that states her date of hire and her salary. [Hart Aff. ¶ 2 (Exh. D).] The term of Rembar's employment was left indefinite. [*Id.*]

3. At or before the time of Rembar's hiring, Alexander Hart gave Rembar a Policy Manual that summarizes many of the personnel procedures at Comcon. [Policy Manual (Exh. A).] The Policy Manual includes one example of a ground for discharging a nonprobationary employee, but it does not explicitly limit Comcon's right to discharge an employee for any other reason. [*Id.* at § IV.]

4. Under the heading *Probationary Employment*, section IV.A of the policy manual provides that "Each employee will work on probationary status during his or her first 60 days of employment. During this probationary period, Comcon reserves the right to terminate the employee for any reason or for no reason at all." [*Id.* at § IV.A.]

5. Under the heading *Nonprobationary Employment*, section IV.B of the policy manual provides that "Comcon reserves the right to terminate the

employment of any employee who is not performing satisfactorily." [*Id.* at § IV.B.]

6. From the beginning of her employment at Comcon, Rembar sought to attract Hart's attentions with casual flirtations, such as references to his appearance and suggestive smiles. Hart returned the flirtations in a similar manner, but no sexual relationship developed between them. Any flirtations directed by Hart toward Rembar were welcomed, and even invited, by her. Hart never demanded sexual favors from Rembar, and he never conditioned any benefits of employment on Rembar's submitting to a sexual demand or otherwise reacting to a flirtation. [Hart Aff. ¶ 3 (Exh. D).]

7. In the fall of 2017, Hart became dissatisfied with Rembar's performance. Specifically, she displayed a negative attitude in her work. Because Comcon consultants must work closely with their clients, a consultant with a negative attitude severely hampers Comcon's business relationships. [Hart Aff. ¶ 4 (Exh. D).]

8. Effective November 2, 2017, Hart terminated Rembar's employment because of her negative attitude. [Nov. 1, 2017 Payroll Action (Exh. C).] Hart communicated the discharge to Rembar in a normal, professional manner. [Hart Aff. ¶ 4 (Exh. D).]

August 5, 2018

Lisa Hall
Kendricks, Hall, & Oats, P.C.
3310 Alma School Rd., Suite 200
Mesa, Arizona 85283
(480) 839-0365
Bar No. 0076089

Exhibit A

POLICY MANUAL
for Employees of Comcon

I. Introduction

The success of Comcon lies in its ability to recruit and retain the best employees available nationally. To promote a stable and productive workforce, Comcon provides attractive terms and conditions of employment, including those set forth in the following policies.

II. Salary

A. Initial Salary. . . .

B. Change in Salary. . . .

III. Holidays, Vacations, Sick Leave

A. Holidays. . . .

B. Personal Leave. . . .

IV. Termination

A. Probationary Employment

Each employee will work on probationary status during his or her first 60 days of employment. During this probationary period, Comcon reserves the right to terminate the employee for any reason or for no reason at all.

B. Nonprobationary Employment

Comcon reserves the right to terminate the employment of any employee who is not performing satisfactorily.

Exhibit B

PAYROLL ACTION

Nature of Action

___X___ New Hire   _____ Change in Pay _____ Termination

Previous Pay ___N.A._____

New Pay ___$5,000/mo._____

Effective Date ___Jan. 1, 2017_____

Reason for Change or Termination

Comments

   Consultant

Date ___Dec. 30, 2016_____

Processed By ___Leslie West_____

Exhibit C

PAYROLL ACTION

Nature of Action

_____ New Hire   _____ Change in Pay ___X___ Termination

Previous Pay ___$5,000/mo._____

New Pay ___N.A._____

Effective Date ___Nov. 2, 2017_____

Reason for Change or Termination

___Negative Attitude_____

Comments

Date ___Nov. 1, 2017_____

Processed By ___Leslie West_____

Exhibit D

AFFIDAVIT OF ALEXANDER HART
IN SUPPORT OF MOTION FOR SUMMARY JUDGMENT

Maricopa County, Arizona

Alexander Hart, under oath, swears to the following information from personal knowledge:

1. I am the sole owner and manager of Comcon, a firm that provides consulting services to businesses on the development and use of computer systems. From January to November 2017, I employed eight employees, the largest workforce that I have employed since I formed Comcon in 2008. Specifically, during that period I employed a secretary, an accountant, and six consultants.

2. Effective January 1, 2017, I hired Charlotte Rembar for the position of consultant. The Payroll Action form identified in this motion as Exhibit B is the only written record of Rembar's hiring and her terms of employment. Rembar and I understood at the time of hiring that her term of employment was indefinite. On or before the time of her hiring, I gave her a Comcon Policy Manual, which reaffirms that Rembar had no definite term of employment or guarantee of continued employment.

3. From the beginning of her employment at Comcon, Rembar sought to attract my attentions with casual flirtations such as suggestive smiles and compliments on my grooming and appearance. She made it clear that she welcomed reciprocation, and I often returned her flirtations with similar smiles and comments. Our personal relationship never advanced beyond these casual flirtations. Specifically, we never had a sexual relationship, and I never made any unwelcome sexual advances toward Rembar, nor did I ever condition any benefits of employment on Rembar's submitting to any sexual demands or otherwise reacting in any way to my flirtations.

4. Sometime in the fall of 2017, I began to notice that Rembar displayed a negative attitude about me, about herself, and about her work. I find it extremely important to maintain a workforce with positive attitudes and pleasant personalities, because the consultants work closely with clients, and our business thus depends on maintaining good personal relationships with clients. To ensure that we maintained those relationships, I discharged Rem-

bar effective November 2, 2017, to rid our workforce of her negativism. I communicated the discharge to Rembar in a normal, professional manner in an office meeting on November 1, 2017.

5. The Payroll Action forms in Exhibits B and C are true copies of records that were prepared and kept under my direction by my personal secretary, Leslie West, in the course of her regularly conducted business activity, which includes maintaining such employment records as a uniform practice. Those forms include information within Ms. West's own knowledge and information that I transmitted to her on matters within my knowledge. The Policy Manual in Exhibit A is a true copy of a manual that I drafted and printed in June 2009 and have since distributed to all employees.

I swear under oath that the foregoing is true:

_____   _____

Alexander Hart   Date

Chapter 6

Motion to Exclude Evidence

Before Trial

Black's Law Dictionary defines "in limine" as: "preliminary; presented to only the judge, before or during trial."[1] The typical motion in limine is a motion to exclude evidence before trial, or at least to require opposing counsel to raise the question of admissibility outside the presence of the jury if the trial is underway. Conversely, but much more rarely, an advocate may use it to move for admission of evidence before trial if she anticipates an objection to the evidence.[2]

Thus, in contrast to the typical motion for summary judgment, a motion to exclude evidence seeks to define the scope of the trial litigation rather than to dispose of the case before trial. It generally is simpler than a motion for summary judgment. If you can strip the mystery away from the popular Latin phrase, you should have little trouble supporting or opposing the motion.

---

1. BLACK'S LAW DICTIONARY 858 (9th ed. 2009).

2. *See* Hon. Robert E. Bacharach, *Motions in Limine in Oklahoma State and Federal Courts,* 24 OKLA. CITY U. L. REV. 112, 114 (1999).

I. Pretrial Exclusion of Evidence

The Federal Rules of Civil Procedure provide that "the admissibility of evidence" is appropriate for consideration and disposition in a pretrial conference.[3] Additionally, those rules and the Federal Rules of Evidence implicitly authorize a trial court to rule on pretrial motions to exclude evidence other than in pretrial conference, or they at least leave undisturbed the court's inherent power to do so.[4]

During trial, attorneys can and do object to evidence offered for admission.[5] However, pretrial rulings on complex, potentially prejudicial, or especially significant evidentiary matters tend to improve the efficiency and quality of the trial proceedings.[6]

For example, suppose a visitor to your client's factory sues your client for injuries sustained at the factory. At trial, the plaintiff's counsel asks a defense witness in front of the jury to confirm that your client offered to pay the plaintiff's medical expenses. You can immediately object that the question seeks a response that may lead the jury to find liability on an improper ground.[7] In most jurisdictions, the judge will sustain your objection and will order the witness not to provide the solicited testimony.[8] However, the damage to your client's case may be irreparable if the question alone improperly influences the jury's deliberations, despite the court's admonishments to the jury to ignore it. You could have protected your client more effectively had you earlier persuaded the judge to exclude the evidence before trial and to order the parties and their attorneys to refrain from referring to the evidence in any way at trial.

Additionally, pretrial litigation of complex evidentiary matters permits more thorough written and oral argument by the parties and more considered deliberation by the court, all without disrupting an ongoing trial. Moreover, pretrial disposition of objections to particularly significant evidence gives the parties an opportunity to modify their trial strategies or to reassess their settlement positions.[9]

---

3. FED. R. CIV. P. 16(c)(2)(C).

4. *See generally* FED. R. EVID. 103(c) ("In jury cases, proceedings shall be conducted, to the extent practicable, so as to prevent inadmissible evidence from being suggested to the jury by any means, such as making statements or offers of proof or asking questions in the hearing of the jury."); Charles W. Gamble, *The Motion* in Limine: *A Pretrial Procedure That Has Come of Age*, 33 ALA. L. REV. 1, 2 & n.6 (1981).

5. *See* FED. R. EVID. 103(a) (unnumbered paragraph following subsections (1) & (2)) (referring to rulings "admitting or excluding evidence, either at or before trial").

6. *See* FED. R. CIV. P. 16(a) (stating objectives of pretrial conference).

7. *See* FED. R. EVID. 409, Advisory Comm. Note. Exclusion of such evidence also promotes a generally humanitarian policy of encouraging such assistance, regardless of liability. *Id.*

8. *See* FED. R. EVID. 409.

9. *See* Gamble, *supra* note 4, at 8-10.

II. Format

Unless local court rules specifically address motions in limine,[10] you should follow procedural rules governing motions generally.[11] Beyond that, the common format is a product of custom and common sense. As with any legal document, you can best support or oppose a motion to exclude evidence if you understand the purposes of your document and draft it accordingly.

III. The Motion

In a motion to exclude evidence, you should simply and clearly state the requested action and briefly summarize the grounds for the motion. In describing the relief requested, you probably should go beyond generally asking for exclusion of certain evidence. To ensure effective protection, you should describe the objectionable evidence as inclusively as possible and should request an order specifically prohibiting the opposing party from referring to the evidence:

The defendant, Axxon Corp., moves for a pretrial order excluding all evidence that Axxon Corp. offered to provide medical care and to pay the medical expenses of the plaintiff, Herb Taylor. The evidence is inadmissible under Federal Rule of Evidence 409.

Specifically, Axxon Corp. requests an order directing Taylor and his counsel (1) to refrain from referring to such an offer in any way in the presence of the jury during voir dire and all subsequent proceedings, and (2) to take all necessary steps to ensure that their witnesses avoid such references.

To oppose a motion to exclude evidence, you need not file a separate motion; you can simply file a brief that opposes the original motion. At the most, you might want to draft a cover page with a caption and a paragraph that parallels the motion in summarizing the ruling you seek and the supporting grounds:

---

10. *See, e.g.*, Ariz. R. Civ. P. 7.2(b), (c) (specifying timing for motions in limine and disallowing reply briefs).

11. *See, e.g.*, D. Ariz. Lrciv. 7.2(a)-(e) (specifying requirements for motions and for opening, answering, and reply briefs in this federal trial court); Ariz. R. Civ. P. 7.1(a) (setting forth general requirements for motions in this state's trial practice).

Plaintiff Herb Taylor opposes Defendant Axxon Corp.'s motion to exclude evidence of Axxon Corp.'s offer to provide and pay for medical care. The evidence is admissible to show the extent of Taylor's injuries. The court should not exclude the evidence for this limited purpose.

IV. The Brief

A brief supporting or opposing a motion to exclude evidence, or any other motion, is often referred to as a "Memorandum of Law." When preparing a brief supporting a motion to exclude evidence, you ordinarily should follow the familiar pattern of Introduction, Argument, and Conclusion. The party opposing your motion should file a responsive brief that directly answers the arguments in your supporting brief. Similarly, if local rules permit a reply brief, the moving party can rebut the counterarguments presented in the opposing brief.[12]

On a motion for summary judgment, you will address at least some of the claims or defenses of the litigation on their merits. In contrast, on a motion to exclude evidence, you will typically focus more narrowly on the admissibility of certain evidence. Consequently, in your supporting or opposing briefs, you should address the merits of claims or defenses only to the extent necessary to address some element of admissibility, such as relevance. This narrow focus affects the scope of the introduction and argument sections of the briefs.

A. The Introduction

In the introductory section of a brief supporting a motion to exclude evidence, you need not include a full statement of facts and procedural history. In light of the motion's focus on an evidentiary issue, your introduction need summarize only those portions of the facts and procedural history necessary to an understanding of that specific issue. You should accompany your motion with any necessary factual support for your assertions, such as affidavits or documents generated during discovery or prepared specifically for the motion. Additionally, you should cite to such attachments or to other parts of the record. Absent a local rule specifying a specific format, any reasonable citation form is acceptable; two examples are presented below. Finally, your introduction should explain why you expect the nonmoving party to attempt to introduce the evidence at trial and why the court should resolve the matter before trial, unless you choose to address those matters in the Argument section.

---

12. *Compare* D. ARIZ. LRCIV. 7.2(b)-(d) (for all motions in this federal trial court, referring to the moving party's brief, the responsive memorandum, and the reply memorandum) *with* ARIZ. R. CIV. P. 7.2(c) (disallowing reply briefs for motions in limine in this state's trial courts).

For example, the brief supporting the motion might begin with the following introductory points:

MEMORANDUM IN SUPPORT OF MOTION TO EXCLUDE EVIDENCE

I. Introduction

Herb Taylor, a sales representative for Corbin Heavy Equipment Co., brought this tort action against Axxon Corp. He alleges negligence in the maintenance of the Axxon manufacturing plant in Albuquerque, New Mexico.

Nature of the case

Specifically, Taylor alleges that, while touring the Axxon plant in January 2009 with Axxon General Manager Jerry Olshon, Taylor lost his footing, fell backwards, and struck his head against a forklift. [Compl. ¶¶ 3, 4.] According to Olshon's deposition testimony, as a humanitarian gesture, Olshon immediately offered on behalf of Axxon to provide transportation to the nearest hospital and to pay for Taylor's medical expenses. [Olshon Dep. 18.] Taylor later developed difficulties with his eyesight, which he alleges are the result of his accident at the Axxon plant. [Compl. ¶ 6.]

Facts

The critical issue in this case is whether Axxon negligently maintained its plant, causing Taylor to fall. Taylor's counsel has examined Olshon extensively during deposition about Olshon's offer to pay medical expenses, leading Axxon to believe that Taylor's counsel will attempt to introduce that evidence at trial.

Belief that evidence will be introduced

Evidence of Olshon's offer to pay medical expenses is inadmissible to establish Axxon's liability, and Axxon will not introduce it for other purposes. The evidence must be excluded before trial, because reference to it even in a question to a witness would indelibly and improperly influence the jury.

Need for pretrial exclusion

When opposing a motion, you should state any facts and procedural history that are material to your argument and that are not fairly stated in the opening brief:

I. Introduction

Issues for trial

Plaintiff Taylor is prepared to prove that Defendant Axxon Corp.'s negligence proximately caused Taylor to lose nearly all sight in his right eye. Axxon apparently seeks to show that Taylor's injuries at the Axxon factory were slight and that Taylor's partial blindness must be unrelated. *See* Answer ¶ 6. Thus, the extent of Taylor's injuries at the factory is in issue.

Relevance of evidence on particular issue

Taylor plans to introduce Axxon Corp.'s offer to provide and pay for medical care as evidence that Axxon's agent at the scene of the accident determined Taylor's injuries to be serious. The evidence is admissible for this purpose and should not be excluded.

B. The Argument

The argument section of a motion to exclude evidence follows the same general pattern discussed in Chapter 2. Each section or subsection within the argument should state a contention in a point heading, analyze the law and the facts, and restate or summarize the contention in a conclusion.

1. Legal Rules

In the statement of legal standards in the opening brief supporting a motion to exclude evidence, you typically will focus on rules of evidence that restrict admissibility. If you prefer a thorough analysis, you may choose to develop the legal standards in some detail:

Even relevant evidence is inadmissible "if its probative value is substantially outweighed by the danger" that it will cause "unfair prejudice, confusion of the issues, or misleading the jury." Fed. R. Evid. 403. Evidence presents such a danger if it has "an undue tendency to suggest a decision on an improper basis, commonly, though not necessarily, an emotional one." *Id.*, Advisory Committee Note.

In this case, evidence of Powell's membership in the Black Panther Party more than 40 years ago has little, if any, probative value....

On the other hand, the general standards for some of the more commonly invoked evidentiary rules are familiar to judges and attorneys. Therefore, you could exercise stylistic discretion to present those standards summarily, or even implicitly, and to move more quickly to the fact analysis:

Evidence of Powell's former membership in the Black Panther Party should be excluded because its probative value is substantially outweighed by its potential for confusion and unfair prejudice. *See* Fed. R. Evid. 403. The F.B.I. file report shows that Powell was a member of the Black Panther Party more than 40 years ago for the brief period of eight months. During that time, Powell participated in political rallies and peaceful protests against police brutality, and he met with other members in political strategy meetings....

2. Application of Rules to Facts

As in any legal argument, the fact analysis should lead to a conclusion by relating the facts to the legal standard:

Purely political activities such as these have little or no probative value on the merits of Powell's position that he did nothing to provoke Officer Beatty's assault. As the record shows, when Powell was a member of the Black Panther Party for less than a year in 1970, he did not espouse violence or engage in any violent activities.	**Little relevance**
The primary effect of evidence of Powell's membership would be to inflame the passions of the jury. Despite the nonviolent role that Powell played as a member of the organization, many view the Black Panther Party as a radical organization that actively sought confrontation with established institutions such as police agencies. Some jurors undoubtedly would react emotionally to the controversial image of the Black Panthers.	**Unfair prejudice**
Moreover, some jurors undoubtedly will confuse the original Black Panther Party, a serious political movement, with an unrelated, less constructive, and more controversial "New Black Panthers Party." ...	

The argument section of an opposing brief or a reply brief will contain similar elements, except that each will be narrowly tailored to respond directly to contentions advanced in the brief that preceded it.

C. The Conclusion

Chapter 2's discussion of conclusions includes examples from sample motions in limine. In summary, you should

1. end each argument in a brief with a conclusion on that argument, and
2. end the entire brief with a general summary of all the arguments and with your request for relief.

This sample Conclusion sums up the theme of a brief that presented a single argument:

III. Conclusion

Officer Beatty is on trial in this civil suit. By offering evidence of Powell's membership in the Black Panther Party, Officer Beatty is inappropriately trying to turn the tables and put Powell on trial for his nonviolent political activities more than four decades ago. The evidence should be excluded because its minimal probative value, if any, is substantially outweighed by the danger of confusion and unfair prejudice.

V. Summary

To prepare a motion to exclude evidence before trial,

1. draft a motion that simply and clearly requests the court to exclude specified evidence and to prohibit the parties from referring to the evidence at trial;
2. draft a supporting brief that
   a. introduces the facts and procedural history relevant to the motion,
   b. argues the law and facts relating to the evidentiary issues, and
   c. states your conclusions; and
3. attach any documentary evidence or affidavits necessary to support your motion, or refer to evidence already in the record.

To oppose a motion to exclude evidence, or to reply to an opposition brief, you need not file a separate motion. Instead, you should submit a brief that responds to the arguments presented in the preceding brief.

For further practice with motions to exclude evidence, complete Assignment 6 in the Appendix.

The following sample is taken from the files of an actual case, although it is reproduced here with lesser line spacing than in the original.

Sample

Deborah E. Driggs
State Bar No. 6081
David L. Keily
State Bar No. 12345
SACKS, TIERNEY, KASEN & KERRICK, P.A.
3300 North Central Avenue, Suite 2000
Phoenix, Arizona 85012-1576
Telephone: (602) 279-4900
Attorneys for Defendants Rayner

SUPERIOR COURT OF ARIZONA
MARICOPA COUNTY

AGUA FRIA SAND & ROCK, INC., an Arizona corporation, Plaintiff, v. Estate of DALE FAY RAYNER, Deceased; JACK RAYNER, JR., Personal Representative of the Estate of DALE FAY RAYNER, Deceased; Estate of JACK RAYNER, JR., Personal Representative of the Estate of JACK RAYNER, SR., Deceased; JACK RAYNER, JR., Defendants.	No. C-531100 MOTION IN LIMINE TO EXCLUDE TESTIMONY AS TO TRANSACTIONS WITH OR STATEMENTS BY JACK M. RAYNER, SR., AND DALE FAY RAYNER (Oral Argument Requested) (Hon. Gloria G. Ybarra)

Defendants Rayner move for an order excluding testimony by the plaintiff or its agents, or questions or statements by its counsel, about transactions with or statements by Jack M. Rayner, Sr., and Dale Fay Rayner. This motion is made pursuant to Arizona's Deadman's statute, Ariz. Rev. Stat. Ann. § 12-2251 (Supp. 1985), and is supported by the attached Memorandum of Points and Authorities.

DATED December 29, 1986.

By _____
Deborah E. Driggs
David L. Keily, for
SACKS, TIERNEY, KASEN & KERRICK, P.A.
Attorneys for Defendants

MEMORANDUM OF POINTS AND AUTHORITIES

I. FACTUAL BACKGROUND

Plaintiff Agua Fria Sand & Rock, Inc. (Agua Fria) brought this suit against defendants for fraud, breach of a duty of due care, and breach of a lease. Agua Fria was the assignee of a leasehold interest in certain real property owned by defendants. On this property, Agua Fria operated a sand and gravel mine. In February 1980, Agua Fria's plant and equipment were destroyed by a flood. After the flood, Agua Fria moved its operations to a new site on the property.

Agua Fria alleges that the defendants wrongfully evicted them from the new site. Although Agua Fria occupied the land as a tenant at will, it alleges that the defendants promised to execute and deliver a written lease for a term of 20 years.

The defendants deny that they had promised to execute and deliver a written lease for a term of 20 years to Agua Fria. They allege that Agua Fria was evicted because it had failed to make rental payments and to satisfy other lease obligations.

Jack M. Rayner, Sr., died on October 14, 1982. Dale Fay Rayner died on April 17, 1984. Jack M. Rayner, Jr., is the Personal Representative of the Estates of Jack M. Rayner, Sr., and Dale Fay Rayner. Agua Fria has sued Jack M. Rayner, Jr., in his capacity as Personal Representative of the estates of Jack M. Rayner, Sr., and Dale Fay Rayner.

Questions, argument, or testimony before the jury regarding alleged oral promises made by either testator will improperly influence the jury, even if objection at trial or related proceedings is sustained. Therefore, this Court should exclude all such references before trial.

II. ARGUMENT

The Arizona Deadman's Statute bars admission of testimony of transactions with, or statements by, Jack M. Rayner, Sr., and Dale Fay Rayner.

To reduce the danger of fraudulent testimony, the Arizona Deadman's statute restricts the admission of testimony about transactions with, or about statements made by, the testator in certain suits:

In an action by or against personal representatives, administrators, guardians or conservators in which judgment may be given for or against them as such, neither party shall be allowed to testify against the other as to any transaction with or statement by the testator, intestate or ward unless called to testify thereto by the opposite party, or required to testify thereto by the court. The provisions of this section shall extend to and include all actions by or against the heirs, devisees, legatees or legal representatives of a decedent arising out of any transaction with the decedent.

Ariz. Rev. Stat. Ann. § 12-2251 (Supp. 1985).

The statute clearly applies to this case. First, Agua Fria has filed suit against Jack M. Rayner, Jr., in his capacity as personal representative of the estates of Jack M. Rayner, Sr., and Dale Fay Rayner. Judgment may be granted for or against Jack M. Rayner, Jr., in his capacity as personal representative. Finally, Agua Fria plans to introduce evidence of an alleged oral agreement by the deceased, Jack M. Rayner, Sr., and Dale Fay Rayner, to execute a written lease with a term of 20 years.

The statute authorizes admission of testimony of transactions with or statements by the deceased if "required . . . by the court." Therefore, such admission ultimately lies within the discretion of the trial court. *Mahan v. First Nat'l Bank*, 139 Ariz. 138, 140, 677 P.2d 301, 303 (Ct. App. 1984). The trial court's determination to admit testimony of transactions with or statements by the decedent will be upheld only if (1) independent evidence corroborates the transaction with the decedent, and (2) an injustice will result if the testimony is rejected. *Id.*

Agua Fria has no independent evidence to support its claims that the deceased promised to execute and deliver a written lease of the premises for a term of 20 years. Instead, Agua Fria rests on the bald assertion that the deceased made such promises. This type of uncorroborated testimony is exactly what the statute was intended to proscribe.

Second, no injustice will result from exclusion of testimony of transactions with or statements by Jack M. Rayner, Sr., and Dale Fay Rayner. The exclusion will apply equally to both parties. Moreover, exclusion of the testimony comports strongly with public policy to render incompetent as witnesses persons who will gain from distortion of transactions with the decedent when death has rendered the decedent incapable of refuting these inaccuracies. *See Carrillo v. Taylor*, 81 Ariz. 14, 299 P.2d 188 (1956). The exclusion will simply preclude Plaintiff Agua Fria from making use of self-serving, uncorroborated declarations about what the deceased supposedly said. Agua Fria should not be able to manufacture lease obligations out of the alleged representations of those who are no longer able to refute them.

III. CONCLUSION

The objectionable testimony in this case is uncorroborated, and its exclusion will not result in an injustice. Therefore, this testimony should be excluded under the applicable Deadman's statute. To prevent evasion of the statute, this Court's order should apply broadly to comments or questions of counsel in front of the jury, as well as to testimony.

December 29, 1986.
SACKS, TIERNEY, KASEN & KERRICK, P.A.

_____
Deborah E. Driggs
David L. Keily
3300 North Central Avenue
Phoenix, Arizona 85012-1576
Attorneys for Defendants

Part III

Appellate
Briefs

Writing appellate briefs differs from most pretrial brief writing in three respects. First, if you have fully tried your case before appeal, you will analyze the issues on appeal on a more complete factual record than was available during the litigation of pretrial motions. Second, in developing your arguments on appeal, you must consider standards of appellate review, which require varying levels of deference to trial court rulings and findings. Third, rules of procedure and local rules typically prescribe a more formal and detailed format for appellate briefs than for most pretrial or trial briefs.

Chapter 7

Standards of
Appellate Review

I. The Record on Appeal

Aside from physical exhibits and some kinds of documentary evidence admitted into court, the proceedings in the trial court are recorded in two records: the trial court clerk's record and the court reporter's transcript.[1] The trial history of a case can usually be most easily traced in the trial court clerk's record, which contains litigation documents filed with the trial court, from the initial pleadings to the notice of appeal. It also includes the written judgment of the court, along with orders reflecting the court's rulings on procedural and other preliminary matters. A docket sheet attached to the clerk's record contains a brief entry for each document in the record. This provides a convenient index to the record and a summary of the history of the litigation.

---

1. *E.g.*, FED. R. APP. P. 10(a).

The reporter's transcript is a record of all the statements made "on the record" in court during the litigation process. It includes oral arguments of the parties on motions, testimony of witnesses, rulings from the bench, and instructions to the jury.

Shortly after a disappointed litigant has filed notice of appeal from the judgment of the trial court, the parties on appeal designate the portions of the clerk's record and reporter's transcript that are necessary for the appeal.[2] In some circumstances, other original documents and physical exhibits admitted into evidence may also be forwarded to the appellate court.[3]

Before writing an appellate brief, you must master the record on appeal because the evidence and arguments presented to the trial court help to define the scope of the appellate court's inquiry. Indeed, when referring to testimony, arguments, rulings, or other portions of the trial history, you should carefully cite to the pages of the clerk's record or reporter's transcript that reflect that information. Although rules of procedure or local rules may specify a different citation form, common abbreviations for citation to, for example, page 134 of the clerk's record are "CR at 134," for "clerk's record." Page 383 of the reporter's transcript is commonly cited as "RT at 383" or "Trial Tr. at 383." If either record is bound in multiple volumes, you must also cite to the volume number in some reasonable fashion. For example, you might cite to page 115 of the third volume of the reporter's transcript as "III RT at 115" or "RT, vol. 3, at 115." In any of these citations, you can omit the "at," or replace it with an abbreviation for "page," depending on your style or applicable rules; for example, "CR 134," "RT p. 115"; or "RT, vol. 3, pg. 115." If separate records are not designated by volume numbers, include the date or other clarifying information. Finally, if the opening brief is accompanied by an appendix containing relevant parts of the record, appellate rules of procedure or local court rules may require citation to the appendix rather than to the underlying record.[4] One might cite to such an appendix in any of several reasonable ways, such as "Appendix p. 42," "Appendix at 42," or "App. 42."

II. Standards of Review in the Federal Courts

A. Overview

An appellate court cannot necessarily reverse a trial court's judgment simply because the appellate judges would have decided the case differently on the same record. The appellate court will sometimes limit the degree to which it subjects a trial court determination to appellate scrutiny. To accom-

---

2. *See, e.g.,* FED. R. APP. P. 10(b).

3. *See, e.g.,* FED. R. APP. P. 11(b)(2).

4. *E.g.,* FED. R. APP. P. 28(e).

Chapter 7. Standards of Appellate Review   127

plish this calibration, the appellate court will apply different standards of review to different kinds of trial court findings or rulings.

For example, on a motion for summary judgment or a motion to dismiss an action for failure to state a claim, a trial court does not resolve any factual disputes; instead, it decides as a matter of law whether alleged or undisputed facts satisfy the applicable legal standards. When reviewing a trial court's granting of such a motion, the appellate court will also be deciding matters of law, rather than fact. It will place itself in the position of the trial court and decide "*de novo*," without deference to the trial court's analysis, whether the moving party satisfied its burden on the motion.[5]

In contrast, a jury's verdict or a trial judge's findings of fact rendered after trial represent the fact finder's resolution of factual disputes. When reviewing such findings, an appellate court will restrict its review, deferring substantially to the fact finder's resolution of conflicting evidence. Not surprisingly, appellate courts rarely overturn findings of fact.

Thus, to effectively argue your case on appeal, you must consider the standard of review, or the degree to which the appellate court will defer to a finding or ruling made in the trial court. Indeed, the outcome of some appeals will depend directly on the standard of review that the appellate court chooses to apply.[6]

Appellate standards of review in the federal court system will serve as a starting point for your understanding standards that apply in a state court. Under the two most important standards—and subject to a "constitutional facts" exception discussed at the end of this chapter—an appellate court restricts its review of questions of fact but not of questions of law.

B. Restricted Appellate Review of Findings of Fact

1. Review of Jury Findings

The Seventh Amendment to the United States Constitution guarantees the right to a jury trial "in suits at common law," and it provides that "no fact tried by a jury shall be otherwise re-examined in any court of the United States, than according to the rules of the common law." Accordingly, a federal appellate court generally will uphold the factual findings of a jury in a civil case unless those findings are not supported by "any substantial

---

5. *See* Experimental Eng'g, Inc. v. United Techs. Corp., 614 F.2d 1244, 1246 (9th Cir. 1980) (reviewing dismissal of action for failure to state a claim); Heiniger v. City of Phoenix, 625 F.2d 842, 843-44 (9th Cir. 1980) (discussing standards of review for summary judgment).

6. *See, e.g.*, Chaline v. KCOH, Inc., 693 F.2d 477, 480 n.3 (5th Cir. 1982); Walsh v. Centeio, 692 F.2d 1239, 1241 (9th Cir. 1982).

evidence."[7] Federal statutes prescribe the same standard of review for the findings of some administrative agencies.[8]

Even though a different set of constitutional considerations applies, an appellate court will also restrict its review of a jury's findings of fact resulting in a criminal conviction. Specifically, rather than reweigh all the evidence, an appellate court may constitutionally uphold a criminal conviction if "the record evidence could reasonably support a finding of guilt beyond a reasonable doubt."[9]

The Seventh Amendment does not apply to state courts. Therefore, some states may permit broader appellate review of jury findings, particularly review of a jury's calculation of damages in a civil suit. New York, for example, has legislatively authorized its state appellate courts to overturn a jury's calculation of damages as excessive or inadequate if the jury award materially deviates from reasonable compensation. More typically, however, a state or federal trial court will set aside a jury's calculation of compensatory damages only if the damages are so excessive as to shock the conscience of the court, and an appellate court typically will overturn the trial court's determination on whether to set aside a jury award only if the trial court abused its discretion.[10]

2. Review of a Judge's Findings of Fact

In civil suits in which the parties have no constitutional or statutory right to a jury, or in suits in which the parties have waived their right to a jury, the trial judge will both find the facts and rule on the law. Under Federal Rule of Civil Procedure 52(a)(6), a federal court of appeals will not overturn the factual findings of a federal trial judge unless the findings are "clearly erroneous." Although Rule 52(a) applies only to civil proceedings and does not directly apply to a trial judge's factual findings on preliminary rulings in a criminal trial, some courts have adopted Rule 52(a)'s "clearly erroneous" standard by analogy for the criminal context.[11]

---

7. *See, e.g.*, Aetna Life Ins. Co. v. Kepler, 116 F.2d 1, 4 & n.1 (8th Cir. 1941). Interestingly, a finding of negligence is not a pure finding of fact, because it requires the jury to define and apply a standard of care, resulting in a mixed conclusion of law and fact. For purposes of appellate review, however, such jury verdicts are treated as findings of fact. Appellate courts distinguish more finely between a trial judge's findings of fact and conclusions of law.

8. *See, e.g.*, 29 U.S.C. §160(f) (2012) (appellate review of factual findings of the National Labor Relations Board); 5 U.S.C. §706(2)(E) (2012) (judicial review of the factual findings of some administrative agency findings, as set forth in the Administrative Procedure Act); *In re* Gartside, 203 F.3d 1305 (Fed. Cir. 2000) (under the Administrative Procedure Act, "substantial evidence" standard of review applies to review of findings of fact of Patent and Trademark Office Board of Appeals).

9. Jackson v. Virginia, 443 U.S. 307, 318 (1979).

10. *See* Gasperini v. Ctr. for Humanities, Inc., 518 U.S. 415, 422 (1996) (comparing earlier judicial standards in New York courts to N.Y. CIV. PRAC. L. & R. §5501(c)(McKinney 1995)). In *Gasperini*, the Court held that the Seventh Amendment is satisfied in a federal diversity action applying New York substantive law if the federal district court reviews the jury's award under the New York statutory standard and if the federal appellate court reviews the district court's determination only for abuse of discretion. *Id.* at 419, 432-39.

11. *See, e.g.*, Ornelas v. United States, 517 U.S. 690, 699 (1996) (in reviewing determinations of reasonable suspicion and probable cause in suppression hearing, appellate

Under Rule 52(a)(1), a trial judge trying a case without a jury will divide his findings into findings of fact and conclusions of law. For example, he may state as a conclusion of law that a federal antidiscrimination statute requires proof of intent to discriminate, and he may state as a finding of fact that the evidence shows no discriminatory intent. On appeal, the appellate court could review without restriction the trial judge's interpretation of the statute to require proof of intent to discriminate; accordingly, it would reverse the trial court's conclusion on that question if it interpreted the statute differently. In contrast, the appellate court would not overturn the trial judge's factual finding of absence of discriminatory intent unless the record showed that finding to be clearly erroneous,[12] even if the appellate judges might have found discriminatory intent had they been the initial fact finders.

One court has defined the clearly-erroneous standard of appellate review in a colorful manner that seems to require great deference to the trial court's findings of fact: "To be clearly erroneous, a decision must ... strike us as wrong with the force of a five-week-old, unrefrigerated dead fish."[13] Under a more conventional measure of clear error, however, the reviewing court simply asks "whether 'on the entire evidence,' it is 'left with the definite and firm conviction that a mistake has been committed.'"[14] At least in theory, the clearly-erroneous standard permits slightly broader appellate review than does the substantial-evidence standard, which is typically applied to findings of juries and some administrative agencies:[15]

> Under the substantial-evidence standard, a reviewing court must uphold the findings of a jury or administrative agency if the record contains sufficient evidence to permit a reasonable person to make those findings. In contrast, the clearly-erroneous standard permits the reviewing court to review the entire record, and to overturn a finding of fact if it is convinced that the finding is clearly wrong, even though a reasonable person could have made the finding.[16]

An appellate court's deference to factual findings made in the trial court is supported by practical and policy considerations that recognize distinctions in the roles of trial and appellate courts. The fact finder in the trial

---

court reviews district court's findings of historical fact for clear error). Of course, the defendant has a right to a jury determination of the ultimate facts regarding criminal liability. *See* U.S. Const. Amend. VI.

12. *See* Pullman-Standard v. Swint, 456 U.S. 273, 287-88 (1982).

13. Parts & Elec. Motors, Inc. v. Sterling Elec., Inc., 866 F.2d 228, 233 (7th Cir. 1988).

14. Easley v. Cromartie, 532 U.S. 234, 235 (2001) (quoting United States v. United States Gypsum Co., 333 U.S. 364, 395 (1948)).

15. *See, e.g.,* Dickinson v. Zurko, 527 U.S. 150, 162-64 (1999) (recognizing that the "clearly erroneous" standard allows for more searching review, but characterizing the difference as subtle, and observing that the choice between the two standards will not often determine the outcome); Loehr v. Offshore Logistics, Inc., 691 F.2d 758, 760-61 (5th Cir. 1982).

16. Charles R. Calleros, *Title VII and Rule 52(a): Standards of Appellate Review in Disparate Treatment Cases—Limiting the Reach of Pullman-Standard v. Swint,* 58 Tul. L. Rev. 411 n.40 (1983) (citations omitted); *see also Zurko,* 527 U.S. at 162 (distinguishing between the "definite and firm conviction" required for clear error and the "reasonable mind" standard for the substantial-evidence test).

court, either the judge or the jury, is generally in a better position than the appellate court to evaluate the evidence. This advantage is strongest when factual findings are based partly on the fact finder's evaluation of the credibility of witnesses. The mannerisms of the witness on the stand may be much more revealing than the cold print of the reporter's transcript. Accordingly, Rule 52(a)(6) specifically directs appellate courts to give "due regard to the trial court's opportunity to judge the witnesses' credibility."

Conversely, the trial court's advantage is weakest when factual findings are based largely on other evidence that is available in identical form to both the trial and appellate courts. Nonetheless, Rule 52(a)(6)'s restricted standard of review applies to "[f]indings of fact, whether based on oral or other evidence," suggesting that restrictions on appellate review must be at least partly based on policies other than a practical advantage enjoyed by the trial court.

In fact, restrictions on appellate review of findings of fact are independently justified by the importance of an appellate court's role in developing general principles of law relative to its role of correcting error in the judgment in a specific case. Admittedly, appellate courts should perform a limited "corrective" function by subjecting each trial judgment to some review for error and thus reducing the risk of injustice.[17] At least as important, however, is the appellate court's "institutional" function of "developing and declaring legal principles that will have application beyond the case that serves as the vehicle for expression of the principles."[18] This institutional function is strongest in the highest appellate court in a jurisdiction.[19] It emphasizes the development of a cohesive body of legal standards rather than the review of evidence supporting findings of fact.

C. Conclusions of Law: Mixed Conclusions of Fact and Law in a Nonjury Trial

In contrast to the restricted appellate review of findings of fact, appellate review of a trial judge's conclusions of law is unrestricted. The appellate court may freely correct the trial court's formulation of legal standards.[20]

Often, however, classifying a finding as more nearly one of law than of fact in a nonjury trial is a difficult task.[21] Without doubt, Rule 52(a)(6)'s clearly-erroneous standard applies to appellate review of a trial judge's findings of historical fact, such as findings about events and actions.[22] It also

---

17. Calleros, *supra* note 16, at 421-22.

18. *Id*. at 420-21.

19. Indeed, under its "two-court rule," the United States Supreme Court will give special deference to a finding of fact made by a trial judge and upheld on appeal in the intermediate court of appeals. *See, e.g.,* Rogers v. Lodge, 458 U.S. 613, 622-27 (1982).

20. *See* Pullman-Standard v. Swint, 456 U.S. 273, 287 (1982).

21. *See id*. at 288.

22. *See, e.g.,* Washington v. Watkins, 655 F.2d 1346, 1352 (5th Cir. 1981).

applies to review of "factual inferences" drawn by a trial court from "undisputed basic facts."[23]

However, some trial court determinations fall between the two extremes of formulation of abstract legal standards and findings of historical fact or factual inference. For example, a trial judge's determination of whether the historical facts satisfy an abstract legal standard is a mixed finding of fact and law, which may contain elements of both factual inference and refinement of the legal standard. Thus, whether a trial court finding is one of fact, subject to restricted appellate review, or one of law, subject to full review, could be subject to dispute and thus be raised as one of the threshold issues on appeal.

1. Review of Discretionary Rulings

Appellate review of a narrow class of mixed findings is restricted under a special standard of review. Specifically, an appellate court will severely restrict its review of certain "discretionary" rulings of a trial judge, such as discovery and evidentiary rulings, the granting or denial of injunctive or declaratory relief, or the determination whether to grant a new trial. Assuming that the trial judge formulated the correct legal rule before applying it to the facts, the appellate court generally will not overturn such a mixed finding of the trial judge unless she abused her discretion.[24]

2. Mixed Findings as Predominantly Fact or Law

Most mixed findings, however, do not fall within this narrow class of discretionary rulings. Instead, for purposes of appellate standards of review, appellate courts must classify the findings under Rule 52(a) as findings of fact or conclusions of law. The proper means of accomplishing this classification is a matter of continuing debate. However, the practical and policy considerations underlying restrictions on appellate review provide some guidance in the debate.

In many cases, the standard of review will turn on the level of court that is in the best position to make the determination. For example, if a mixed question of fact and law requires the application of a simple, noncontroversial legal rule to complex historical facts, its resolution will require the trial judge primarily to refine her understanding of the facts rather than

---

23. Commissioner v. Duberstein, 363 U.S. 278, 291 (1960) (citing United States v. United States Gypsum Co., 333 U.S. 364, 394 (1948)).

24. *See, e.g.,* Gen. Elec. Co. v. Joiner, 522 U.S. 136 (1997) (district court's evidentiary rulings—including those on admission or exclusion of scientific evidence—are reviewed only for abuse of discretion); Browning-Ferris Indus. of Vt. v. Kelco Disposal, Inc., 492 U.S. 257, 279 (1989) (district court's decision whether to grant new trial or remittitur after jury award is reviewed for abuse of discretion), *cited with approval in* Gasperini v. Ctr. for Humanities, Inc., 518 U.S. 415, 435 (1996) (review of district court's decision whether to set aside jury award of damages in a diversity suit); Wilton v. Seven Falls Co., 515 U.S. 277, 289-90 (1995) (abuse of discretion standard for reviewing district court's decision whether to entertain a declaratory judgment action); Los Angeles Mem'l Coliseum Comm'n v. Nat'l Football League, 634 F.2d 1197, 1200 (9th Cir. 1980) (abuse of discretion standard for reviewing district court's decision whether to grant injunctive relief).

to interpret the legal rule. The trial judge normally is in the best position to make such a determination, and review of the factual record is more in keeping with the trial court's customary role than with the appellate court's institutional function of clarifying the law.[25] Therefore, an appellate court should view the finding as more nearly a finding of factual inference than a conclusion of law, and it should restrict its review accordingly.

Consider, for example, a trial judge's ruling in one case that an employer's series of early retirement offers to employees did not amount to a "plan" subject to regulation under the federal Employee Retirement Income Security Act. The meaning of the statutory term "plan" adopted by the trial judge was a matter of law subject to unrestricted review; however, the mixed question of whether the early retirement offers satisfied the legal test for constituting a "plan" primarily required analysis of the factual characteristics of the offers. The appellate court thus treated this mixed question as "principally a question of fact," and it applied the restrictive "clearly erroneous" standard to its review of the trial judge's finding on that issue.[26]

Conversely, if a mixed question of fact and law requires the application of complex, uncertain, or highly controversial legal standards to simple historical facts, the trial judge's resolution of the question will primarily reflect refinement of her understanding of the content of the legal rules. De novo review of such a mixed finding produces the "normal law-clarifying benefits [of] an appellate decision on a question of law."[27] Accordingly, an appellate court should view such a finding as more nearly a conclusion of law, subject to unrestricted review, than one of factual inference.

Consider, for example, the question in one United States Supreme Court case of whether the government presented "clear, unequivocal and convincing" proof that a naturalized citizen had fraudulently procured his certificate of naturalization during World War II by falsely renouncing his allegiance to Nazi Germany and falsely swearing allegiance to the United States. Because of the technical nature of the special standard of proof, along with the uncertain and politically sensitive nature of the legal concept of "allegiance," this mixed question was primarily one of law. Therefore, the appellate courts could review the trial court's determination without restriction.[28]

3 Constitutional Facts Doctrine

Similarly, courts will freely review the mixed question of whether a jury award of punitive damages violates constitutional guarantees of due process[29] or whether certain speech falls within a category protected by the First

---

25. *See* Pierce v. Underwood, 487 U.S. 552, 559-60 (1988).

26. Belanger v. Wyman-Gordon Co., 71 F.3d 451, 453-56 (1st Cir. 1995).

27. *Pierce,* 487 U.S. at 561.

28. Baumgartner v. United States, 322 U.S. 665 (1944).

29. Cooper Indus. v. Leatherman Tool Group, Inc., 532 U.S. 424 (2001).

Amendment.[30] Judicial determinations on these mixed questions necessarily reflect choices about the scope of important constitutional rights.

Indeed, to safeguard constitutional guarantees of freedom of speech, courts have adopted a limited "constitutional facts" exception to the normally restricted review of findings of historical fact discussed above in Section II.B. In such cases, courts may examine the underlying record and freely review even some purely factual findings of a jury or trial court judge, if the facts are critical to the First Amendment analysis.[31] Even when freely reviewing findings of constitutional fact, however, the appellate court will defer to the fact finder's determinations of witness credibility.[32]

III. Summary

An appellate court will freely review a lower court's statement or formulation of a legal rule, without deference to the lower court's interpretation of the law. In contrast, an appellate court will substantially restrict its review of findings of fact in the trial court, with the precise standard of deference varying with the context. On appellate review, a trial judge's application of law to facts will be treated in some courts either as a ruling of law or a finding of fact, depending on whether the trial court's analysis on that point is predominantly one of clarifying the legal rule in a factual context or one of drawing legally relevant factual inferences. Finally, an appellate court will restrict its review of a trial judge's exercise of discretion on certain kinds of issues.

The following chart summarizes widely adopted standards of appellate review for various kinds of trial rulings or findings. You should view the chart as only a starting point in your analysis of appellate review, because the precise standard of review in any category can vary between state and federal courts and between states.

---

30. *See, e.g.,* Bose Corp. v. Consumers Union, 466 U.S. 485, 504-06 (1984).

31. *Id.* at 499-514 (freely reviewing district court's finding of actual malice in defamation case and referring to other cases and contexts, including independent review of the record in jury cases); *see also id.* at 515 (White, J., dissenting) (interpreting majority's analysis as applying to a pure question of fact); *id.* at 515 (Rehnquist, J., dissenting) (same); *id.* at 518 n.2 (Rehnquist, J., dissenting) (arguing that full independent review of constitutional facts found by state jury is less controversial than freely reviewing the careful, written findings of a district court judge); Adam Hoffman, *Corralling Constitutional Fact: De Novo Fact Review in the Federal Appellate Courts,* 50 DUKE L.J. 1427 (2001).

32. *Bose,* 466 U.S. at 499-500; Harte-Hanks Commc'ns, Inc. v. Connaughton, 491 U.S. 657, 688 (1989).

TRIAL COURT DETERMINATION	APPELLATE STANDARD OF REVIEW
Finding of fact by civil jury and some administrative agencies	Affirmed if supported by substantial evidence
Finding of guilt by jury in criminal prosecution	Affirmed if rational basis or reasonable support in the evidence for a finding that prosecution met its burden of proof
Trial judge's exercise of discretion	Affirmed unless trial judge abused discretion
Trial judge's finding of fact	Affirmed unless clearly erroneous
Trial judge's ruling on the law or instructions on law to jury	Reviewed without restriction and rejected if appellate court disagrees on the merits
Trial judge's mixed finding of law and fact	Treated as finding of fact or conclusion of law, often depending on whether legal or factual questions predominate

Chapter 8

The Brief—Effective Appellate Advocacy

I. Overview of Appellate Briefs: Formats and Filing

Rules of procedure and local court rules typically prescribe more formal and detailed formats for appellate briefs than for motions memoranda and other briefs. As the following examples illustrate, you must follow the latest version of applicable rules in the appropriate jurisdiction to ensure that the clerk's office of the court will accept your brief for filing.

A. Components of the Opening Brief

When you represent the "appellant" (bringing an appeal as a matter of right) or the "petitioner" (if you must petition the court to accept the case for discretionary review), you will file the opening brief, seeking reversal of the judgment below. At a minimum, typical rules will require this brief to include the following substantive components:

1. a statement of the issues raised on appeal;

2. a statement of the procedural history of the case (frequently entitled "Statement of the Case" or "Proceedings Below");

3. a statement of the facts relevant to issues raised on appeal;

4. an argument (often preceded by a summary of the argument, either as mandated by applicable rules or as a matter of the brief writer's discretion); and

5. a conclusion.

In addition, rules of procedure or court rules typically require other substantive and formal components such as a table of contents, an alphabetically arranged table of authorities, and statements of jurisdiction and of standards of review. For example, United States Supreme Court Rule 24.1 requires nine components in opening briefs to that court, along with a table of contents and a table of authorities in all but very short briefs:

Rule 24. Briefs on the Merits: In General

1. A brief on the merits for a petitioner or an appellant ... shall contain in the order here indicated:

(a) The questions presented for review ....

(b) A list of all parties to the proceeding in the court whose judgment is under review ....

(c) If the brief exceeds 1,500 words, a table of contents and a table of cited authorities.

(d) Citations of the official and unofficial reports of the opinions and orders entered in the case by courts and administrative agencies.

(e) A concise statement of the basis for jurisdiction in this Court, including the statutory provisions and time factors on which jurisdiction rests.

(f) The constitutional provisions, treaties, statutes, ordinances, and regulations involved in the case, set out verbatim with appropriate citation....

(g) A concise statement of the case, setting out the facts material to the consideration of the questions presented, ...

(h) A summary of the argument, suitably paragraphed....

(i) The argument, exhibiting clearly the points of fact and of law presented and citing the authorities and statutes relied on.

(j) A conclusion specifying with particularity the relief the party seeks.

For briefs filed with a United States Court of Appeals, Federal Rule of Appellate Procedure 28(a) specifies eight components for the appellant's opening brief, with two others required in certain circumstances. As amended in 2013, Rule 28(a)(6) now combines two previously separate components into a single "statement of the case," which includes both the procedural history and the statement of facts. Rule 28(a) now requires the following format for the opening brief:

Rule 28. Briefs

(a) Appellant's Brief. The appellant's brief must contain, under appropriate headings and in the order indicated:

(1) a corporate disclosure statement if required by Rule 26.1;

(2) a table of contents, with page references;

(3) a table of authorities—cases (alphabetically arranged), statutes, and other authorities—with references to the pages of the brief where they are cited;

(4) a jurisdictional statement, including:

(A) the basis for the district court's or agency's subject-matter jurisdiction, with citations to applicable statutory provisions and stating relevant facts establishing jurisdiction;

(B) the basis for the court of appeals' jurisdiction, with citations to applicable statutory provisions and stating relevant facts establishing jurisdiction;

(C) the filing dates establishing the timeliness of the appeal or petition for review; and

(D) an assertion that the appeal is from a final order or judgment that disposes of all parties' claims, or information establishing the court of appeals' jurisdiction on some other basis;

(5) a statement of the issues presented for review;

(6) a concise statement of the case setting out the facts relevant to the issues submitted for review, describing the relevant procedural history, and identifying the rulings presented for review, with appropriate references to the record (see Rule 28(e));

(7) a summary of the argument, which must contain a succinct, clear, and accurate statement of the arguments made in the body of the brief, and which must not merely repeat the argument headings;

(8) the argument, which must contain:

(A) appellant's contentions and the reasons for them, with citations to the authorities and parts of the record on which the appellant relies; and

(B) for each issue, a concise statement of the applicable standard of review (which may appear in the discussion of the issue or under a separate heading placed before the discussion of the issues);

(9) a short conclusion stating the precise relief sought; and

(10) the certificate of compliance, if required under Rule 32(g)(1) [*e.g.*, if the brief satisfies length requirements through word or line count under Rule 32(a)(7)(B), rather than through page limitations].

B. Components of Answering and Reply Briefs

If you represent the "appellee" or "respondent," the party seeking a ruling affirming the judgment of the court below, you must file an answering brief. In the United States Courts of Appeals, for example, Federal Rule of Appellate Procedure 28(b) provides that the appellee's answering brief should include all the components listed for the appellant's opening brief except for subsection (a)(9); however, the appellee may adopt the statements of jurisdiction, issues, case, facts, and standard of review presented in the appellant's brief if the appellee is satisfied with them.

According to subsection Rule 28(c), the appellant may respond to the appellee's answering brief with a reply brief, but the reply brief can dispense with most of the statements set forth in the appellant's opening brief. In addition to an argument responding to the answering brief, the reply brief need contain only a table of contents and a table of authorities.

C. Formatting and Other Formal Requirements

Rules of procedure or local court rules typically specify additional formal requirements regarding such things as typeface, line spacing, margins, overall length, and the color of the cover sheets for the opening, answering, and reply briefs.[1]

The specified form for the information on the cover of an appellate brief varies in different jurisdictions. In some jurisdictions, the cover sheet includes the caption of the case in the same basic format as it appeared in trial pleadings and briefs, as illustrated by the sample briefs at the end of this chapter and Chapters 4 through 6. In other jurisdictions, including the United States Courts of Appeals, rules of procedure require the cover to include certain identifying information, which attorneys usually present on several widely spaced lines that are centered on the cover page.[2]

D. Filing the Brief in Hard Copy and Electronically

Court rules traditionally contemplated that appellate advocates will provide multiple copies of briefs in "hard copy," printed or typewritten on paper. More recently, however, most federal courts and many state courts have adopted rules that permit or require parties to file briefs electronically, and some court rules permit electronic briefs to include hyperlinks that connect citations in the brief to cited authorities or to parts of the record.[3]

---

1. *See, e.g.,* FED. R. APP. P. 32(a).

2. *See* FED. R. APP. P. 32(a)(2).

3. *See, e.g.,* FED. R. APP. P. 25(a)(2)(D) (authorizing federal courts of appeals to adopt local rules permitting electronic filing of briefs and other documents); 9TH CIR. R. 25-5 (requiring electronic filing of briefs by attorneys, with listed exceptions); 2D CIR. R. 25-1(i) (permitting hyperlinks).

United States Supreme Court rules require briefs submitted to that court to be filed both electronically and in hard copy.[4]

II. Statement of Issues

The art of stating issues in a student case brief or an office memorandum is discussed in detail in Section III of Chapter 6 and Section III.A of Chapter 7. You should review those principles now as a starting point for drafting the statement of issues in your appellate brief. When drafting an issue statement in a brief, however, you should additionally strive to phrase the issue in a way that suggests a favorable response or otherwise serves to advocate your client's case.

A. Issue Statements as Preliminary Advocacy

Your statement of the issue can invite the court to apply an analytical framework or standard of review that best suits your client's arguments. Of course, you should develop that strategy primarily in the argument section of the brief. However, you can make the judge more receptive to your approach by initially exposing her to the theme of your brief in your statement of the issues.

For example, suppose that you represent an appellant who appeals from a trial judge's decision to deny a preliminary injunction. You know that the appellate court will overturn that decision only if the trial judge abused her discretion, provided that the trial judge applied the proper legal standards to the facts.[5] However, you believe that her ruling leaves some room for questions about the content of the legal rules governing injunctions that she applied to the facts. Accordingly, you might use the statement of the issue to invite the appellate court to find error in the trial judge's formulation of the legal rules, which formulation would be subject to unrestricted review, as discussed in Chapter 7:

In denying Surge Corp.'s request for a preliminary injunction, did the trial judge apply an incorrect legal rule by requiring a showing of likelihood of success on the merits, rather than using a "sliding-scale" test that would justify a preliminary injunction upon a showing of especially great irreparable harm and at least substantial questions on the merits?

---

4. U.S. S. Ct. R. 29.7 (excepting briefs filed by *pro se* litigants).

5. *See, e.g.,* Los Angeles Mem'l Coliseum Comm'n v. Nat'l Football League, 634 F.2d 1197, 1200 (9th Cir. 1980).

The opposing counsel could argue that the trial judge applied a sliding-scale test and that the judge's balancing of the facts does not reflect an abuse of discretion under the most flexible of legal rules. Nonetheless, he might frame the issue so that it emphasizes the restricted standard of review of the ultimate ruling and refers only abstractly to potential questions about choices among legal rules:

Did the trial judge properly exercise her discretion to deny preliminary injunctive relief on the ground that Surge Corp. failed to make the requisite showing on the merits under applicable legal rules?

Of course, the nature of the opportunity to promote a favorable approach in the statement of the issue will vary with the circumstances of each appeal. For example, an appeal in a contract dispute might raise a purely legal question about whether the peculiar facts of an exceptional case justify a special exception to the general common law requirement of consideration for contract formation. If so, the parties might use their statements of the issue, as well as their arguments, to appeal either to the appellate judges' senses of fairness and justice or to their appreciation of the benefits of certainty in the law.

In those circumstances, if you represent the party who would benefit from an exception to the general rule, you might use the statement of the issue to promote the value of fairness by vividly and concretely emphasizing the peculiar facts of the case:

Does McGowin's moral obligation to perform his promise to pay Webb for past services give rise to a legal obligation in light of the serious physical injuries suffered by Webb and the immeasurable benefit he gave to McGowin in heroically saving McGowin's life?

This statement of the issue appeals to the appellate court's corrective function: reaching a just result on the unique facts of the case before it, even if that requires a departure from general principles.[6]

In contrast, if you represent the party who would benefit from application of the general rule, you would advance a different theme. Specifically, you might use the statement of the issue to promote the consideration rule in its abstract form or to emphasize the general policies supporting the rule:

---

6. *See generally* Webb v. McGowin, 168 So. 196, 199 (Ala. Ct. App. 1936) (Samford, J., concurring) (departing from "strict letter of the rule" in the interests of justice).

Did the trial court correctly reject a vague and uncertain "moral obligation" exception to the fundamental principle that a promise made in recognition of past services lacks consideration and therefore is unenforceable?

This issue appeals to the appellate court's institutional function: the wisdom of applying the rule in nearly every context, the importance of maintaining the vitality of a long-standing rule, and the need for certainty and predictability in the law.[7]

B. Credibility of the Advocate

In phrasing the statement of the issue to advocate an approach or a conclusion, you should not be so anxious to invite a favorable response that you state a false issue. For example, assume that you represent a criminal defendant who appeals from a state conviction for illegal possession of cocaine. The applicable criminal statute defines "possession" as contemporaneous intent and ability to exercise physical control over the substance. If the trial judge correctly instructed the jury on the applicable legal rules and definitions, you might still argue that substantial evidence did not support the jury finding of ability to exercise control over the cocaine. If so, the following statement of the issue would not effectively advance your client's cause:

Is proof of ability to control an illegal substance a requisite element of a conviction for illegal possession of that substance?

Under currently accepted legal definitions in the state, an appellate judge would readily agree that the question presented by this statement of the issue must be answered affirmatively. However, she would object that the question does not fairly characterize any genuine issue on appeal. Because the trial judge correctly instructed the jury on the applicable legal standards, your implicit attack on the completeness of the instructions would be futile. Instead, your issue statement must fairly address your client's true contention on appeal:

Is the jury's finding of Wade's ability to control the cocaine unsupported by the evidence in light of undisputed testimony that the officers found Wade standing outside the locked automobile containing the cocaine, without a key to the automobile?

---

7. See generally Mills v. Wyman, 3 Pick. 207 (Mass. 1825) (rejecting "moral obligation" exception in the interests of maintaining universal application of the consideration doctrine).

Thus, you must recognize limits on your efforts to invite a favorable response to a statement of the issue. Specifically, you must maintain credibility and must fairly link the statement of the issue to your genuine argument on appeal.

III. Statement of Procedural History

Rules of procedure or local court rules will specify whether you must state the procedural history in a separate section or combine it with the historical facts. If the rules require you to state the procedural history in a separate section, they typically designate the section as the "Statement of the Case." If the rules instead require you to combine the facts and procedural history, they typically designate the combined section as either the "Statement of the Case" or the "Statement of Facts." With either format, the essential elements of a statement of procedural history are brief descriptions of "the nature of the case, the course of proceedings, and the disposition below."[8]

In the opening paragraph of the statement of procedural history, you should introduce the parties and generally describe the claims and defenses that they presented in the trial court. Next, you should chronologically recite the portions of the trial history and the rulings of the court that are relevant to the issues on appeal, including the trial court's final judgment and the appellant's filing notice of appeal. In a brief to a second-level court of appeal, you should also summarize the ruling of the intermediate appellate court. As described in Section I above, court rules in some jurisdictions might require you to discuss additional matters.

Once you have identified parties as the appellant and the appellee in your brief, you would do well in any jurisdiction to follow federal appellate rules for referring to parties:

> References to Parties. In briefs and at oral argument, counsel should minimize use of the terms "appellant" and "appellee." To make briefs clear, counsel should use the parties' actual names or the designations used in the lower court or agency proceeding, or such descriptive terms as "the employee," "the injured person," "the taxpayer," "the ship," "the stevedore."[9]

IV. Statement of Facts

A. Telling a Compelling Story

The opening statement of facts in a brief can play a surprisingly important role in your advocacy. A persuasive statement of facts near the begin-

---

8. FED. R. APP. P. 28(a)(6).
9. FED. R. APP. P. 28(d).

ning of your brief may incline a judge to rule in favor of your client even before the judge has considered the legal analysis. If so, the judge may take advantage of the flexibility or uncertainty in the legal principles to reach the result that the facts show to be just, provided that she can do so without departing from clearly controlling precedent or otherwise upsetting the orderly development of a coherent body of law. A persuasive opening statement of facts will help make the judge receptive to the legal and factual analyses in the argument section of your brief.

As you can imagine, the appellant's statement of facts and the appellee's statement of facts should evoke very different reactions in the reader. Each brings the client's story to the fore while stating the facts accurately, fairly, and completely.

Good examples of fact statements appear in the opening and answering appellate briefs at the end of this chapter, taken from a case in which a shopper sued a department store and others for wrongfully detaining him after accusing him of shoplifting. The fact statement in each brief tells the story from a very different perspective than that advanced in the opposing brief. The brief for the shopper emphasizes facts that show how events unfolded from the shopper's perspective, detailing how he entered the store twice and made three separate purchases during those visits. The brief for the department store emphasizes facts that show how events unfolded within the perception of store employees, who were confused by the shopper's multiple purchases, some placed in the same shopping bag.

Each brief states the facts fairly, accurately, and completely, with citations to the record. Yet, each also succeeds in presenting the client's perspective in an engaging manner that holds the reader's attention. A simple trip to the store for farm tools unfolds as a drama, complete with the shopper's flirtation with a store employee, tough talk between the shopper and security guards, and a shoving match between the shopper and a police officer resulting in the shopper stumbling head first through a wall of the store's security room.

Not every case will present such dramatic events; consequently, it will not always be easy to present your facts in a way that "commands the reader's attention" and "compels the reader to keep reading."[10] Nonetheless, if you develop a good theme as discussed in Chapter 2, if you employ the techniques of persuasive writing style explored in Chapter 3, and if you emphasize facts that tell the story from your client's perspective, any case can lend itself to telling a compelling story.[11]

B. Constraints That Build Trust

To present the facts persuasively, you might be tempted to slant the record misleadingly in favor of your client's case or to introduce legal

---

10. Mark K. Osbeck, *What Is "Good Legal Writing" and Why Does It Matter?*, 4 DREXEL L. REV. 417 (2012).

11. For much more on telling your client's story, in both legal and factual argument, see Ruth Anne Robbins, Steve Johansen & Ken Chestek, YOUR CLIENT'S STORY (2013).

arguments and conclusions in the statement of facts. Neither technique will succeed. They will only undermine your credibility with the court. Conversely, if you combine persuasive themes and writing style with accuracy and completeness, judges likely will turn to your statement of facts as a trustworthy reference.

1. Advocacy with Credibility

If you riddle your statement of facts with exaggerations or misleading omissions, you will simply diminish your credibility. Instead, your statement of facts should display your client in a favorable light while reflecting a concern for completeness and accuracy. If the judge is convinced that your statement is accurate and complete, he may repeatedly turn to it for a fair summary of the record, resulting in maximum exposure of the subtle advocacy of your statement.

a. Organization of Facts

Rather than omit unfavorable facts, you should place them in a context that minimizes their impact and that helps you emphasize favorable facts. In addition to the techniques of persuasive writing discussed in Chapter 3, you can use the organization of the entire fact statement to emphasize the favorable facts. Chronological order of facts may be the clearest and most logical; it is certainly the order most often recommended by judges. However, you can increase the impact of favorable events by describing them in the places of greatest emphasis: the beginning and end of the fact statement. If you can do so without unduly sacrificing clarity and continuity, you can justify departing from chronological order or at least supplementing a chronological statement with a second reference to a critical and favorable fact at the beginning or end.

For example, if a defendant in a murder case has pled not guilty and is seeking to suppress evidence of an illegal search, the defendant's chronology normally should not begin with the death of the victim, but perhaps with the illegal search. The prosecution in that case, on the other hand, might begin with the defendant's relationship with the victim prior to the victim's death.

b. Variation in Emphasis

You can also emphasize favorable facts by using specific, concrete descriptions and strong verbs in active voice. Conversely, you can lessen the impact of unfavorable facts by describing them in general, abstract terms.

For example, suppose that Samuel Hughes, convicted of first-degree murder, had sought at trial to mitigate the offense by showing that he was intoxicated at the time of the crime and therefore could not have premeditated the killing. On appeal, he hopes to persuade the court to interpret the statutory requirement of premeditation in a restrictive manner so that it will apply only to deliberation with a relatively clear mind.

As appellate counsel for Hughes, you could emphasize the intoxication, while referring to the murder with a light touch, even though you must concede that Hughes struck the fatal blow, as established by several eyewitnesses:

When he fatally injured the decedent, Samuel Hughes was staggering from the effects of a full pint of whiskey.

This statement refers to both the killing and the victim in abstract terms and in a subordinate clause. Moreover, it humanizes the defendant in the main clause by referring to him by name and describing his intoxication vividly.

Conversely, as the prosecutor on appeal, you could deemphasize Hughes's intoxication by referring to it generally, and you could emphasize his aggressive conduct by describing it in gruesome detail:

While under the influence of self-induced intoxication, the defendant murdered Grace Smith by bludgeoning her from behind with a baseball bat.

This statement relegates the defendant to anonymity by referring to him with a procedural label. In contrast, it names the victim, thus inviting the reader to recognize her as a person, rather than a statistic. Moreover, the description of the attack as one from behind tends to portray the victim as particularly sympathetic and defenseless. The statement not only refers to the defendant's impaired state of mind abstractly and in a subordinate phrase, it invites the reader to reject intoxication as a mitigating factor by characterizing it as self-induced. Finally, powerful verbs—"murdered" and "bludgeoning"—convey the horror of the assault.

Neither of these statements directly addresses the legal issue of statutory interpretation. Both are designed, however, to remind the judge of the concrete factual context in which the statute will apply in this case. Each statement portrays the event in a light that could make the judge more or less receptive to a restrictive interpretation of the statute.

2. Premature Legal Argument

If your fact statement crosses the line between presenting facts in a favorable light and prematurely introducing legal argument, you may undermine its effectiveness as a vehicle for making the judge receptive to your main argument. A judge knows that the legal argument of a brief will be one-sided, and he generally reserves judgment on legal conclusions until he has read both briefs. But he may be more willing to develop an immediate impression of the case from an apparently complete and accurate statement of facts.

For example, if the prosecutor's statement of facts specifically character-izes an act as premeditated, thus assuming a favorable interpretation of that statutory element, the judge may react defensively; he may warn himself that he should resist such a mixed conclusion of law and fact until he has thoroughly studied the arguments in both briefs. On the other hand, if the prosecutor's statement of facts vividly describes the convicted defendant as seething from a humiliating insult and then selecting a baseball bat as a weapon for retaliation after rejecting a cue stick as insufficiently weighty, the judge is invited to draw his own conclusion that the statutory element of premeditation does not require a restrictive interpretation to account for intoxication. Even if tentative or subconscious, that conclusion could pre-dispose the judge at an early stage to accept the prosecutor's explicit legal arguments and conclusions in the argument section of the prosecutor's brief.

Conversely, when the judge reaches the argument section of the brief, he may resist arguments supporting conclusions that you had bluntly attempted to force on him in the statement of facts. He will be more comfortable with arguments that confirm conclusions he had reached on his own after reading apparently non-argumentative facts.

3. Permissible Sources for the Facts

Your statement of facts on appeal is subject to two further limitations. First, except for matters within common knowledge or otherwise subject to judicial notice,[12] the appellate court and the litigants are constrained by the trial court record as the exclusive source of the facts of the dispute. In a fully tried case, those facts are reflected in testimony recorded in the reporter's transcript, in documentary evidence admitted at trial, and in any physical evidence admitted at trial and retained by the trial court clerk. If the trial court disposed of the case on the pleadings or on summary judgment, the facts are reflected in the allegations of the pleadings or in the preliminary presentation of evidence on the motion for summary judgment. Rules of procedure and local court rules will set forth the responsibilities of the par-ties, primarily the appellant, in forwarding all or part of the trial court record to the appellate court and in filing relevant portions in an appendix to the appellate briefs.[13]

Second, if findings of fact are made by a jury or by the trial court, those findings take on greater significance than the underlying record of testimony and other evidence because of the restricted appellate review of such find-ings, as discussed in Chapter 7. If the appellant wishes to challenge the find-ings of fact, the appellant should refer to the underlying record of evidence

---

12. *See, e.g.,* FED. R. EVID. 201 and advisory committee note on subsection (f) (judicial notice of adjudicative facts in trial and on appeal); United States v. Pink, 315 U.S. 203, 216 (1942) (appellate judicial notice of record in other case); Ellie Margolis, *Beyond Brandeis: Exploring the Uses of Non-Legal Materials in Appellate Briefs,* 34 U.S.F. L. REV. 197 (2000) (arguing for effective use of nonlegal materials to establish "legislative facts" on appeal, as well as at trial).

13. *E.g.,* FED. R. APP. P. 10 (the record on appeal), 11 (forwarding the record), 30 (appendix to the briefs), 32(b) (form of appendix).

to support the challenge; however, the findings will stand unless they are clearly erroneous or unsupported by substantial evidence. If the appellant instead chooses to limit the attack to a challenge of the trial judge's formulation of legal standards or the judge's application of those standards to facts, the appellant must rely on the lower court's findings of fact. Such an argument may include supplementary references to illuminating evidence, but only if consistent with the findings. The appellee should focus on either the findings or the underlying evidence supporting the findings, depending on which response most appropriately meets the appellant's challenge. These strategic considerations are illustrated in Section V.D.1, below.

As discussed in Chapter 7, Section I, when you refer to facts or procedural history in any section of your appellate brief, you must cite to the source. Applicable rules may require you to cite directly to the underlying record on appeal or to an appendix that contains excerpts of the record.[14]

C. Summary and Perspective

To ensure that your opening statement of facts increases the judge's receptivity to your main argument, you should

1. tell a compelling story from your client's perspective;
2. state the facts completely and accurately, drawn from permissible sources;
3. emphasize favorable facts and deemphasize unfavorable ones through sentence structure, varying levels of specificity and concreteness, and general organization; and
4. avoid premature legal argument.

V. The Argument

Earlier chapters and exercises have provided you with the basic information and skills you need to formulate, organize, and express your arguments in any brief. In summary, for each issue you should

1. state the conclusion you want the court to adopt in an argumentative point heading,
2. argue for a favorable interpretation of legal authority,
3. apply the legal rules to the facts, and
4. state the conclusion that you want the appellate court to reach.

---

14. *E.g.,* FED. R. APP. P. 28(e), 30(c)(2); *see also* Han v. Stanford Univ., 210 F.3d 1038 (9th Cir. 2000) (appeal dismissed for failure to correct opening and reply briefs' omission of citations to the record). For a guide to preparing an appellate appendix containing excerpts of the record on appeal, see Roger J. Miner, *Essay: Common Disorders of the Appendix and Their Treatment,* 3 J. APP. PRAC. & PROCESS 3954 (2001).

This section will supplement the earlier chapters by examining some characteristics that are peculiar to appellate arguments.

A. Summary of Argument

Some rules of procedure and local court rules will require, or at least permit, appellate advocates to include a summary of the argument immediately before the main argument.[15] If applicable rules do not require a summary, you should include one in a separate section if your brief is sufficiently complex that an overview of your arguments will substantially enhance your reader's comprehension. If a summary in a separate section is neither required nor appropriate, you nonetheless should consider beginning your argument with an overview paragraph that outlines your arguments and conveys the theme of your brief.

If you do include a summary of argument in a separate section of your brief, you should place it under a section heading entitled "Summary of Argument." United States Supreme Court Rule 24.1(h) calls for a "clear and concise condensation of the argument made in the body of the brief," and it contemplates a multi-paragraph summary, because it states that the summary should be "suitably paragraphed."

The summary, however, should not stretch into several pages. A summary should do no more than briefly explain your major points in a few paragraphs, citing only to the most significant authorities. Along with the collection of point headings in your Table of Contents, the Summary of Argument can provide your reader with a general road map of her journey through your brief. If the summary delves into your argument in even moderate detail, however, it will make the main argument seem repetitive, to the irritation of your reader.

B. Standard of Review

Standards of appellate review are examined in detail in Chapter 7, and their significance to appellate strategy and argument is evident throughout the current chapter. Not surprisingly, the standard of review for each issue on appeal is a matter of great interest to the court as well as to the advocates. Consequently, even if applicable court rules do not require it, you should state the standard or standards of review, either in a separate section of the brief or at the outset of your argument for each issue on appeal. Your statement might be as simple as a single sentence, such as the following reference to unrestricted review: "This Court will engage in *de novo* review of the district court's summary judgment for the defendant. *See Heininger* ...."

Occasionally, the standard of review will be a matter of dispute between the parties; if so, you should devote a section of your argument to this topic, just as you develop other arguments in your brief. In an appeal by your client from a nonjury trial in federal court, for example, the parties might dispute

---

15. *E.g.*, FED. R. APP. P. 28(a)(7).

whether the trial judge correctly classified a finding as one of law or fact. You might have reason to argue that a finding classified as a "finding of fact" should be treated instead as a mixed finding of law and fact in which questions about the boundaries of the legal rule predominate. If the appellate court agrees with your description of the finding, it might review the finding without restriction, as a question of law rather than as a finding of fact.

C. Arguing the Law—The Role of Policy Analysis

1. When the Question Is One of First Impression

On questions of first impression in a jurisdiction, courts of all levels will consider policy arguments in an effort to develop the law in a way that best suits the social needs and existing legal framework of the jurisdiction. If the parties advance competing legal approaches from other jurisdictions, or novel approaches based on scholarly commentary, a court typically will seek to determine which proposed rule will best promote the values and policies that are reflected in existing case law or enacted law.

For example, prior to the Supreme Court's recognition of a constitutional right to marriage equality in *Obergefell v. Hodges,* lower courts wrestled with difficult questions relating to the scope of existing precedent and the appropriate standard of constitutional scrutiny of state statutes that barred same-sex marriage. The outcome in these cases, however, was often influenced by broad policy considerations regarding the appropriate role of the judiciary. When lower courts rejected challenges to legislative bans, they frequently invoked a policy of deferring to elected members of the legislature and to democratic deliberation on questions of great social import; in contrast, courts that struck down same-sex marriage bans frequently emphasized equality principles and the duty of the courts to uphold constitutional rights.[16]

2. The Enhanced Role of Policy Analysis on Appeal

Appellate briefs differ in style from pretrial and trial briefs, partly because they examine the underlying policies of legal standards more frequently or to a greater extent. Depending on the procedural posture and other circumstances of an appeal, this difference in approach may be reflected in such factors as the restrictions on appellate review of factual findings, the appellate court's institutional function of developing a cohesive body of law, and the varying degrees to which stare decisis controls decisions at various levels of the court system.

Unless the appellant assumes the difficult burden of challenging factual findings made in the trial court, the appellate briefs likely will explore questions about the content of legal rules, either in the abstract or in the

---

16. *See* Charles R. Calleros, *Advocacy for Marriage Equality: The Power of a Broad Historical Narrative During a Transitional Period in Civil Rights,* 2015 MICH. ST. L. REV. 1249, 1282-86, 1289-90, 1309-13.

process of determining whether the accepted facts satisfy the rules. Because the appellate court can overrule its own precedents, it will consider policy arguments that favor or oppose extending, limiting, modifying, or overruling those precedents.

The institutional function of the appellate courts further encourages policy analysis in appellate brief writing. For two reasons, this effect is greatest in the highest court of a jurisdiction. First, unlike an intermediate court of appeals, the highest court is not bound by the precedent of any court within that jurisdiction. Second, the highest courts in many jurisdictions will accept review of some kinds of lower court decisions only after a discretionary determination that appellate resolution would help develop a cohesive body of law or otherwise would significantly affect the outcome of many cases other than the one that serves as the vehicle for addressing the questions.

Thus, more often than in trial briefs, appellate advocates will allocate substantial portions of their arguments to the policies underlying legal rules and to the social and jurisprudential consequences of retaining or abandoning those rules. Moreover, these characteristics typically will be even more pronounced in a court of last resort than in an intermediate court of appeals.

For example, the following two passages are excerpts of arguments about the proper application of precedent of the state supreme court, the highest court in the state. The first argument could be addressed to the trial court or even to the intermediate court of appeals. Because neither court can overrule the state supreme court precedent, the argument focuses on the applicability of the precedent to the facts of the dispute:

B. The trial judge erred in instructing the jury that Bramwell could be liable for the tort of wrongful discharge if he discharged Kirkeide in "bad faith" rather than in violation of public policy.

Introduction to argument

The trial court's instruction on the tort of wrongful discharge fails to distinguish between conduct that violates a public policy and conduct that might strike the employee as unfair or unwarranted in the context of a specific employment relationship. This instruction permitted the jury to award damages against Bramwell for conduct that is not a tort in this state.

General legal rule

The New Maine Supreme Court has recently recognized a cause of action in tort for wrongful discharge. However, it carefully limited its holding to discharges that violate public policy:

> Thus, an employer is liable in tort for wrongful discharge if it discharges an employee for a reason that violates an important public policy of the state. Pronouncements of public policy will

most often be found in our state's constitution and its legislation.

Blass v. Arcon Co., 337 N. Me. 771, 776 (1996).

In *Blass*, the employer discharged a truck driver in retaliation for the driver's refusal to transport toxic wastes in unsafe containers. The employer was liable in tort for wrongful discharge because its conduct violated the policies of state environmental and occupational safety statutes. *See id.* at 777.

In-depth case analysis

In contrast to *Blass*, Bramwell's discharge of Kirkeide in this case did not violate any public policy. At most, Bramwell acted hastily and exercised poor business judgment, but not in a way that implicates public policy. Yet, the trial court's instruction permitted the jury to impose liability . . . .

Application to facts

In the preceding illustration, the *Blass* decision did not need to address whether a discharge can be tortious for reasons other than a violation of public policy; therefore, it does not preclude future extensions of the new tort of wrongful discharge. Nonetheless, the brief writer has reasonably assumed that a trial court or intermediate court of appeals would not readily extend a newly recognized tort beyond the terms of the Supreme Court's holding. Thus, the brief writer concentrates on explaining the holding of the *Blass* decision and distinguishing it.

In contrast, the following passage is addressed to the New Maine Supreme Court, the mythical author of the *Blass* decision. Because that court can overrule, limit, or extend its own precedent, the argument spends more time on policy analysis. Specifically, it argues that, as a matter of policy, the court should not broaden the tort of wrongful discharge beyond the holding of the *Blass* decision.

B. The trial judge erred in instructing the jury that Bramwell could be liable . . . .

The trial court's instruction on the tort of wrongful discharge fails to distinguish between conduct that violates a public policy and conduct that . . . .

Introduction to argument

Although this Court has recently recognized a cause of action in tort for wrongful discharge, it carefully limited its holding to discharges that violate public policy:

General legal rule

Thus, an employer is liable . . . .

Blass v. Arcon Co., 337 N. Me. 771, 776 (1996).

In *Blass*, the employer discharged a truck driver in retaliation for the driver's refusal to transport toxic wastes in unsafe containers. . . .

In-depth case analysis

Policy analysis

   This court should reject Kirkeide's invitation to extend the tort of wrongful discharge beyond the holding of *Blass*. This state has long promoted the policy of freedom of contract, permitting contracting parties to shape their own rights and obligations. *See, e.g., Snell v. Abundes*, 128 N. Me. 217, 221 (1970). Even if limited to violations of public policy, the tort of wrongful discharge effectively limits the parties' freedom to create a contract that is terminable at the will of either party. Any further restriction on the freedom to contract would require courts to review nearly every contested business decision that affects the tenure of an employee. To preserve freedom of contract and to conserve judicial resources, this Court should narrowly tailor the tort of wrongful discharge to impose liability only for discharges that offend the values of society as a whole, and not for employment decisions that merely reflect a failed relationship between two private parties.

Application to facts

   In our case, the trial court's instruction, approved by the court of appeals, extended the tort of wrongful discharge beyond the holding of *Blass*. By permitting an award of damages for a "bad faith" discharge, ...

  In a final example, the author of an amicus brief, Professor Ralph Brill, helped to persuade the Illinois Supreme Court to broaden the exceptions to the traditional common law rule that a landowner owed no duty of care to protect a trespasser from serious harm. The opening paragraphs of the Argument section of the amicus brief equated the traditional rule with outdated doctrines of property law that courts had already abandoned:

  Primogeniture has long ago been abolished. The doctrines of Worthier Title and the Rule in Shelly's Case have faded into history. No longer does a landowner own upward to the heavens and downward to the center of the earth; aircraft may fly overhead without trespassing, and utilities may gain easements for their wires and pipes. The rule of caveat emptor has been tempered or abolished; in fact, sellers now impliedly warrant the habitability of the property they sell. And landlords no longer are free to avoid responsibility for protecting their tenants from harm.

  These and other ancient doctrines derived from our English heritage have been altered or replaced out of recognition of their purely feudal origins, and their inconsistency with modern life, mores, practices and problems.

However, one major vestige of these bygone times has remained, at least in theory, the limitation on the landowner's duty to trespassers on the land....

3. The Persuasive Value of Warning about Negative Consequences

Of course, an advocate should always explain to a judicial panel why the holding desired by the advocate is consistent with precedent, logical analysis, and sound policy. But advocates should not overlook the persuasive power of combining this positive argument with a negative story about the undesirable consequences of the holding sought by the opposing party.

Judges normally are relatively cautious creatures. When creating precedent, they are sensitive to the risk of taking the law on a path that will be difficult to traverse in future cases, or one that may lead to an undesirable destination. Accordingly, an advocate frequently can dissuade a judge from adopting a proposed holding by describing the difficulties of applying the resulting rule to other factual contexts, or by explaining how the holding could lead to an absurd result if logically extended. In this fashion, the advocate can make the judge more receptive to the holding sought by the advocate's client. Indeed, a negative argument against an adverse holding may pack even more persuasive punch than the advocate's positive description of the virtues of the holding desired by the advocate.

For example, in a sample passage in the preceding subsection, the writer warns that expansion of the tort of wrongful discharge would launch the judiciary on a path of inappropriately assessing whether every challenged discharge is consistent with sound business practices. Such a path not only would erode the established policy of freedom of contract, it also would divert judicial resources from matters more appropriately assigned to the judiciary.

In a different case, an advocate for the plaintiff might warn of the future repercussions of a holding that fails to recognize a claim on the plaintiff's facts. The advocate might explain that the plaintiff's case is not an isolated one and that a negative holding will lead to numerous injustices:

Defendant correctly points out that this court has not yet based a finding of substantive unconscionability solely on price disparity. Nonetheless, such a finding represents a natural extension of existing precedent and is necessary to vindicate important policies favoring consumer protection. Failing to find unconscionability in grossly inflated and unfair pricing would leave countless consumers at the mercy of unscrupulous vendors, many of them highly trained and experienced in high-pressure sales tactics.

D. Arguing the Law and the Facts

1. Strategic Choices

The appellant will seek to overturn unfavorable findings or conclusions of the trial court. As explained in Section V.B above, the appellant will benefit from unrestricted appellate review of conclusions of law. Moreover, the appellate court is not bound by the trial court's characterization of a finding as one of fact or law. Accordingly, if you represent the appellant, you should try to characterize unfavorable mixed findings of fact and law in a nonjury trial as conclusions of law, which are reviewable on appeal without restriction. In a jury trial, on the other hand, a jury's mixed finding of fact and law normally will be treated as a finding of fact for purposes of restricted appellate review.

If an unfavorable finding is undeniably one of fact, you must make some strategic choices among alternative approaches on appeal. As counsel for the appellant, you must decide whether to challenge the unfavorable finding of fact under a restricted standard of review, argue that the trial court applied the wrong legal rule to the facts, or both.

For example, suppose the plaintiff in a federal civil rights suit won an award for compensatory and punitive damages against your client, a police officer, for false arrest in violation of the Fourth Amendment. At trial, the judge gave the following instructions to the jury over your objection:

If you find that Officer Mullins arrested Ms. Wong without probable cause, you must find that Officer Mullins violated Ms. Wong's clearly established constitutional rights, and you must award Ms. Wong compensatory damages in the amount of her actual injuries. Furthermore, if you find that Officer Mullins was grossly and inexcusably careless regarding Ms. Wong's constitutional rights, you may exercise discretion to award Ms. Wong punitive damages in an amount that will punish Officer Mullins and discourage him and others from similar violations.

Applying these instructions to the facts, the jury found Officer Mullins liable and awarded Ms. Wong $25,000 in compensatory damages and $100,000 in punitive damages. The trial court also awarded Ms. Wong her reasonable attorneys' fees.

Your client, Officer Mullins, has appealed. As one of your arguments on appeal, you wish to challenge the award of punitive damages, which is necessarily premised on a jury finding that Officer Mullins was "grossly and inexcusably careless." You can attack the award in either or both of two ways.

First, to take advantage of unrestricted appellate review of matters of law, you can try to persuade the appellate court that the trial judge incorrectly instructed the jury on the law:

A. Officer Mullins is entitled to a new trial because the trial judge erroneously instructed the jury that it could award punitive damages for conduct less culpable than reckless disregard for constitutional rights.

General legal rule

The United States Supreme Court has established a recklessness standard for punitive damages in federal civil rights actions:

> We hold that a jury may be permitted to assess punitive damages in an action under §1983 when the defendant's conduct is shown to be motivated by evil motive or intent, or when it involves reckless or callous indifference to the federally protected rights of others.

Smith v. Wade, 461 U.S. 30, 56 (1983).

A standard based on reckless misconduct or callous indifference requires a greater showing of culpability than simple negligence. *See Johnson v. Lundell* .... In *Johnson* ....

Related legal rules

The extraordinary nature of punitive damages justifies close scrutiny of the trial judge's instructions to ensure that they recognize even fine distinctions in culpability. Otherwise ....

Policy analysis

In this case, the trial court instructed the jury that it could award punitive damages if it found that Officer Mullins was "grossly and inexcusably careless." (III R.T. 52.) This instruction did not adequately convey the requisite standard: reckless or callous disregard of constitutional rights.

Application to facts: the instruction

Even when coupled with the adjective "grossly," the word "careless" connotes only a breach of duty rising to the level of negligence....

Further analysis of instruction

The trial court improperly instructed the jury on the standard for punitive damages. Officer Mullins is entitled to a new trial so that the jury may apply the proper legal standard to the facts.

Conclusion

Alternatively, if you are prepared to labor against a restricted standard of review, you can try to persuade the appellate court to overturn the jury's implicit finding that Officer Mullins was "grossly and inexcusably careless." Under this approach, you must review the underlying evidence, such as the testimony at trial, and explain why the jury's finding is not supported by substantial evidence:

B. Alternatively, this court should vacate the award of punitive damages because substantial evidence does not support the jury's finding that Officer Mullins acted with the requisite culpability to justify punitive damages.

Introduction to argument

Even if the trial court's instructions adequately conveyed the culpability required for an award of punitive damages, the jury did not properly find such culpability on the part of Officer Mullins. At most, the evidence supports the conclusion that Officer Mullins made a reasonable mistake in judgment in chaotic circumstances. Therefore the trial judge erred in denying Mullins's Motion for Judgment Notwithstanding the Verdict on the issue of punitive damages, and this Court should overturn the jury's award of punitive damages.

Rules governing review of jury's findings

This Court may overturn a finding of the jury if the finding is unsupported by substantial evidence in the record so that no reasonable juror could have made the finding on the evidence. *See* .... This substantial-evidence standard permits appellate courts to review jury findings to guard against verdicts based on bias, passion, or incompetence. *See* .... To satisfy the purposes of such review, this court should scrutinize the record for ....

Examination of facts: the testimony

Officer Mullins's uncontradicted testimony establishes the reasonableness of his actions. He testified that the report over his squad car radio identified the robbery suspect only as a young man of slight build with dark, shoulder-length hair. (II RT at 335-36.) One block from the robbery site, Officer Mullins spotted Ms. Wong walking at a very brisk pace away from the robbery site. *Id.* at 336. He initially passed her by because he was looking for a male suspect. *Id.* at 337. However, when he found no other suspects in the vicinity, he realized that Ms. Wong fit the description of the robbery suspect except for her gender. *Id.* at 339. He remembered that Ms. Wong was wearing jeans and a sweatshirt, and he realized that an agitated witness might have been mistaken about her gender. *Id.* at 339-40. Consequently, he turned his squad car around, found Ms. Wong again, and stopped her for questioning. *Id.* at 340.

Other testimony supports Officer Mullins's version of the events. Ms. Wong herself testified that she had been walking at an unusually brisk pace. (I RT at 327.) She also admitted that she had trouble answering Officer Mullins's questions. *Id.* at 331. Although in her testimony Ms. Wong offered innocent explanations for her hurried pace and her inability to communicate effectively with Officer Mullins, *id.* at 360, nothing in the record shows that these explanations were apparent to Officer Mullins at the time of the arrest....

Analysis of testimony: permissible inferences

In sum, the evidence leads inescapably to one conclusion: In his eagerness to fulfill his duties as a police officer, Officer Mullins mistakenly arrested the wrong person, but he did not recklessly disregard anyone's constitutional rights in doing so. Quite the contrary, he took steps at several stages to safeguard Ms. Wong's rights.

The record simply does not contain substantial evidence supporting the jury's finding of sufficient culpability to justify an award of punitive damages. Apparently, the jurors misunderstood or ignored the trial court's instructions and based their verdict on irrelevant factors.

Conclusion

For these reasons, this Court should overturn the jury's award of punitive damages. The evidence does not support this extraordinary award.

Counsel for the appellee can respond to either of these arguments directly. In response to the first sample argument, for example, she can argue either that (1) the law permits an award of punitive damages for culpability less than recklessness, perhaps because "callous indifference" denotes a lower standard that equates to gross and inexcusable carelessness, or (2) the trial judge's instructions adequately conveyed the requisite standard of recklessness. In response to the second sample argument, she can (1) emphasize the restricted standard of appellate review, (2) describe evidence in the record that supports a jury finding of recklessness or callous indifference, and (3) explain why that evidence should be viewed as "substantial."

2. Varieties of Fact Analysis

As illustrated in the preceding subsection, the appropriate nature and depth of fact analysis on appeal will depend in part on two factors: (a) the nature of the appellant's challenge to the trial court's judgment, and (b) the procedural posture of the case when the trial court disposed of it.

a. Nature of Appellant's Challenge

For an example of the first factor, suppose that you represent the appellant and that you choose to challenge the trial judge's instructions on the law, as in the first sample passage in Subsection 1 above. Your arguments on such a challenge will often focus on the law and include only modest fact analysis. Specifically, after your arguments on the law, your application of the law to the facts could include no more than a comparison of the correct legal rule to the actual instruction and a statement about the need for a new trial with proper instructions to the jury:

In this case, the trial court instructed the jury that it could award punitive damages if it found that Officer Mullins was "grossly and inexcusably careless." (III R.T. 52.) This instruction did not adequately convey ....

... Officer Mullins is entitled to a new trial so that the jury may apply the proper legal standard to the facts.

In contrast, detailed fact analysis will be mandatory if the appellant challenges the findings of fact of the trial judge or jury, as did the appellant in the sample briefs at the end of this chapter. As illustrated in the second sample passage in Subsection 1 above, the parties then must review the record and argue whether the evidence supports the finding of fact under the applicable standard of review:

Officer Mullins's uncontradicted testimony establishes the reasonableness of his actions. He testified that the report over his squad car radio ....

Other testimony supports Officer Mullins's version of the events. Ms. Wong herself testified that she had been walking at an unusually brisk pace. (I RT at 327.) She also admitted ....

In sum, the evidence leads inescapably to one conclusion: ....

The record simply does not contain substantial evidence supporting the jury's finding of sufficient culpability to justify an award of punitive damages....

---

b. Procedural Posture

Your fact analysis may also vary with the second factor: the procedural posture of the case at the time of trial disposition. Specifically, dispositions at different pretrial and trial stages will lead to appellate analyses of different kinds of facts.

For example, suppose that the trial court dismissed the action for failure of the complaint to state a claim for relief. On appeal, you can argue the law, but you will have no findings of fact or even underlying evidence in the record to which to apply the law. Instead, you must argue whether the factual allegations of the complaint state a claim for relief under the correct interpretation of the law.

On appeal from summary judgment, on the other hand, you ordinarily will have a record of preliminary showings of fact with documents, affidavits, and other discovery materials. Therefore, you can argue whether the evidentiary materials submitted by both parties created a genuine issue of fact for trial under the applicable law.

Finally, the record will include formally introduced evidence if either party has appealed from the trial judge's denial of a motion for a directed verdict or for a judgment notwithstanding the verdict after presentation of the evidence in a jury trial. Moreover, on appeal from judgment after a full trial, the record will include both the evidence and the findings of the judge or jury. As explored above, the record in either case may provide a fertile source for fact analysis, depending on the appellant's strategic choices and the nature of her challenge to the ruling or judgment in the trial court.

VI. The Conclusion

The discussion in Section III.C of Chapter 2 about the conclusion section of a brief applies with full force to appellate briefs. At the least, your conclusion must briefly restate the action that your client requests the appellate court to take. In a complex case, your conclusion may also include a brief summary and synthesis of the arguments presented in your brief.

VII. Summary

When preparing an appellate brief, you should

1. follow rules of procedure and local court rules governing format,
2. state the issues and facts in a manner that invites a favorable conclusion but that maintains credibility and accuracy, and
3. argue the case with attention to the law, the facts, and policy considerations.

Exercise 8-1

In addition to responding to the appellant's arguments on appeal, an appellee may file its own "cross-appeal" to affirmatively challenge aspects of a lower
court's decision. The following appellate briefs are the Opening Brief, Answering
Brief, and Reply Brief on a cross-appeal filed by the appellee of the main appeal.
The briefs reproduced below appear in their original form, with the exception of
corrections of minor typographical errors, the reduction of line spacing, the dele-
tion of some references to the main appeal, and the omission of a procedural issue
and a portion of the arguments on punitive damages.

The briefs depart in many ways from standard citation form and from the writing style recommended in this book, perhaps illustrating that a variety of styles
can effectively communicate or persuade. As you read these briefs, consider what
changes you would make to conform the writing to your own style, and consider
the following questions.

1. Statements of the Case

Study the procedural history traced in the statements of the case in the opening brief and the answering brief. Identify the trial court rulings challenged by
each party. Is it clear why both Koepnick and Sears were dissatisfied, resulting in
cross-appeals? What standard did the trial court apply in reaching its decision on
the point appealed from on the cross-appeal? What standard of review should the
appellate court apply?

2. Statements of Fact

Study the statements of fact in the opening and answering briefs. Could you
identify the author of each statement if you read no other parts of the briefs? Does
each fact statement successfully present an apparently complete and neutral summary of the facts while placing the advocate's client in the best possible light?

Consider the points of conflict between the two fact statements. In what
instances is the apparent conflict simply a reflection of each advocate using techniques of writing style to emphasize some facts and deemphasize others? In what
instances is the conflict rooted in genuine disagreement about the factual conclusions that find support in the record? What is the legal significance on appeal of
conflicting evidence in the record on a material point, given the procedural posture of this case?

3. Statements of Issues

Study the statements of the issues in the opening and answering briefs. Does
each advocate successfully phrase each issue in a way that invites a favorable
response for his client? Does either state a false issue that easily invites a favorable response but that does not fairly identify the real issue on appeal?

4. Arguments

Study the arguments in all three briefs. How important is fact analysis to the arguments in each brief ? Would the brief allocate more time to discussion of legal rules if the appellant were appealing from the trial court's rejection of a novel legal theory of recovery? Would the main point headings be easier to read if they did not capitalize the first letter of nearly every word in each heading?

5. Responsive Arguments

Does the answering brief effectively respond to the opening brief ? Does the reply brief effectively respond to the answering brief ?

6. Writing Style

How would you change the writing style or presentation of authority in any of the briefs? Explain the reasons for your editing.

7. Format

How well do the briefs conform to the following formats for appellate briefs that were prescribed by the version of the Arizona Rules of Civil Appellate Procedure in effect when the briefs were filed? (But note that the line spacing is less than typically required by court rules, to reduce the space occupied by the sample briefs in this book.)

Rule 13. Briefs

13(a) Brief of the Appellant. The brief of the appellant shall concisely and clearly set forth under appropriate headings and in the order here indicated:

1. A table of contents with page references.
2. A table of citations, which shall alphabetically arrange and index the cases, statutes and other authorities cited, with references to the pages of the brief on which they are cited.
3. A statement of the case, indicating briefly the basis of the appellate court's jurisdiction, the nature of the case, the course of the proceedings and the disposition in the court below.
4. A statement of facts relevant to the issues presented for review, with appropriate references to the record ....
5. A statement of the issues presented for review ....
6. An argument, which shall contain the contentions of the appellant with respect to the issues presented, and the reasons therefor, with citations to the authorities, statutes and parts of the record relied on. The argument may include a summary ....
7. A short conclusion stating the precise relief sought.
8. An appendix if desired.

13(b) Brief of the Appellee. The brief of the appellee shall conform to the requirements of the preceding subdivision, except that a statement of the case, a statement of the facts or a statement of the issues need not be included unless the appellee finds the statements of the appellant to be insufficient or incorrect.

13(c) Reply Brief. The appellant may file a reply brief, but it shall be confined strictly to rebuttal of points urged in the appellee's brief. No further briefs may be filed except as provided in Rule 13(e) or by leave of court....

13(e) Briefs in Cases Involving Cross-Appeals. A party who files a cross-appeal may combine in one brief his brief as appellee and his brief as cross-appellant. If the appellant wishes to file a further brief, he may combine in one brief his reply brief as appellant and his brief as cross-appellee. The cross-appellant may file a reply brief on the issues of the cross-appeal.

Fred Cole
Roger W. Perry
Gust, Rosenfeld, Divelbess & Henderson
3300 Valley Bank Center
Phoenix, Arizona 85073
Attorneys for Defendant-Appellee/Cross-Appellant

IN THE COURT OF APPEALS
STATE OF ARIZONA

Division One

MAX KOEPNICK,
 	
  Plaintiff-Appellant
 	
  Cross-Appellee,
 	
v.
 	
SEARS, ROEBUCK & COMPANY,
 	
  Defendant-Appellee
 	
  Cross-Appellant.
	1 CA-CIV 9147
	
	MARICOPA County Superior Court
	
	No. C-502081

OPENING BRIEF ON CROSS-APPEAL

TABLE OF CONTENTS

TABLE OF AUTHORITIES

APPELLEE'S OPENING BRIEF ON CROSS-APPEAL

STATEMENT OF THE CASE

Plaintiff-appellant Max Koepnick ("Koepnick") commenced this action by fil-ing a complaint on December 5, 1983 (C.T. at 1). The defendants named in the complaint were defendant-appellee Sears, Roebuck & Company ("Sears") and the City of Mesa ("Mesa"). The complaint set forth claims in six counts, which were all alleged to have arisen out of an incident that occurred at the Sears store at Fiesta Mall in Mesa, Arizona on December 6, 1982. Sears was named as defendant in only four of the counts. These were Count One for false arrest, Count Four for trespass to chattel, Count Five for invasion of privacy and Count Six for malicious pros-ecution. Mesa was named as defendant in Count Two for false arrest and Count Three for assault and battery. Mesa was also named as a co-defendant with Sears in Counts Five and Six.

Prior to trial, Mesa moved for summary judgment on Count Two for false arrest (C.T. at 55). The court granted Mesa's motion on that count based on the court's determination that probable cause existed for Mesa to detain Koepnick (Minute entry dated January 9, 1986).

Trial to a jury on the other counts of Koepnick's complaint commenced on January 10, 1986. At the close of Koepnick's case-in-brief, Sears moved for a directed verdict on all counts asserted against it (7R.T. at 13). Plaintiff stipulated to the dismissal of Count Six for malicious prosecution against Sears, and the court granted Sears a directed verdict on Count Four for invasion of privacy (Min-ute entry dated January 21, 1986). Mesa made a similar motion and was granted directed verdicts on Count Two for false arrest, Count Five for invasion of privacy, Count Six for malicious prosecution, and all plaintiff's claims for punitive dam-ages (Minute entry dated January 21, 1986).

At the close of evidence, Sears and Mesa again moved for directed verdicts on all the remaining claims against them. These motions were denied (8R.T. at 84-92). The remaining claims were submitted to the jury. The jury returned ver-dicts against Sears for $25,000.00 in compensatory damages and $500,000.00 in punitive damages on Count One for false arrest and $100.00 in compensatory dam-ages and $25,000.00 punitive damages on Count Four for trespass to chattel (9R.T. at 101-03). The jury also returned verdicts against Mesa for $50,000.00 on Count Three for assault and battery and $100.00 on Count Four for trespass to chattel (9R.T. at 101-03). Judgment was entered on the verdicts on February 25, 1986 (C.T. at 97; Appendix A).

Sears filed motions for judgment notwithstanding the verdicts and for a new trial on Counts One and Four on March 11, 1986 (C.T. at 100). Mesa filed a motion for a new trial on March 11, 1986 (C.T. at 101) and a motion for judgment not-withstanding the verdict or, in the alternative, for a new trial and for remittitur on

March 12, 1986 (C.T. at 104). An amended motion for judgment notwithstanding the verdicts and for new trial was filed by Sears on April 16, 1986 (C.T. at 113).

A hearing on the post-trial motions was held on April 17, 1986. Upon consideration of the motions, the court granted Sears' and Mesa's motions for judgment N.O.V.[17] on Count Four for trespass to chattel and granted Sears' motion for new trial on Count One for false arrest. The court granted judgment N.O.V. for defendants on the trespass to chattel claim as Koepnick failed to present evidence that the alleged trespass caused any damage or injury, which is an essential element of an actionable claim. The court granted a new trial on the false arrest claim as the court determined that reasonable cause to detain Koepnick existed as a matter of law and that, therefore, it had erred in instructing the jury on the issue of reasonable cause (Minute entry dated May 14, 1986; Appendix B).

A second hearing occurred on June 24, 1986, pertaining to further post-trial motions .... The final order setting forth the court's disposition of the post-trial motions, ... was entered July 23, 1986 (C.T. at 125; Appendix D).

Koepnick filed a notice of appeal on July 24, 1986, with respect to the trial court's order granting Sears' motion for judgment notwithstanding the verdict on Count Four for trespass to chattel and for a new trial on Count One for false arrest (C.T. at 124). Sears filed a notice of cross-appeal with respect to the portions of the judgment dated February 24, 1986, granting judgment in favor of Koepnick and the portions of the order dated July 18, 1986, denying Sears' motion for judgment notwithstanding the verdict on Count One for false arrest and conditionally denying defendant Sears' motion for new trial on Count Four for trespass to chattel (C.T. at 128). No appeal was taken by either Koepnick or Mesa with respect to the adjudications of the claims asserted by Koepnick against Mesa. Accordingly, Mesa is not a party to this appeal.

The parties stipulated to waiving the posting of cost bonds on the appeals. This court has jurisdiction of the appeal and cross-appeal pursuant to A.R.S. §12-1201 B and F.

STATEMENT OF FACTS

On December 6, 1982, Koepnick drove to the Sears store located at Fiesta Mall to get some screwdrivers (4R.T. at 145-47). He arrived at approximately 5 p.m. (4R.T. at 145). Once in the store, he was assisted by Mara Thomas, a sales clerk in the hardware department (4R.T. at 147; 8R.T. at 36). After Koepnick selected the tools he wanted, Thomas carried them to the cash register (4R.T. at 148). Koepnick was waited on at the cash register by Bruce Rosenhan, another sales clerk, who

---

17. [Author's note: "N.O.V." is an abbreviation for the Latin term *non obstante veredicto*, which means "notwithstanding the verdict," the phrase used earlier in the Statement of the Case. A judgment notwithstanding the verdict refers to a ruling by the judge that the jury's verdict on an issue is not supported by the evidence presented at trial and should be replaced by the court's contrary judgment on that issue.]

rang up the tools for Koepnick (4R.T. at 150-51; 7R.T. at 88). These tools consisted of a set of screwdrivers, a wrench set, a nut-driver set, an open-end wrench set and a set of pliers (7R.T. at 88-89; Ex. 11). Koepnick asked Rosenhan for an itemized receipt (4R.T. at 151; 7R.T. at 88). Rosenhan bagged Koepnick's purchases, stapling the bag closed with the receipts on the outside (4R.T. at 151; 7R.T. at 89). Koepnick left the cash register area (4R.T. at 171; 7R.T. at 89).

After waiting on Koepnick, Rosenhan went out to work on the sales floor (7R.T. at 90). Rosenhan saw Koepnick again in the hardware department approximately 15 minutes after he had waited on him (7R.T. at 90-91). Koepnick came over to where he and Thomas were in the back of the department (7R.T. at 90). Rosenhan saw Koepnick speak to Thomas and pull a large wrench out of the shopping bag Rosenhan had earlier stapled closed (7R.T. at 91). At that time, Koepnick's bag was open and there were no receipts in view on it (7R.T. at 91). Rosenhan realized that the wrench Koepnick pulled out of the bag was not one of the wrenches from the sets that he sold to Koepnick (7R.T. at 91). When Rosenhan finished with the customer he was helping, he asked Thomas if Koepnick put the wrench back in his bag and whether she had sold it to him (7R.T. at 92). Thomas told him that Koepnick put it back in his bag and that she had not sold that wrench to him or had anything to do with it (7R.T. at 92). Rosenhan asked all the other employees present in the department whether they had sold that particular wrench to Koepnick and learned that none of them had either (7R.T. at 92).

Rosenhan went to the front register and used the phone to call security (7R.T. at 92). He spoke with Steve Lessard, one of the security agents on duty at that time in the store (4R.T. at 77). It was approximately 5:35 to 5:40 when Lessard received the call from Rosenhan (4R.T. at 83). He informed Lessard that he believed that there was a customer in the store who was a shoplifter (4R.T. at 77). Lessard told him to meet in the sewing machine department, which is located next to hardware (4R.T. at 77-78). When Rosenhan and Lessard met, Rosenhan explained what had occurred with the purchase of the tools and the subsequent incident of the large wrench being observed in the bag (7R.T. at 93; 4R.T. at 78-79). Lessard radioed to Dave Pollock, another security agent on duty at Sears, and requested that he come and assist him (4R.T. at 79).

When Pollock arrived, Lessard explained what he had learned from Rosenhan and asked him to watch Koepnick while he spoke with the other employees (4R.T. at 79-80). Lessard went around the hardware department and spoke with each of the employees present there (4R.T. at 80). Among the employees he spoke with was Mara Thomas, who informed Lessard of her contacts with Koepnick and confirmed the fact that she did not sell or help Koepnick with the large wrench he had in his bag (4R.T. at 80-81; 8R.T. at 41).

After Lessard had spoken with all of the employees in the hardware department and confirmed that none of them sold the wrench in question, he observed

Koepnick in the socket aisle (4R.T. at 82). Koepnick picked out some sockets and then put the bag he was carrying down at the cash register (4R.T. at 82). Koepnick went back to the socket aisle and picked up another socket (4R.T. at 82). While Koepnick was away from the cash register area, Lessard instructed Pollock to go by the shopping bag and confirm that the large wrench in question was still in it (4R.T. at 82). When Pollock went over to the bag, he observed that the bag was pulled open and the wrench was inside (7R.T. at 41). No receipts were seen in or on the bag by Pollock (7R.T. at 41, 84). Pollock reported back to Lessard and told him what he saw (7R.T. at 41).

Lessard and Pollock observed as Koepnick returned to the cash register and purchased some sockets (7R.T. at 42; 4R.T. at 82-83). As Koepnick began to leave the store, Lessard went to the clerk at the cash register and asked what items had been purchased, verifying that Koepnick had not paid for the crescent wrench in question at that time (7R.T. at 83-84). Lessard and Pollock followed Koepnick out of the store (4R.T. at 84). At no time did either observe Koepnick take any receipts off the shopping bag he was carrying (4R.T. at 84). As they followed Koepnick out of the store, they discussed the information they had and decided to stop Koepnick with respect to the large wrench in question (4R.T. at 84).

Koepnick estimated that it was approximately 6:15 P.M. when he exited the east door of the store (5R.T. at 72). Lessard approached Koepnick as he walked into the parking lot area approximately 20 to 25 feet from the door of the store (4R.T. at 87). Koepnick refused to stop when Lessard first spoke to him (5R.T. at 178; 4R.T. at 87-88). Koepnick testified that Lessard then came around in front of him, pulled the wrench in question out of the bag and told him that he did not have a receipt for it (4R.T. at 178). Koepnick was also told he was under arrest for shoplifting (4R.T. at 178). Both Koepnick and Lessard testified that Koepnick was shown identification by Lessard, although Koepnick testified that he did not see it clearly (4R.T. at 179-80; 4R.T. at 87-88). Koepnick did not show a receipt for the wrench when Lessard stopped him (4R.T. at 91; 5R.T. at 63).

Koepnick initially refused to return to the store with Lessard and Pollock (4R.T. at 179). Koepnick was informed that he had to return to the store with them (4R.T. at 180). After some further discussion, Koepnick was escorted up to the security office in the Sears store (4R.T. at 179-81; 5R.T. at 70-72). He was not handcuffed or physically injured in any way by the Sears employees (5R.T. at 70, 72). Once in the security office, Koepnick was instructed to sit down to wait for the police to arrive (4R.T. at 183).

In the security office, Lessard examined the shopping bag Koepnick had been carrying and found receipts for the purchase of the sockets (4R.T. at 94; 5R.T. at 72-73). No other receipts were found in or on the bag (4R.T. at 95). Although Koepnick had the receipts for his other purchases in his front shirt pocket, he never attempted to show them to the Sears employees (5R.T. at 63, 66). While waiting for the police to arrive, Koepnick asked if he could get a drink of water or go down to his truck, but those requests were refused (4R.T. at 183).

While Pollock watched Koepnick, Lessard continued his investigation and began to prepare his report of the incident (4R.T. at 97-98). Lessard telephoned the hardware department and spoke to Kim Miller, the hardware department manager. Lessard called the hardware department as he needed the stock number for the wrench in question (8R.T. at 72). He also wanted to have the audit tape on the cash register checked as there were no receipts in the shopping bag for the tool sets that Rosenhan had told him he had rung up for Koepnick (8R.T. at 72).

Officer Michael Campbell of the Mesa Police Department arrived at 6:30 P.M., approximately 15 minutes after Koepnick had been brought to the security office (6R.T. at 67; 4R.T. at 186). Campbell and Lessard stepped across the hall to permit Lessard to inform the officer as to what he had observed (4R.T. at 186; 4R.T. at 101-102). As Lessard was talking with Officer Campbell, Koepnick attempted to walk out of the security office (4R.T. at 187; 4R.T. at 58). Officer Campbell came out into the hallway and met Koepnick at the door to the security office (4R.T. at 187; 4R.T. at 59). Koepnick and Officer Campbell became involved in an altercation, resulting in Koepnick striking his head against the back wall of the security office (4R.T. at 187-88; 4R.T. at 60-64). After that occurred, Officer Campbell was able to handcuff Koepnick (6R.T. at 96-98).

Officer Campbell had made the decision to arrest Koepnick when the altercation started (6R.T. at 93). While he was being handcuffed by Officer Campbell, Koepnick took the receipts that had been in his shirt pocket and stuffed them inside his shirt (4R.T. at 189; 6R.T. at 96-97). Once Koepnick was handcuffed, Officer Campbell removed the receipts he had observed Koepnick stuffing inside his shirt (4R.T. at 66; 6R.T. at 100). The receipts that were found on Koepnick were examined and matched to the various tools Koepnick had in his shopping bag (4R.T. at 191; 4R.T. at 68).

During the altercation, Officer Campbell had instructed Pollock to use his radio to call for assistance (6R.T. at 98). Sergeant Reynolds and Officer Gates came to the Sears security office in response to the request (6R.T. at 108).

Lessard learned after the altercation that another sales clerk, Jeff Ward, had also been working in the hardware department that day (4R.T. at 103-104). Ward, however, had left the sales floor before Rosenhan observed Koepnick with the wrench in the shopping bag and called Lessard down to investigate the situation (8R.T. at 9-10). When Ward later returned to the hardware department, Miller informed him of the call from Lessard and that security had some questions about whether a customer paid for a certain wrench (8R.T. at 110). Ward told Miller that he had rung up such a wrench for a customer (8R.T. at 11). Miller took Ward up to the security office (8R.T. at 11). They arrived about the time the altercation occurred between Koepnick and Officer Campbell (4R.T. at 103; 8R.T. at 12).

Once Lessard became aware of Ward's contact with Koepnick, he interviewed Ward (4R.T. at 104). Ward stated that he had first observed Koepnick as Koepnick walked up to the cash register and pulled the receipt off a shopping bag that was lying on the counter (4R.T. at 104; 8R.T. at 6). Ward asked him if that was his package and Koepnick said it was (4R.T. at 104; 8R.T. at 6). Koepnick had a large combination wrench and a smaller set of wrenches with him to purchase (4R.T. at 104; 8R.T. at 6). Ward rang these items up, and Koepnick paid for them (4R.T. at 104). Ward then bagged these wrenches in a smaller brown bag, which Koepnick placed inside the larger shopping bag he already had (4R.T. at 104; 8R.T. at 104; 8R.T. at 8). Koepnick then placed the receipts Ward had prepared for the wrenches in his shirt pocket and left (8R.T. at 8). Ward did not see Koepnick again on the sales floor that night (8R.T. at 9). After Ward finished ringing up the other customers at the cash register, he left the sales floor (8R.T. at 9, 24). Ward told Lessard he had been on a break (4R.T. at 72). Ward could not recall at trial exactly where he went when he left the sales floor (8R.T. at 9).

After questioning Ward, Lessard discussed with the police officers the possibility that Koepnick had taken the wrench he purchased from Ward out to his truck and brought the shopping bag back in and put another wrench in it (4R.T. at 69-70). Lessard was familiar with this method of shoplifting through his work as a security agent (4R.T. at 105). The information Lessard had that caused him to believe that this was a possibility was (1) Ward's statement that he had bagged the large wrench in a separate brown bag that was not present in the large shopping bag Koepnick had when he was stopped, (2) Rosenhan's statement that there was a period of 15 minutes from the time he last saw Koepnick after his first purchase until he saw him again in the hardware department with the wrench, and (3) Koepnick's actions in not exhibiting the receipts for his purchases when he was detained (4R.T. at 105-06, 111).

The police officers made the decision to search Koepnick's truck (6R.T. at 101-02; 6R.T. at 128). Officer Campbell testified that he asked Koepnick for permission to search the truck and Koepnick consented (6R.T. at 130). Koepnick testified that he consented to the search only on the condition that he be allowed to go with them (4R.T. at 194). Lessard accompanied Officer Gates down to Koepnick's truck (4R.T. at 107). Officer Gates opened the vehicle and Lessard assisted him in looking in the truck (4R.T. at 107). No Sears merchandise was found (4R.T. at 107). The search of the truck lasted about two minutes (4R.T. at 72-73). Nothing was taken or damaged in the search (4R.T. at 110-11, 197).

Once Officer Gates and Lessard returned to the security office, the police officers discussed what action they would take (4R.T. at 197-98). Sergeant Reynolds made the decision to cite Koepnick for disorderly conduct for his actions in striking Officer Campbell (6R.T. at 130). After Koepnick received the citation, he was released by the Mesa Police Department (4R.T. at 198).

ISSUES PRESENTED

1. Did the trial court err in denying Sears' motion for judgment notwithstanding the verdict on the claim for false arrest when the evidence is insufficient to support a finding by the jury that plaintiff was detained by Sears in an unreasonable manner or for an unreasonable length of time?

2. Did the trial court err in denying Sears' motion for judgment notwithstanding the verdict on the punitive damage claims where the evidence fails to establish a *prima facie* case for such damages?

ARGUMENT

I. Sears' Motion for Judgment Notwithstanding the Verdict on the Claim for False Arrest Should Have Been Granted by the Trial Court.

A. Applicable Standard of Review.

The standard of review for determining the appropriateness of the granting of a judgment N.O.V. is whether the evidence is sufficient that reasonable men could discern facts to support the verdict. *Rancho Pescado, Inc. v. Northwestern Mutual Life Insurance Co.*, 140 Ariz. 174, 680 P.2d 1235 (App. 1984). In reviewing a judgment N.O.V., the appellate court views the evidence most favorably to sustaining the verdict. *Lerner v. Brettschneider*, 123 Ariz. 152, 598 P.2d 515 (App. 1979). When the evidence is insufficient to meet the burden of proof to establish the claim, entry of judgment N.O.V. is proper. *Rancho Pescado, Inc. v. Northwestern Mutual Life Insurance Co.*, 140 Ariz. at 186, 680 P.2d at 1247; *Lerner v. Brettschneider*, 123 Ariz. at 155, 598 P.2d at 518.

B. There Was Insufficient Evidence to Justify Any Finding of Liability on the Claim of False Arrest.

A.R.S. §13-1805C sets forth the statutory shopkeeper's privilege for detaining a suspected shoplifter. A detention is deemed privileged under this statute if it is made with reasonable cause for a proper purpose and done in a reasonable manner and for reasonable time. *Gortarez v. Smitty's Super Valu, Inc.*, 140 Ariz. 97, 680 P.2d 807 (1984). The undisputed evidence established the existence of all the elements necessary for this privilege. Therefore, Sears' motion for judgment notwithstanding the verdict on plaintiff's claim of false arrest should have been granted by the trial court.

1. Reasonable Cause.

The existence of reasonable cause and the reasonableness of the detention, both as to time and manner, are for the court to decide as a matter of law where there is no conflict in the evidence. *Id.* at 104. The trial court determined as a matter of law that reasonable cause did exist for plaintiff's detention in granting of the motion for new trial. The propriety of that decision is discussed in Section

I.E of Sears' response brief, which is incorporated herein by reference to avoid duplication.

The remaining elements of A.R.S. §13-1805C that must be established for the privilege to exist are (1) a proper purpose for the detention, (2) the reasonableness of the time of the detention, and (3) the reasonableness of the manner of the detention. *Id. Gortarez*, 140 Ariz. at 104.

2. Proper Purpose.

A.R.S. §13-1805C sets forth two purposes for which a privileged detention may be made under the statute. They are (1) questioning the subject, or (2) summoning a law enforcement officer. Given Koepnick's testimony at trial, which must be accepted for the purposes of deciding a motion for judgment N.O.V., there is plainly a dispute in the evidence as to what questioning, if any, occurred during Sears' detention of him. Koepnick's testimony was that he was not questioned at all (4R.T. at 184-85). There is, however, no question about the existence of the alternative purpose authorized by the statute for Koepnick's detention—summoning a law enforcement officer. It is undisputed that the Mesa Police Department was contacted by Sears and requested to respond to where plaintiff was being detained (Opening brief, p. 8). Thus, this element of the privilege is unquestionably present in this case.

3. The Length of Detention.

The reasonableness of the length of Koepnick's detention is also undisputedly established by the evidence. There is no evidence in the record that creates any issue of fact as to the reasonableness of the length of Sears' detention of Koepnick. The undisputed evidence is that plaintiff was taken to the Sears security office and the police called without any undue delay on the part of Sears. No evidence of anything to the contrary is present in the record. Upon Officer Campbell's arrival, Lessard immediately began to explain the situation to him. Before he could even finish, the altercation between Koepnick and Officer Campbell occurred. At that time, Koepnick was placed under arrest by Officer Campbell independently of any shoplifting and taken into the custody of the Mesa Police. From that point on plaintiff was no longer in Sears' custody.

These facts are undisputed. There is nothing in the evidence which would permit the jury to conclude that the length of Koepnick's detention by Sears for the express statutory purpose of summoning a law enforcement officer was unreasonable. Indeed, there was no way Sears could make Koepnick's detention for that purpose any shorter. The length of that detention was determined by the amount of time it took the Mesa Police to respond to the Sears store. This is something that Sears had no control over; in any event, there is no evidence to permit a jury to find that the actual amount of time it took the officer to respond was in any way unreasonable. Accordingly, the trial court should have determined that the length of Koepnick's detention by Sears was reasonable as a matter of law.

4. The Manner of Detention.

Neither is there any evidence in the record that creates any issue of fact as to the reasonableness of the manner of Koepnick's detention by Sears. The evidence is again undisputed that Koepnick was stopped by Lessard, escorted up to the Sears security office and detained there until the police arrived. The Arizona Supreme Court in *Gortarez* stated that reasonable force may be used to detain a suspected shoplifter. 140 Ariz. at 104, 680 P.2d at 814. There is no evidence that any unreasonable force was ever used on plaintiff by Sears employees. Sears employees never struck or fought with Koepnick (5R.T. at 70-72). They did not even handcuff or search him (4R.T. at 96; 5R.T. at 70). Koepnick confirmed in his testimony that he was not physically injured in any manner by Sears employees (5R.T. at 72). In short, there is absolutely no evidence to indicate that the manner of plaintiff's detention by Sears was unreasonable.

As indicated above, the reasonableness of the detention, both as to time and manner, is one for the court to decide as a matter of law where there is no conflict of the evidence. *Id.* As there was no conflicting evidence presented at trial as to these elements that would support a finding that the manner and length of Sears' detention of Koepnick was unreasonable, the trial court should have determined that the detention was reasonable as a matter of law and not submitted any issue of this claim to the jury. Accordingly, Sears' motion for judgment notwithstanding the verdict on the claim of false arrest should have been granted by the trial court.

II. Sears' Motion for Judgment Notwithstanding the Verdict on the Claims of Punitive Damages Should Have Been Granted by the Trial Court.

A. The Applicable Standard.

The Arizona Supreme Court has recently modified the standard for determining whether there has been a *prima facie* showing permitting the assessment of punitive damages. The decisions discussing and applying this new standard include *Filasky v. Preferred Risk Mutual Insurance Co.*, No. CV-86-0237-T (filed March 2, 1987); *Gurule v. Illinois Mutual Life and Casualty Co.*, No. CV-86-0488-PR (filed March 2, 1987); *Rawlings v. Apodaca*, 151 Ariz. 149, 726 P.2d 565 (1986); and *Linthicum v. National Life Insurance Co.*, 150 Ariz. 326, 723 P.2d 675 (1986). The portion of the *Linthicum* decision setting forth the new standard is quoted at length in Section IV.B of Appellee's response brief, which is incorporated herein by reference to avoid duplication.

Although the trial court denied Sears' motion for judgment N.O.V. with respect to punitive damages before the Supreme Court announced the more stringent standard in *Linthicum v. National Life Insurance Co.*, that standard applies to cases upon appellate review. *See, e.g., Hawkins v. Allstate Insurance Co.*, No. CV-86-0010-PR (filed February 26, 1987) (applying standard announced in *Linthicum* to trial court's pre-*Linthicum* ruling on motion for judgment notwithstanding the verdict).

Under the new standard, plaintiffs are not automatically entitled to an instruction on punitive damages upon the showing of a *prima facie* intentional tort. To recover punitive damages, something more is required over and above the "mere commission of a tort." *Rawlings v. Apodaca*, 151 Ariz. at 162, 726 P.2d at 587. There must be a showing of either an intent to injure the plaintiff or a conscious pursuit of a course of conduct knowing that it creates a substantial risk of significant harm to others. *Linthicum v. Nationwide Life Insurance Co.*, 150 Ariz. at 330, 723 P.2d at 679. The requirement of this "something more" or "evil mind" is to assure that punitive damages are awarded only where the purposes of deterrence are furthered. *Gurule v. Illinois Mutual Life and Casualty Co.*, slip op. at 3. The punishment resulting from punitive damage is appropriate only where there is "some element of outrage similar to that usually found in crime." *Rawlings v. Apodaca*, 151 Ariz. at 161, 726 P.2d at 578, *quoting* Restatement (Second) of Torts, §908, comment b (1979).

B. The Evidence Fails to Show a *Prima Facie* Case for Punitive Damages with Respect to the Claim of False Arrest.

As discussed in Section I.B of this cross-appeal brief, the evidence in the record is insufficient to make out a *prima facie* case of false arrest, let alone rise to the level necessary to permit the assessment of punitive damages. There is absolutely no evidence that suggests that Sears intended to injure Koepnick or that it consciously pursued a course of conduct knowing that it created a substantial risk of tremendous harm to him. As the trial court determined, the facts are uncontradicted that Lessard actually and reasonably believed that when Koepnick left the store he had merchandise for which he had not paid. Acting on that reasonable belief, Lessard stopped Koepnick . . . .

. . . .

C. The Evidence Fails to Establish a *Prima Facie* Case for Punitive Damages with Respect to the Claim of Trespass to Chattel.

. . . .

CONCLUSION

The trial court was correct in finding that reasonable cause existed as matter of law for Sears' detention of Koepnick. The court erred, however, in ruling that there was sufficient evidence to submit to the jury the issues of the reasonableness of the time and manner of the detention. Accordingly, the trial court's order of July 23, 1986 should be reversed to the extent that it provides for a new trial on these issues. The trial court should be instructed to enter judgment notwithstanding the verdict in favor of Sears on the false arrest claim.

The evidence was also insufficient to submit the issue of punitive damages to the jury on either of the claims of false arrest or trespass to chattel. Accordingly, Sears is entitled to judgment notwithstanding the verdict on the issue of punitive damages as well.

Respectfully submitted this 13th day of April, 1987.

GUST, ROSENFELD, DIVELBESS & HENDERSON

By _____
          Fred Cole
          Roger W. Perry
          Attorneys for Defendant-Appellee/Cross-Appellant

Thomas J. Quarelli, Esq.
1832 E. Thomas Road
Phoenix, Arizona 85016
William J. Monahan, P.C.
340 E. Palm Lane, Suite 130
Phoenix, Arizona 85004
Paul G. Ulrich, P.C.
3030 N. Central, Suite 310
Phoenix, Arizona 85012
Attorneys for Plaintiff-Appellant/Cross-Appellee

IN THE COURT OF APPEALS
STATE OF ARIZONA
DIVISION ONE

MAX KOEPNICK,	
Plaintiff-Appellant	No. CA-CIV 9147
Cross-Appellee,	MARICOPA County Superior Court
v.	No. C-502081
SEARS, ROEBUCK & COMPANY,	
Defendant-Appellee	
Cross-Appellant.	

APPELLANT'S CROSS-APPEAL ANSWERING BRIEF

TABLE OF CONTENTS

TABLE OF AUTHORITIES

APPELLANT'S CROSS-APPEAL ANSWERING BRIEF

STATEMENT OF THE CASE

On December 5, 1983, Plaintiff/cross-appellee Max Koepnick sued Defendant/ cross-appellant Sears, Roebuck & Co. ("Sears") and the City of Mesa ("Mesa") for false arrest, assault, trespass to chattel (by further detaining him while searching his truck), invasion of his right of privacy and malicious prosecution. These claims all arose out of Koepnick's arrest for alleged shoplifting on December 6, 1982 (Appendix A, C.T. at 1). The counts in Koepnick's complaint alleging invasion of privacy against both defendants and alleging malicious prosecution, false arrest and punitive damages against Mesa were all disposed of by directed verdicts (Appendix B, C.T. at 97). Those issues are not involved in this appeal.

The remaining portions of Koepnick's complaint were tried to a jury on January 13-22, 1986. The jury awarded Koepnick $25,000 in compensatory damages and $500,000 in punitive damages against Sears for false arrest. It awarded him $100 in compensatory damages against both Sears and Mesa and $25,000 in punitive damages against Sears for trespass to Koepnick's personal property. The jury also awarded Koepnick $50,000 in compensatory damages against Mesa for assault (9R.T. at 101-03). Judgment was entered against both defendants pursuant to those jury verdicts on February 25, 1986 (Appendix B, C.T. at 97).

On March 11, 1986, Sears filed motions for judgment notwithstanding the verdicts and for new trial (C.T. at 100). Mesa also filed a motion for a new trial on March 11, 1986 (C.T. at 101). Mesa then also moved for judgment notwithstanding the verdict and, in the alternative, for new trial and for remittitur on March 12, 1986 (C.T. at 104). Sears thereafter filed an amended motion for judgment notwithstanding the verdicts and for new trial on April 16, 1986 (C.T. at 113). Koepnick filed responses to Mesa's and Sears' motions on March 20 and 25, 1986, respectively (C.T. at 107, 108, 109). Both Sears and Mesa filed reply memoranda in support of their respective motions on April 16, 1986 (C.T. at 114, 115).

On May 14, 1986, the trial court entered the following minute orders: (1) granting Sears' motion for new trial on Koepnick's false arrest claim; (2) granting Sears' and Mesa's motions for judgment N.O.V. with respect to Koepnick's claim of trespass to personal property; and (3) denying Mesa's motion for new trial or for judgment N.O.V. with respect to Koepnick's assault claim. On June 27, 1986, the trial court clarified its May 14, 1986 minute order by denying Sears' motion for judgment N.O.V. on Koepnick's false arrest claim to the extent it granted Sears' motion for a new trial concerning that issue. Having granted a new trial on Koepnick's false arrest claim, the trial court also vacated his judgment against Sears for punitive damages. A formal written order incorporating all those rulings and directing that it be entered as a final judgment was filed on July 23, 1986 (C.T. at 124).

On July 24, 1986, Koepnick filed a notice of appeal only from the portions of the trial court's order granting Sears' motion for new trial on his false arrest claim and for judgment N.O.V. on his claim of trespass to chattel (C.T. at 124). The portion of the litigation involving Mesa has been settled. Mesa is therefore not a party to this appeal and has not filed a cross-appeal. Sears filed a notice of cross-appeal with respect to other portions of the judgment on August 5, 1986 (C.T. at 128). The parties have stipulated that the cost bonds for their respective appeals are waived. This Court has jurisdiction concerning this appeal pursuant to A.R.S. §12-2101(F)(1).

STATEMENT OF FACTS

I.   Koepnick and His Purchases.

Max Koepnick was a manager, foreman, and mechanic for a large Queen Creek farming operation whose assets exceed $2,500,000 (4R.T. at 145, 6R.T. at 21). His lawsuit resulted from his detention and arrest for shoplifting while he was purchasing tools for the farm at the Sears store in Fiesta Mall, Mesa, Arizona, on December 6, 1982 (4R.T. at 145-47). Koepnick paid cash for those tools and had the receipts for all of them in his possession when he was arrested, including the receipt for a 1 5/16 open-end crescent wrench. That wrench was the precipitating cause of his arrest.

Koepnick drove to Sears in the farm pickup truck he used for business purposes (4R.T. at 145-46). He entered the store at approximately 5:00 P.M. (4R.T. at 145, 5T 68). Business in the Sears store happened to be slow at that particular time (3R.T. at 13). Koepnick proceeded to the hardware department. He first purchased a five-wrench set, a nut-driver, an open-end wrench set, a plier set, and a set of screwdrivers (Ex. 11). Bruce Rosenhan, Sears hardware department manager, rang up those purchases on a cash register and stapled portions of the Sears seven-part handwritten receipt used at customers' requests for cash purchases to the outside of the bag (4R.T. at 149, 173). Sears' policy was to staple the register receipt and the original of the seven-part receipt to the outside of the bag (3R.T. at 22, 4R.T. at 45). The customer's purchases were also recorded automatically on the cash register tape (3R.T. at 18-19). The other six copies of the handwritten receipt may have been placed in a trash can on one of the shelves below the cash register (3R.T. at 21).

Koepnick then left his purchases at the cash register counter to look for a wrench (4R.T. at 151). During this time he flirted with a salesperson, Mara Thomas, who showed him various tools. Ms. Thomas then escorted him to the register where he purchased a 1 5/16 open-end crescent wrench. Sales clerk Jeff Ward made this sale. At that time, Ward prepared another handwritten seven-part form, since this sale was also for cash (8R.T. at 8-9, Ex. 12). As had occurred with

Koepnick's first purchases, the crescent wrench was bagged and stapled together with the receipt. This bag was placed inside the first, with the wrench handle sticking out (4R.T. at 173). At trial, Koepnick denied the wrench was ever put into a separate brown bag (4R.T. at 173, 174). He also testified all the receipts were stapled onto the original bag (4R.T. at 17). Jeff Ward then left the hardware department to take a break (3R.T. at 12, 8R.T. at 9).

Koepnick picked up the bag from the register counter and started to leave. However, he then remembered he needed some spark plug sockets (4R.T. at 174). He therefore went back to the register, set the bag down and proceeded to look for the sockets (4R.T. at 175).

During this time, manager Rosenhan contacted Sears security guards Steve Lessard and Dave Pollock, who began observing Koepnick. Lessard spoke with all four hardware department employees then on the floor about whether there was a receipt for the open-end crescent wrench (3R.T. at 9). None could remember ringing it up. However, Lessard failed to ask those employees if anyone else was then on a break (id.). He simply assumed those four employees were the only ones on duty (3R.T. at 10-11). Moreover, no one checked either the register tape or the receipts tray behind the counter (3R.T. at 34). Doing so would have confirmed that Koepnick had in fact paid for the crescent wrench, since the cash register tape could have been checked against the wrench's stock number (3R.T. at 19-20). Lessard also admitted at trial that he also could have searched for the six discarded copies of Koepnick's three sets of receipts that were probably in the trash container below the cash register (3R.T. at 21-22).

Meanwhile, Lessard had Pollack walk past the bag on the counter to confirm visually that the wrench in the bag was a Sears product (3R.T. at 28). Pollack could see a price tag sticker on the end of the wrench. However, although the stapled receipts on the bag were also in plain view, they were not checked against the merchandise (4R.T. at 175). Lessard himself admitted that Pollack had an "easy view" of the receipts (3R.T. at 29-30).

Lessard himself also saw the bag on the counter. However, he did not notice the handwritten receipts and cash register tape stapled to the top of the bag (3R.T. at 27). He also testified at trial he could not dispute testimony that the register receipts and handwritten receipts were stapled to the top of the bag (id.). He "didn't recall" whether anyone bothered to look for those receipts on the bag before Koepnick was stopped, although he conceded that it would have been a "fairly reasonable thing to do" (3R.T. at 30).

While this "investigation" was occurring, Koepnick located and purchased the sockets, returned to the register counter, picked up his bag from the counter, tore off all the receipts, placed them in his shirt pocket and left the store. Lessard and Pollack followed him (4R.T. at 177). Lessard estimated that he had between 20 and 25 minutes to make his investigation before he stopped Koepnick outside the store (3R.T. at 14). He even had time to discuss with Pollack that they had "done a thorough investigation" (3R.T. at 34).

II. Koepnick's Detention, Arrest, Assault, and Eventual Release.

Koepnick placed the time and location of his stop and arrest by Lessard and Pollack at 6:15 P.M., in a dark, dimly lighted area of the Sears parking lot (5R.T. at 72). Koepnick's version of the facts was that in that dimly lighted area two punks accosted him, yelled "Hey," and positioned themselves on each side of him (4R.T. at 178). They then jerked the wrench out of the bag stating, "You don't have a receipt, do you?" (4R.T. at 180-81).

Koepnick thought he was being hustled. He asked who his captors were. Their response was, "We're security guards." (4R.T. at 179). Koepnick asked them to "prove it." In response, one of the guards flashed his badge (*id.*). However, Koepnick could not see it clearly (4R.T. at 179-80). Koepnick was then told that he was going with the guards and that he was under arrest for shoplifting (4R.T. at 180).

Koepnick was escorted to an upstairs security room, denied a drink of water, and seated, with no inquiry as to whether he had a receipt for the wrench (4R.T. at 180). The Mesa police were called. When Koepnick attempted to enter the hallway to obtain a drink of water, he and Officer Campbell (who was wearing a bulletproof vest) got into a pushing match. As a result, Koepnick fell or was thrown head first through the wall of the security room, causing him to incur neck and other injuries (4R.T. at 60-64).

Koepnick was then handcuffed. While he was recovering from the blow to his head, the Mesa police and the Sears security staff verified every item he had purchased against every receipt on the table of the security room (4R.T. at 68). Lessard had also verified with Jeff Ward that Koepnick had in fact purchased the crescent wrench. The bag which supposedly contained the wrench had already been accounted for in the security office. However, despite all of Koepnick's purchases being fully accounted for, the Mesa police continued to detain him at Sears' insistence while Lessard conducted a non-consensual, unescorted search of his truck, looking for an alleged "brown bag" (4R.T. at 71). Koepnick had approximately $1,200-1,400 in cash and all of his business records in the truck (4R.T. at 197). The search, which required approximately 15 to 20 minutes, proved fruitless (4R.T. at 197-98). During this time, Koepnick remained under detention. Had Lessard not decided to search Koepnick's truck, Koepnick would simply have been cited immediately for disorderly conduct and then released (6R.T. at 115). Instead, after the search, Koepnick was then freed of his handcuffs and cited for disorderly conduct (4R.T. at 198). He was finally permitted to leave the Sears security room at about 7:00 P.M. (4R.T. at 199).

ISSUES PRESENTED

1. Did the trial court properly deny Sears' motion for judgment notwithstanding the verdict on Koepnick's false arrest claim where the evidence, viewed most favorably to him, was disputed as to each element of the statutory shopkeeper's privilege, A.R.S. §13-1805(C)?

2. Did the trial court properly deny Sears' motion for judgment notwithstanding the verdict on Koepnick's false arrest punitive damage claim where the evidence presented reasonably established a *prima facie* case for such damages?

3. Was the evidence supporting punitive damages as to Koepnick's trespass to chattel claim sufficient to submit that issue to the jury as well?

ARGUMENT

I. The Trial Court Properly Denied Sears' Motion for Judgment Notwithstanding the Verdict with Respect to Koepnick's False Arrest Claim.

A. The Applicable Standards of Review.

In reviewing the trial court's denial of a motion for judgment notwithstanding the verdict, the appellate court will review the evidence to determine whether it was of sufficient character that reasonable minds could differ as to inferences to be drawn from the facts. *Adroit Supply Co. v. Electric Mutual Liability Insurance Co.*, 112 Ariz. 385, 542 P.2d 810 (1975); *Marcal Limited Partnership v. Title Insurance Co. of Minnesota*, 150 Ariz. 191, 722 P.2d 359 (App. 1986). In doing so, this Court will view the evidence in the light most favorable to sustaining the verdict. It then must review the evidence to determine whether the evidence would permit a reasonable person to reach the challenged verdict. *Maxwell v. Aetna Life Insurance Co.*, 143 Ariz. 205, 693 P.2d 348 (App. 1984).

When the sufficiency of evidence to sustain the jury's verdicts is questioned on appeal, every conflict in the evidence and every reasonable inference therefrom will be resolved in favor of sustaining the verdict and judgment. *See McNelis v. Bruce*, 90 Ariz. 261, 367 P.2d 625 (1961). On appeal, a reviewing court must take the evidence in the light most favorable to upholding the jury's verdict. *Miller v. Schafer*, 102 Ariz. 457, 432 P.2d 585 (1967). Applying these standards to the evidence in this record, Koepnick submits the trial court properly denied Sears' motion for directed verdict with respect to his false arrest claim.

B. Requirements to Sustain the Statutory Shopkeeper's Privilege.

A.R.S. §13-1805(C) provides that a merchant "with reasonable cause may detain on the premises in a reasonable manner and for a reasonable time any person suspected of shoplifting ... for questioning or summoning a law enforcement officer." The statute thus states four elements, all of which must be established to sustain the shopkeeper's privilege: (1) reasonable cause for detention; (2) reasonable manner for detention; (3) reasonable time; and (4) proper purpose (for questioning or summoning a law enforcement officer). Koepnick submits that a directed verdict in Sears' favor with respect to his false arrest claim would not be justified unless the evidence satisfied the applicable standard of review previously stated with respect to all four elements required to establish the statutory privilege. Viewing the evidence most favorably to Koepnick, this record simply does not permit that conclusion.

Each of the elements of Sears' defense also required Sears to prove the affirmative of the issue. *E.g., Black, Robertshaw, Frederick, Copple & Wright, P.C. v. United States*, 130 Ariz. 110, 634 P.2d 398 (App. 1981); *Yeazell v. Copins*, 98 Ariz. 109, 402 P.2d 541 (App. 1965). Unless Sears could persuade a jury by a preponderance of the evidence and reasonable inferences therefrom that each statutory element had been satisfied, Sears thus could not prevail.

1. Reasonable Cause.

Given the facts and reasonable inferences therefrom most favorable to Koepnick, he was clearly entitled to have the reasonable cause issue submitted to the jury. In the first place, Lessard testified he had 20 to 25 minutes to make an investigation before Koepnick left the Sears store and stated that he had made a thorough investigation. He therefore did not have to make a "snap" decision based on incomplete evidence to detain someone who might be hurriedly leaving. Koepnick testified that all of the handwritten receipts for the tools he bought were stapled to the outside of his shopping bag in plain view. However, neither Lessard nor Pollack ever attempted to read them to determine whether the open-end crescent wrench was listed. Lessard was also unable to dispute Koepnick's testimony in this regard, and admitted that looking at the receipts would have been a reasonable thing to do.

Lessard also failed to make the basic inquiry whether there were other hardware department employees then on duty other than the four he interviewed. The possibility that another employee might have been on a break was certainly a reasonable one to be explored. The security guards also never looked for the extra copies of the seven-part receipt, although they might well have been found either in the receipts tray behind the counter or in a trash container on one of the shelves below the cash register. No one ever checked the register tape which would have shown the stock number for the open-end wrench Koepnick had paid for. Given all these deficiencies in the security guards' investigation, there was certainly a reasonable basis for disputing Sears' position that it had reasonable cause to detain Koepnick. Moreover, pursuant to A.R.S. §13-1805(d), "reasonable cause" is a defense to a false arrest claim. Sears therefore had the burden of proving the affirmative of this issue. *E.g., Black, Robertshaw, Frederick, Copple & Wright,*

P.C. v. United States, 130 Ariz. 110, 634 P.2d 398 (App. 1981); *Yeazell v. Copins*, 98 Ariz. 109, 402 P.2d 541 (1965). Unless it could persuade a jury by a preponderance of the evidence and reasonable inferences therefrom that the nature and extent of its investigation was appropriate under the circumstances, Sears could not prevail. Given all the deficiencies in the security guards' investigation and in view of the relatively lengthy time available for them to pursue the simple additional inquiries that could have been made, the trial court could not properly remove the "reasonable cause" issue from the jury in Sears' favor.

2. *Proper Purpose.*

Sears' Cross-Appeal Opening Brief at p. 3 concedes there was a factual dispute concerning what questioning, if any, occurred during Sears' detention of Koepnick. The statutory purpose of "questioning the subject" was thus admittedly not satisfied for purposes of obtaining a directed verdict. The other possible proper purpose permitted by A.R.S. §13-1805(C) for privileged detention is "summoning a law enforcement officer." Koepnick acknowledges that Sears did contact the Mesa Police Department, but only after he was detained by Sears employees. He was not necessarily detained for that purpose. Moreover, after Officer Campbell's investigation, the officer testified he would simply have cited Koepnick immediately for disorderly conduct and then let him go (6R.T. at 115). Instead, Lessard, Sears employee, insisted that Sears search Koepnick's truck even after all the receipts for his purchases had been accounted for (6R.T. at 101, 102). Koepnick remained in detention for at least 15 to 20 minutes more while Lessard and Officer Gates searched his truck (4R.T. at 197). His handcuffs were not removed until this search had been completed (4R.T. at 197). Koepnick submits that this continuation of his detention was improper because it was motivated by Lessard's desire to search his truck, not for any legitimate reasons connected with the police officers' investigation. There was therefore an issue presented as to whether a proper purpose existed throughout the entire time in which Koepnick was detained.

3. *Length of Detention.*

Koepnick contends that the length of his detention was reasonable only until the Sears employees and Mesa police officers had completed their investigation. Once that occurred, Koepnick should have been released immediately. Instead, he was then detained for an additional 15 to 20 minutes at Lessard's request so Lessard could search his truck. Although Koepnick technically may have been in the police officers' custody during that additional period of time, the evidence clearly established that this additional period of detention would not have occurred but for Lessard's request. Under these circumstances, there is also a factual issue as to the propriety of the length of time Koepnick was detained so far as Sears is concerned.

4. *Manner of Detention.*

Factual disputes were also presented as to the manner in which Koepnick was detained by Sears. To begin with, he was accosted by Lessard and Pollack in an accusatory manner. Koepnick testified they stated, "You don't have a receipt, do you?" (4R.T. at 180-81) rather than asking to see a receipt. Then, although Koepnick responded that he had a receipt, he was nevertheless detained for shoplifting without further questioning on that subject. Koepnick submits the manner of his initial detention was thus improper for that reason.

Koepnick was then escorted to an upstairs security room where he was denied a drink of water and seated with no inquiry as to whether he had a receipt for the wrench (4R.T. at 180). When Koepnick entered the hallway to obtain a drink of water, he and Officer Campbell got into a pushing match which resulted in Koepnick falling or being thrown head first through the wall of the security room, causing him to incur neck and other injuries (4R.T. at 60-64). Koepnick was then handcuffed. However, had Koepnick been offered a drink of water and had the proper inquiries been made by Sears employees initially, his injuries arguably would not have occurred.

Koepnick submits these facts all raise factual issues as to whether the manner of his detention was reasonable. Based on these facts, a jury could reasonably have found that Sears security guards did not handle his detention in a reasonable manner.

II. The Trial Court Properly Denied Sears' Motion for Judgment Notwithstanding the Verdict as to Koepnick's Punitive Damages Based on his False Arrest Claims.

A. The Applicable Standards of Review.

The recent Arizona appellate decisions modifying the standard for determining whether there has been a *prima facie* showing permitting the assessment of punitive damages do not necessarily require that all prior jury verdicts awarding such damages be reversed. For example, *Filasky v. Preferred Risk Mutual Insurance Co.*, 152 Ariz. 591, 734 P.2d 76 (1987), instead recognizes that "a jury's decision to award punitive damages should be affirmed if any reasonable evidence exists to support it." *Gurule v. Illinois Mutual Life and Casualty Co.*, 152 Ariz. 600, 734 P.2d 85 (1987), also states that the appellate court must review the facts in a light most favorable to the party obtaining a punitive damage award and affirm the jury's verdict if a reasonable juror could conclude that the defendant either intended to violate his rights or consciously pursued a course of conduct knowing that it created a substantial risk of doing so. 734 P.2d at 88.

Of the various recent decisions, both *Hawkins v. Allstate Insurance Co.*, 152 Ariz. 490, 733 P.2d 1073 (1987), and this Court's Opinion in *Carter-Glogau*

Laboratories, Inc. v. Construction, Production & Maintenance Labors Local 383, (1 CA-CIV 8107, 8128 filed October 30, 1986, *review denied*, May 12, 1987), have affirmed punitive damages awards where the evidence presented met the standards stated in *Linthicum v. Nationwide Life Insurance Co.*, 150 Ariz. 326, 723 P.2d 675 (1986). *Rawlings v. Apodaca*, 151 Ariz. 149, 726 P.2d 565 (1986), also remanded for further proceedings as to punitive damages where it was uncertain whether the trial judge had applied the appropriate standards.

According to *Gurule, supra*, the "evil mind" required for punitive damages may be satisfied by "defendant's conscious and deliberate disregard of the interests and rights of others." 152 Ariz. at 602, 734 P.2d at 87. It may also be established by defendant's expressed statements or inferred from his expressions, conduct or objectives. *Id.* If a defendant conducts himself in an outrageous or egregiously improper manner, the inference is permitted that he intended to injure or consciously disregarded the substantial risk that his conduct would cause significant harm. The "evil mind" may also be inferred if a defendant "deliberately continued his actions despite the inevitable or highly probable harm that would follow." *Id.*

B. Applying These Standards, the Evidence Demonstrated a *Prima Facie* Case for Punitive Damages with Respect to Koepnick's False Arrest Claim.

Numerous deficiencies in Sears' investigation support a jury's finding that its employees acted with conscious and deliberate disregard of Koepnick's rights and interests. The "bottom line" of Lessard's investigation at the time Koepnick left the Sears store was that he and Pollack "felt we had done a thorough enough investigation for us to ask [Koepnick] if he had a receipt for the wrench" (3R.T. at 35). Significantly, Lessard himself apparently did not then believe he had sufficient cause to detain Koepnick for shoplifting at that time without further questioning. Yet Lessard and Pollack accosted Koepnick in a hostile and threatening manner in a dark corner of the parking lot and accused him of not having a receipt, instead of asking in a more normal manner whether he had a receipt. Then, even though Koepnick told Lessard and Pollack in response to their accusations that he did have a receipt, he was ordered under arrest for shoplifting without further discussion or inquiry (4R.T. at 178-81). These facts clearly could support a reasonable conclusion that Sears employees had the required "evil mind" in making their initial decision to detain Koepnick without adequate investigation or proper inquiry concerning whether he in fact had the receipts they should be seeking....

C. The Evidence Supporting Koepnick's Punitive Damages with Respect to His Trespass to Chattel Claim Was Sufficient to Submit That Issue to the Jury as Well.

    ....

CONCLUSION

For all the foregoing reasons, the trial court properly denied Sears' motions for judgment notwithstanding the verdict as to Koepnick's claim for false arrest, for punitive damages with respect to the false arrest, and for punitive damages with respect to Koepnick's trespass to chattels claim. The trial court's rulings concerning the issues properly before this Court should therefore be affirmed.

DATED this day 11th of May, 1987.

Respectfully submitted,
THOMAS J. QUARELLI, ESQ.
WILLIAM J. MONAHAN, P.C.

By _____
William J. Monahan
and
PAUL G. ULRICH, P.C.

By _____
Paul G. Ulrich
Attorneys for Appellant
Cross-Appellee

Fred Cole
Roger W. Perry
Gust, Rosenfeld, Divelbess & Henderson
3300 Valley Bank Center
Phoenix, Arizona 85073
Attorneys for Defendant-Appellee/Cross-Appellant

IN THE COURT OF APPEALS
STATE OF ARIZONA
DIVISION ONE

MAX KOEPNICK,	
Plaintiff-Appellant	1 CA-CIV 9147
Cross-Appellee,	MARICOPA County Superior Court
v.	No. C-502081
SEARS, ROEBUCK & COMPANY,	
Defendant-Appellee	
Cross-Appellant.	

APPELLEE'S REPLY BRIEF ON CROSS-APPEAL

TABLE OF CONTENTS

TABLE OF AUTHORITIES

ARGUMENT

I. Sears Is Entitled to Judgment Notwithstanding the Verdict on the False Arrest Claim.

Koepnick fails to demonstrate any valid issue of fact that would preclude the granting of judgment in favor of Sears on the false arrest count. All four of the necessary elements for a privileged detention under A.R.S. §13-1805 C are undisputedly established in the record. On the element of reasonable cause, the trial court, after hearing all the evidence, determined that reasonable cause existed for Koepnick's detention. This ruling was a proper exercise of the trial court's discretion and is fully justified by the evidence. There is no basis for this court to reverse the trial court's determination on this issue. To avoid duplication, Sears incorporates all its proper arguments on this issue by this reference.

The evidence also undisputedly establishes a proper purpose for Koepnick's detention pursuant to the statute. It is uncontroverted that Sears detained Koepnick to summon the Mesa police concerning the suspected shoplifting. Indeed, Koepnick never made any claim or offered any jury instruction with respect to some other purpose for his detention by Sears. For Koepnick to now make the bald, totally unsupported statement in his response brief that "He was not necessarily detained for that purpose" is ridiculous (Cross-appeal answering brief, p. 5). Koepnick does not even suggest any other purpose in support of this statement. As for the period of time after the police arrived, the evidence is also undisputed that Koepnick was legitimately in the Mesa police department's custody, not Sears'. Probable cause existed for the police to detain Koepnick during this period, and Sears had no control over whether or how Koepnick was kept in detention by the police.

There is also no dispute concerning the reasonableness of the length of time Sears detained Koepnick. Koepnick concedes that the length of his detention in Sears' custody until the police arrived and investigated was reasonable (Cross-appeal answering brief, p. 6). As stated above, from that point on, Koepnick was in the Mesa police department's custody, not Sears'. Koepnick was under arrest for his altercation with Officer Campbell. Prior to trial, the trial court ruled that probable cause existed for the Mesa police department's detention of Koepnick during that period for the alleged assault on Officer Campbell. (*See* Minute entry dated January 9, 1986.) Koepnick has never raised any issue or objection with respect to that ruling.

Although Koepnick repeatedly states that Steve Lessard "requested" his continued detention by the Mesa police department during this period, such statements have no support in the record. Koepnick fails even to cite to the record when making such assertions of "fact." (*See, e.g.,* cross-appeal answering brief, p. 6.) The uncontroverted evidence is that Lessard simply told the police the information and knowledge he had in his possession (4R.T. at 105-06). This information included the fact that the bag Jeff Ward stated he had wrapped the wrench in before placing it in the larger shopping bag was missing (4R.T. at 104-05). Contrary to Koepnick's statements in his briefs, that bag was never accounted for in the security office (4R.T. at 104-05). It was the police officers who made the decision to search Koepnick's truck (6R.T. at 128). Lessard had no control over whether Koepnick was detained or released by the police during that period (8R.T. at 59-60).

Finally, the element of the reasonableness of the manner of Sears' detention of Koepnick is also undisputedly established by the record. Koepnick's arguments in trying to explain why Sears' detention of him should be viewed as unreasonable are nothing less than frivolous. Koepnick's first argument revolves around the fact that, according to Koepnick's testimony, Lessard approached him and said, "You don't have a receipt, do you?" rather than asking to see his receipt. Even accepting all of Koepnick's testimony as true, as we must on this appeal, there is still no evidence of any abusive conduct that would rise to the level of a tortiously unreasonable specific manner of detention. If the court were to accept Koepnick's argument, potential liability would exist any time a subject stopped pursuant to A.R.S. §13-1805 did not like the manner in which he was addressed. It is inconceivable that the legislature intended such a result when referring to a "reasonable manner" of detention in A.R.S. §13-1805 C. Much more substantial conduct is required for liability to exist for false arrest.

Koepnick further argues that the manner of his detention was unreasonable in that he should have been questioned by Sears. A.R.S. §13-1805 C, however, indicates that store personnel are not required to question a subject; they can simply detain for the purpose of summoning a law enforcement officer to handle the investigation.

Finally, Koepnick stretches so far as to attempt to attribute the injuries he received in his altercation with Officer Campbell in the hallway to the fact that the Sears employees declined to give him a drink of water. Koepnick's need for such a nonsensical argument makes readily apparent the total lack of any factual basis for any claim that Sears detained Koepnick unreasonably. The undisputed facts show that Koepnick was simply stopped outside the store and then taken to the security office to await the arrival of the police. According to even Koepnick's testimony, he was not physically or verbally abused by the Sears employees. As such, there is no evidence that would warrant submitting this issue to the jury.

As all the elements for a privileged detention under A.R.S. §13-1805 C are undisputedly established in the record, Sears is entitled to have judgment entered in its favor on the false arrest claim.

II. Sears Is Entitled to Judgment Notwithstanding the Verdicts on the Punitive Damage Claims.

As Koepnick acknowledges in citing *Filasky v. Preferred Risk Mutual Insurance Co.*, 152 Ariz. 591, 734 P.2d 76 (1987), and *Gurule v. Illinois Mutual Life and Casualty Co.*, 152 Ariz. 600, 734 P.2d 85 (1987) (en banc), a punitive damage award will only be sustained on appeal when there is reasonable evidence to support it. In discussing the nature of an act necessary to permit punitive damages, the Arizona Supreme Court observed that "[p]unishment is an appropriate objective in a civil case only if the defendant's conduct or motive involves 'some element of outrage similar to that usually found in a crime.'" *Gurule*, 734 P.2d at 86 (quoting *Rawlings v. Apodaca*, 151 Ariz. 149, 162, 726 P.2d 565, 578 (1986)).

Where a trial court submits the issue of punitive damages to the jury on slight and inconclusive evidence of such conduct, an appellate court may correct the error. *Filasky*, 734 P.2d at 84. In both *Filasky* and *Gurule*, the Supreme Court found that the evidence did not measure up to the requisite standard and reversed the awards of punitive damages. The same conclusion should be reached in this appeal.

A.   The False Arrest Claim.

Koepnick attempts to support the punitive damage award on the false arrest claim based on alleged "deficiencies" in the initial investigation and Lessard's alleged "request" that the Mesa police officers continue to detain Koepnick while his truck was searched. Both of these arguments ignore the uncontroverted facts in the record and fail to demonstrate a level of conduct sufficient to justify an award of punitive damages. First, Koepnick's assertion that the investigation by Lessard was inadequate and unreasonable is belied by the trial court's ultimate determination that reasonable cause existed for Sears' detention of Koepnick. Inherent in the trial court's ruling that reasonable cause existed for Koepnick's detention is the determination that the pre-stop investigation conducted by Lessard was reasonable. If the facts and investigation relied on by Sears were unreasonable, reasonable cause could not exist for the detention. It would be completely illogical for the same evidence that the trial court found to establish reasonable cause for the detention to also be deemed sufficient to support an award of punitive damages for the same detention.

. . . .

B.   The Trespass to Chattel Claim.

. . . .

CONCLUSION

The trial court properly granted Sears' judgment notwithstanding the verdict on the claim of trespass to chattel. The trial court erred, however, in not doing the same on the claim of false arrest. There are no issues of fact present to justify submitting this claim to the jury. This court should therefore reverse the trial court's ruling that denied Sears' motion for judgment N.O.V. on this count.

Furthermore, there was no evidence to justify the submission of the claims for punitive damages on either of the two counts submitted to the jury. Thus, regardless of the ultimate decisions on the trespass to chattel and false arrest counts, Sears is entitled to have the trial court instructed to grant it judgment N.O.V. on the punitive damage claims.

Respectfully submitted this 8th day of June, 1987.

GUST, ROSENFELD, DIVELBESS & HENDERSON

By _____
    Fred Cole
    Roger W. Perry
    Attorneys for Defendant-Appellee/Cross-Appellant

Part IV

Writing to Parties: Contracts

and Correspondence

As a practicing attorney, you will communicate not only with judges and other attorneys but also with your clients and other parties. For example, you might draft a written contract that the parties adopt as the final and complete expression of their negotiated agreement. If your client later complains that the other party has breached the contract, you might draft an "advice letter" to your client, advising her of her legal rights and recommending certain action. Depending on your client's assessment of her options, you might then send a "demand letter" to the opposing party, demanding that he take certain action to satisfy your client's claims.

Part IV examines contracts and letters as examples of drafting directed to parties. It does not proceed on the premise that your immediate audience will invariably be the parties themselves. On the contrary, if you know that the other party is represented by counsel, you will ordinarily address your contract proposal or your demand letter to counsel. Similarly, if you or your law firm is the outside counsel for a corporation, you might address your advice letter to the corporation's in-house counsel. Nonetheless, more so than with office memoranda and briefs, contracts and letters are directed ultimately to the parties themselves.

Contracts and letters can be useful at various stages of litigation. For example, a contract might lead to a dispute, or it might express the parties' agreement to settle a dispute that has already proceeded through pretrial, trial, or even appellate litigation. Similarly, although you will often draft advice and demand letters at the earliest stages of litigation, you may use them at any stage of the litigation that raises new questions or that creates a new opportunity to state your demands.

Chapter 9

Contracts

I. Basic Approaches

With some limitations, parties can privately shape their legal rights and obligations by exchanging enforceable promises in a contract. Each party's promises impose contractual duties on that party and create contractual rights in the other.

The authors of one contracts casebook believe that the contractual promise is the greatest human invention, even greater than the wheel, the lever, and the pulley:

> [F]or it is the promise that breaks the ultimate physical restraint. It permits us to live a bit of the future today. When two or more employ the tool of promise in concert, they create a unique social engine—the *bargain*.[1]

---

1. Daniel W. Fessler & Pierre R. Loiseaux, CONTRACTS, MORALITY, ECONOMICS AND THE MARKETPLACE (CASES AND MATERIALS) 1 (1982).

Although this claim may provoke some debate about the relative merits of the promise and the pulley, none will dispute that enforceable contracts are indispensable to modern commerce.

Moreover, you need not reinvent the wheel with every contract. Some law firms produce high-quality form contracts for common transactions and maintain them in computer files. Whether you find a form contract in your office, online, or in a library, you can use it effectively by following a methodical process like that recommended by Wayne Schiess:

1. Study the entire form contract to secure general understanding of its scope and content.
2. Compose an outline of the component parts of the form contract.
3. Revise the list or outline to conform it to the needs of your client's transaction, such as by:
   - eliminating unnecessary provisions,
   - reorganizing other provisions as needed, and
   - noting the need for additional provisions.
4. As necessary, revise the language of the form contract to:
   - tailor it to the needs of your client's transaction,
   - avoid ambiguities and state the terms in plain English, and
   - add language or provisions needed for your client's transaction but missing from the form.
5. Proofread the entire document for mistakes, and edit the layout and language as needed to ensure readability and flow.[2]

You can best tailor those forms to new transactions if you understand the purposes of each section of a contract and have the drafting skills to express an agreement in plain, simple, clear English. Moreover, for contracts that do not lend themselves to a computerized form system, you should feel comfortable drafting "from scratch" without reliance on a form. You can draft with confidence if you understand the fundamental components of a contract.

II. Fundamental Components

A. General Format

A written contract should always contain the following provisions:

1. an introduction identifying the parties to the transaction,
2. a section describing the rights and obligations of the parties, and
3. signature lines showing the parties' agreement to the terms of the contract.

---

2. Adapted from Wayne Schiess, PREPARING LEGAL DOCUMENTS NONLAWYERS CAN READ AND UNDERSTAND (ABA 2008).

Among other things, a contract may also include:

1. a statement of "recitals," which describes the background of the transaction and the parties' reasons for entering into the contract,
2. a glossary of defined terms, and
3. a section of miscellaneous provisions addressing such topics as termination or modification of the contract, the relationship of the contract to other transactions, or the parties' choice of law or forum in the event of a dispute.

B. Introduction to the Contract

In the first lines after the title of a contract, you should identify the parties as simply and clearly as possible. If more than two parties join in the transaction, or if at least one of the parties is a complex entity, you should set the parties' names apart from each other on the page.

For example, you can start with a descriptive section heading and use paragraphing to separate the parties' names:

I.   PARTIES

The parties to this contract for the purchase and sale of sand are:

1. SOONER SAND CO., a general partnership consisting of Harley T. Price and W. M. McMichael, general partners, and

2. BASSI DISTRIBUTING CO., a joint venture of Bassi Trucking Co. and Hardcore Rock & Gravel, Inc.

If you use this format for the introduction, you can refer to the parties throughout the contract by the formal names of their business entities: SOONER SAND CO. and BASSI DISTRIBUTING CO. Alternatively, you can assign descriptive labels to the parties, such as Seller and Buyer:

1. Sooner Sand Co. ("Seller"), a general . . . .

2. Bassi Distributing Co. ("Buyer"), a joint . . . .

Many drafters also like to assign a label to the contract itself and to include the date of the agreement in the introductory sentence:

This contract for the purchase and sale of sand (the "Agreement") is entered into on May 1, 2006, by the following parties:

C. Recitals

Although not essential to an enforceable contract, a statement of the factual background of the transaction, popularly known as a statement of "recitals," can help a neutral party interpret the contract if the parties dispute its meaning. Recitals can even help establish consideration for the contract by showing the parties' reciprocal inducements or by providing a basis for implying obligations. For example, in the celebrated contracts case *Wood v. Lucy, Lady Duff-Gordon*,[3] Justice Cardozo of the New York Court of Appeals relied partly on the recitals of a written contract to imply an obligation by an exclusive agent to use reasonable efforts, thus satisfying the consideration requirement.

Recitals in an outdated contract are easy enough to spot. Each recital of a background fact appears in a clause beginning with the word "whereas" and is strung together with other recitals in a single, unmanageably long run-on sentence. To provide better guidance to your reader, you should (1) introduce the recitals with a section heading, such as "Recitals" or "Background" and (2) state your recitals in conventional sentences within numbered paragraphs:

II. RECITALS

1. Seller is engaged in the business of selling and shipping sand from Phoenix to various customers in the State of Arizona but has not developed markets outside of Arizona. Seller desires to supply sand wholesale to a distributor with customers outside the state.

2. Buyer has an established business . . . .

When used in a traditional manner, recitals state only the background of the transaction and the motivations of the parties, not the actual obligations that the parties have assumed by their agreement and have stated with precision in a different section of the written contract. Drafters of some contracts, however, have expressly incorporated their Recitals section into their statement of mutual rights and obligations, either by reference or by making it a subsection of a portion of the contract devoted to mutual promises. In doing so, the drafter hopes to legally bind the parties to the recitals, making the recitals the equivalent of warranties of the stated facts.

D. Statement of Reciprocal Promises

The heart of any contract is the parties' statement of their reciprocal promises. Those promises define the parties' mutual rights and obligations, which form the consideration for the agreement.

1. Introductory Clause; Recital of Consideration

Perhaps in an excess of caution, many drafters still begin their statements of reciprocal promises with outdated recitals of consideration such as the following:

---

3. 118 N.E. 214 (N.Y. 1917).

NOW, THEREFORE, in consideration of the mutual covenants herein contained, and other good and valuable consideration the receipt of which is hereby acknowledged, the parties hereby agree . . . .

Aside from displaying an antiquated writing style, in most cases the reference to "the receipt" of "other . . . consideration" is simply false and is an exceedingly poor way to establish consideration. Expressing a promise in a signed writing raises a presumption of consideration in some states,[4] but a recital of consideration has no additional legal effect under the majority rule.[5]

Especially antiquated is the reference to "good and valuable" consideration. Centuries ago, conventional consideration with economic value— such as money, goods, or services—was known as "valuable consideration," and a familial or other personal relationship with the other party was viewed as "good consideration" for a promise to that party, but the latter form of consideration has long been abandoned by the common law.[6]

Under modern theory, the consideration in a typical contract consists of the parties' mutual promises, exchanged for one another with reciprocal inducement.[7] Rather than pompously recite the existence of consideration, you should simply state the mutual promises under a descriptive section heading and a simple introductory clause that refers to the promises as "mutual" or "reciprocal," or otherwise as part of a "bargained-for exchange":

III. MUTUAL RIGHTS AND OBLIGATIONS

Seller and Buyer agree to the following exchange of reciprocal promises:

1. *Supply.* For a period of five years from the date of formation of this contract, Seller will supply Buyer with all the sand that Buyer requires. . . .

2. *Delivery.* . . .

3. *Quality.* . . .

4. *Price.* For each ton of sand delivered, Buyer will pay Seller a sum equal to . . . .

Some drafters are tempted to begin each statement of an obligation with a phrase such as "Seller promises to supply" or "Seller agrees to supply." The reference to "promises" or "agrees," however, is unnecessary. If you begin your section with an appropriate heading, such as "Mutual Rights and Obligations" or "Mutual Promises," and if you follow immediately with an umbrella statement such as "Seller and Buyer agree to the following bargained-for exchange:" you need not repeatedly invoke the word "agree" in each statement of a promise. Moreover, to state a promise, you need not

---

4. *See, e.g.,* CAL. CIV. C. §1614 (West 1982).

5. *See* John D. Calamari & Joseph M. Perillo, CALAMARI AND PERILLO ON CONTRACTS §4.6, at 158 n.3 & accompanying text (6th ed. 2009).

6. *See* Eugen Bucher, ENGLAND AND THE CONTINENT: DISTINGUISHING THE PECULIARITIES OF THE ENGLISH COMMON LAW OF CONTRACT 54 (Tony Weir, trans., 2009).

7. *See* RESTATEMENT (SECOND) OF CONTRACTS §71 (1981).

use the word "promise." If preceded by the appropriate section heading and umbrella statement, words such as "will" and "must" in the statements of obligation will appropriately convey a party's intent to commit to a future performance:

IV. MUTUAL RIGHTS AND OBLIGATIONS

The parties agree to the following exchange of mutual promises:

1. Bank will approve a construction loan application submitted by Contractor, if the application satisfies the following requirements: . . . .

In such a construction, the term "will approve" is an obligation, and not just a prediction or statement of intention, because it follows an umbrella term introducing it as one of several mutual "promises." Thus, it is the equivalent of: "1. Bank promises that it will approve . . . ." On the other hand, the permissive term "may" would denote the granting of a discretionary power or authority under the contract:

---

12. If Tenant commits a major default as defined in Section 11, Landlord may demand acceleration of the remaining rent pursuant to Section 13 or may demand liquidated damages pursuant to Section 14, at its option.

Other authors and drafters are wary of the term "will approve" to denote a mandatory obligation. They advocate use of "shall," "must," "may," and "will" to serve different roles in expressing, respectively: mandatory duties, predicates to asserting contractual rights, authorizations of discretionary action, and statements about future events. If you find that such terms help you differentiate between different kinds of contract provisions, you will find support in sample contracts and in drafting books that explore drafting challenges in greater depth than is possible in this chapter.[8] If you employ terms consistently, and if you accurately and precisely express your meaning, you likely can achieve your drafting goals with any of several approaches. If you are concerned that a party or court will attach an unintended meaning to one of these terms, you can always include a definition or umbrella statement that clarifies the function you are assigning to a term.

2. Precision in Drafting

a. Simplicity; Terms of Art

The terms of the exchange are a matter of negotiation between the parties. If you represent your client in the negotiations, you can participate in shaping the substance of the bargain. As part of that process, you might draft proposed contract provisions to serve as offers or counteroffers to the other

---

8. *See, e.g.,* Tina L. Stark, Drafting Contracts: How and Why Lawyers Do What They Do (2007).

party. In other cases, your client might ask you to prepare a formal written document expressing a bargain that the parties have previously negotiated. In either case, one of your primary tasks as drafter of the final document is to express the parties' negotiated rights and obligations as precisely as possible to reduce the risk of misunderstanding and costly disputes during performance of the contract.

To draft precisely, you should take advantage of helpful terms of art but avoid unnecessary jargon. For example, the provisions below refer to the buyer's "requirements," a legal term of art that has special meaning and legal consequences under the Uniform Commercial Code.[9] Similarly, the parties could belong to a trade that widely recognizes helpful industrial terms of art, which might earn a place in your contract as well. Otherwise, however, the contract language should be in plain, simple English:

1. *Supply.* For a period of five years from the date of formation of this contract, Seller will supply Buyer with all the sand that Buyer requires for Buyer's business of selling and shipping sand to customers outside the State of Arizona.

2. *Delivery.* Buyer may order sand as Buyer's requirements arise by sending a written purchase order to Seller. . . .

Some legal terms are not necessarily terms of art but may be generally helpful and inoffensive. In the following passage, for example, the seller makes a special kind of promise by "warranting" the quality of the goods:

3. *Quality.* Seller warrants that the quality of the sand that is delivered to Buyer will be at least equal to that of sand of corresponding grades sold by other sand companies in the City of Phoenix, Arizona.

The word "warrants" in this passage is not a necessary term of art under the Uniform Commercial Code. The seller would undertake the same legal obligation by simply promising that

Seller will deliver to Buyer sand of a quality that is at least equal . . . .[10]

Nonetheless, drafters typically and reasonably use the term "warrants" or "warranty" to draw attention to the special nature of a promise that goods or services will meet certain standards.

Similarly, many drafters use special phrases to draw attention to statements of "conditions," which qualify or limit contractual duties. In a standard insurance contract, for example, the insured will assume an absolute

9. U.C.C. §2-306(1) (2011).
10. *See* U.C.C. §2-313(1)(a), (2) (2011).

obligation to pay premiums to the insurer, but the insurer will pay money to the insured only if the insured suffers a loss covered by the insurance contract. You could introduce the insurer's conditional promise with the simple word "if":

If Insured suffers a covered loss as defined in section VI above, Insurer will reimburse Insured for ....

Many insurers, however, like to emphasize the conditional nature of their promises with special phrases, such as "on the condition that" or "in the event that":

In the event that Insured suffers a covered loss as defined in section VI above, Insurer ....

---

b. Deliberate Imprecision

Occasionally, precision is neither feasible nor desirable. In some cases, for example, the parties may have failed to reach precise agreement on some difficult issue, even though they are ready to go forward with their general transaction. If so, you might be forced to express their imperfect agreement on the difficult issue in terms that are sufficiently imprecise to encompass the range of interpretations that describes their divergent positions.

For example, imagine that the buyer of factory equipment demands during negotiations that the seller agree to repair or replace defective parts within 10 days after receiving notice of the defect. Imagine further that the seller counteroffers to repair or replace defective parts within 45 days after receiving notice of the defect. If the parties cannot agree to a time period measured by a specific number of days, they might instead agree to the vague language "within a reasonable time in light of all the circumstances," realizing that they might not share the same interpretation of that language in particular applications.

Language such as this might save the deal if negotiations are stalled on a contentious issue. Moreover, if performance of the contract proceeds smoothly, the parties will never test their divergent interpretations of the language. On the other hand, if adverse circumstances place a strain on performance, the lack of perfect agreement on the precise meaning of the provision could erupt into a serious dispute. Thus, during the negotiation of such a deal, you must help your client weigh the benefits of reaching general agreement against the risks of subsequent disputes over the meaning of vague language.

c. Plain English: Perfection and Pitfalls

A student once told me that his law school training in plain English paid great dividends during a summer clerkship with a law firm. On behalf of its client, the firm had conveyed proposed terms for an international licensing agreement, but the other party had declined to accept or otherwise respond in any meaningful way for many months. The student, who had prior professional experience in the subject matter of the contract, redrafted it in plainer English and simpler sentence structure, while cutting its length in half. When his firm conveyed the redrafted version as an offer, the other party accepted almost immediately. The first version was so formal, dense, and complicated that it intimidated the other party. The revised version was much easier to read and understand, putting the readers at ease and allowing them to be persuaded that the proposed enterprise would be mutually beneficial.

When you replace stuffy jargon with simpler, plain English, however, beware of potential pitfalls. What appears to be needless jargon will sometimes amount to a term of art that carries a precise meaning in an industry. Moreover, a seemingly antiquated legal term can carry special force if courts have interpreted and applied it in numerous contexts over many years, thus reducing the risk of a genuine dispute over its meaning in the current context. Accordingly, when updating a form contract to replace antiquated language with modern prose, you should take steps to ensure that the new language is sufficiently clear and precise that it reliably protects your client's interests and conveys the agreement of the parties.[11] In some cases, you can assure that a party or court will give your intended meaning to a plain-language provision by including plain English definitions to key words or phrases.

If you can revise a form contract by improving its style while also *tailoring* it to the current transaction and *reducing* the risk of dispute or unintended judicial interpretation, then you will be realizing the full potential of plain English in drafting.

3. Merger Clauses and Parol Evidence

As an example of a typical miscellaneous provision, a "merger clause" states that the written contract is the exclusive statement of the parties' agreement. If the other party subsequently asserts that the total agreement includes rights and obligations not expressed in the written contract, you can refer to the merger clause and seek to exclude evidence of the alleged unwritten obligations under the "parol evidence rule." With some exceptions, the common law parol evidence rule views the final and complete written agreement as the exclusive statement of the terms of the parties' agreement, thus excluding prior written notes or testimony about prior oral statements if offered to alter or add to the written terms.

A typical merger clause refers only generally to the subject matter of the agreement:

---

11. *See* Lori D. Johnson, *The Ethics of Non-Traditional Contract Drafting*, 84 U. Cin. L. Rev. 595 (2016) (as a matter of professional responsibility, drafters should conduct appropriate research and inform the client of the risks of replacing antiquated language).

XXV. *Prior Agreements Superseded*—This written contract constitutes the parties' complete and exclusive statement of their agreement on the subject matter covered by this contract, and it supersedes all previous agreements, promises, or representations regarding that subject matter.

Unfortunately, such a clause does not eliminate the risk of litigation of a common question under the parol evidence rule: Does an alleged additional agreement address topics within the subject matter of the main written contract so that the main contract supersedes it, or does the additional agreement address unrelated topics so that it can stand separately as an independent, enforceable contract?[12]

For example, suppose that on July 1 the parties signed a written contract for the lease of restaurant space with a fully equipped kitchen. The lessee later asserted that the lessor also orally agreed on June 28 to sell dining tables and chairs to the lessee at the spectacularly low price of $450. The lessor denies the oral agreement. He also points to the merger clause and argues that, assuming he did tentatively agree on June 28 to sell the dining furniture, such an agreement was simply part of continuing negotiations that the parties abandoned and superseded in their July 1 agreement.

However, to successfully invoke the merger clause to exclude evidence of the oral agreement, the lessor must demonstrate that the alleged agreement to sell dining furniture falls within the subject matter of the July 1 contract; otherwise, the alleged June 28 agreement can stand outside the field occupied exclusively by the July 1 contract. Unfortunately, the merger clause cannot help the lessor much because it fails to define the subject matter of the contract.

If you intend a written contract to broadly supersede prior agreements or promises on related transactions, you must describe the subject matter of your contract expansively so that the merger clause can have the intended effect. If you anticipate specific problems stemming from failed negotiations on collateral matters, you can address those matters explicitly:

XXV. *Prior Agreements Superseded*—This written contract constitutes the parties' complete and exclusive statement of their agreement on all matters relating to the lease of the Scottsdale premises, the operation of a restaurant on those premises, and the furnishings and equipment needed for the operation. This contract supersedes all previous or contemporaneous agreements, promises, or representations regarding that subject matter.

This merger clause expresses the parties' intent to abandon any prior agreement for the sale of restaurant furnishings or equipment and to replace it with the terms of the lease agreement. To dispel any doubt about this scope of exclusion, the merger clause could specifically identify previous agreements by name and date, stating that the current contract supersedes

---

12. *See, e.g.*, Gianni v. R. Russell & Co., Inc., 126 A. 791 (Pa. 1924).

them. Alternatively, a separate provision entitled "Rescission and Replacement of Previous Agreements" could state the parties' intentions to rescind specified prior agreements and replace them with the current agreement.

E. Signature Line

You may end your contract with any reasonable means of presenting the parties' signatures as evidence of their agreement to the terms of the contract. You do not need to invoke formalistic jargon such as: "In witness whereof, the said parties have hereunto set their hands and seals the day and year first above written."

Instead, you may simply precede the signature lines with the single word "Signed." At most, you might introduce the signatures with a clause such as, "The undersigned parties agree to these terms."

If you have not already dated the contract at the beginning, you can include a space for the date next to each party's signature. The latest date on a signature line will correspond to one party's acceptance of the other party's offer and normally will identify the date of contract formation.

III. Summary

To draft a simple contract, you should

1. identify the parties in an introductory provision,
2. recite the background facts, if helpful,
3. state the reciprocal promises of the parties as precisely as possible, and
4. provide signature lines as a means for the parties to express their assent to the terms of the contract.

Exercise 9-1

1. Sample Requirements Contract

Study the following contract. Does it require any greater complexity to perform its function?

REQUIREMENTS CONTRACT

I. PARTIES

The parties to this contract for the purchase and sale of sand are:

1. Sooner Sand Co. ("Seller"), a general partnership consisting of the general partners Harley T. Price and W. M. McMichael, and

2. Bassi Distributing Co. ("Buyer"), a joint venture of Bassi Trucking Co. and Hard-core Rock & Gravel, Inc.

II. RECITALS

1. Seller is engaged in the business of selling and shipping sand from Phoenix to various customers in the State of Arizona but has not developed markets outside of Arizona. Seller desires to supply sand wholesale to a distributor with customers outside the state.

2. Buyer has an established business in Phoenix selling and shipping sand to various customers in several states outside Arizona, including California, Nevada, Utah, and Colorado. Buyer desires a stable source of supply of sand for that business.

III. MUTUAL RIGHTS AND OBLIGATIONS

Seller and Buyer agree to the following bargained-for exchange:

1. *Supply.* For a period of 5 years from the date of formation of this contract, Seller will supply Buyer with all the sand that Buyer requires for Buyer's business of selling and shipping sand to customers outside the State of Arizona.

2. *Delivery.* Buyer will order sand as Buyer's requirements arise by sending a written purchase order to Seller. On receipt of such a purchase order, Seller will deliver the ordered sand within 10 days to Buyer's facility at 1531 Range Road in Glendale, Arizona.

3. *Quality.* Seller warrants that the quality of the sand that is delivered to Buyer will be at least equal to that of sand of corresponding grades sold by other sand companies in the City of Phoenix, Arizona.

4. *Price.* For each ton of sand delivered, Buyer will pay Seller a sum equal to 60% of the market price per ton of concrete in the City of Phoenix at the time of Seller's delivery to Buyer.

5. *Term of Payment.* Seller may give an invoice to Buyer for sand on or after Seller delivers the sand to Buyer. Buyer will pay the full amount of such an invoice within 30 days of its receipt of the invoice.

Signed:

_____   _____
SELLER—Authorized Agent for Sooner Sand Co.   Date

_____   _____
BUYER—Authorized Agent for Bassi Distributing Co.   Date

2. Format for More Complex Agreement

a. Compare the following outline of a sample contract with the sample contract in Problem 1 above. The sample below displays an alternative introductory section, and it contemplates more complex provisions that must be subdivided into more numerous subsections.

b. In section 4.2 of the contract, draft a merger clause that identifies your document as the complete and exclusive statement of the parties' agreement. In particular, be certain to supersede prior failed negotiations in which Seller proposed to lease trucks to Buyer for the transportation of the sand to other states.

CONTRACT FOR PURCHASE AND SALE OF
REQUIREMENTS FOR SAND

This contract for the purchase and sale of sand (the Agreement) is entered into on [Date]_____ by the following parties:

1. Seller—Sooner Sand Co., a general partnership consisting of Harley T. Price and W. M. McMichael, general partners, and

2. Buyer—Bassi Distributing Co., a joint venture of Bassi Trucking Co. and Hardcore Rock & Gravel, Inc.

RECITALS

1. Seller is engaged . . . .

2. Buyer has an established . . . .

MUTUAL RIGHTS AND OBLIGATIONS

Seller and Buyer agree to the following bargained-for exchange:

Article I – Definitions

1.1 *Grades of sand*—. . . .

1.2 *Market price*—. . . .

Article II – Supply of Sand

2.1 *Quantity*—. . . .

2.2 *Quality*—. . . .

2.3 *Delivery*—. . . .

Article III – Payment

3.1 *Price*—. . . .

3.2 *Terms of Payment*—. . . .

Article IV – Miscellaneous Provisions

4.1 *No Oral Modification*—. . . .

4.2 *Prior Negotiations Superseded*—. . . .

4.3 *Mandatory Arbitration of Disputes*—. . . .

Signed

_____   _____

Chapter 10

Advice Letters

As counselor and advocate, you will draft many kinds of letters to your client or to others on your client's behalf. Two of the most important are advice letters and demand letters. These letters are closely related to two kinds of documents examined in Volume I and in previous chapters of this book: office memoranda and briefs. Like an office memorandum, an advice letter communicates a balanced legal analysis of a dispute or proposed action, predicts an outcome, and recommends a course of action. In contrast, a demand letter is like a brief in that it advocates a position and usually requests the addressee to take specific action. This chapter examines advice letters; Chapter 11 examines demand letters.[1]

---

1. Many of the ideas in Chapters 10 and 11 are taken with permission from lecture materials prepared by Frank M. Placenti and Mark Hileman, shortly before submission of the first edition of this book in 1989, when they worked for the Phoenix law firm Streich, Lang, Weeks & Cardon, P.A., which later merged with the law firm of Quarles & Brady.

I. Advice Letters Distinguished from Opinion Letters

Many attorneys and commentators use the term "opinion letter" to refer to any letter addressed to a client that offers a legal analysis, opinion, or recommendation. Within this general class of letters, however, are two important subcategories, each of which warrants a narrowly descriptive label. The term "opinion letter" best describes highly specialized letters that provide clients with formal opinions on certain kinds of legal questions. The term "advice letter" accurately describes the far more common kind of letter in which you will more generally analyze a legal problem and advise your client about the relative merits of alternative courses of action.

More specifically, an opinion letter is a formal document that expresses your definite conclusion, or that of your law firm, about whether a specified act is legally valid. For example, you might issue to a corporate client your formal opinion that the corporation has validly issued certain stock under applicable laws and under the articles and bylaws of the corporation. An opinion letter may also be used by your client to demonstrate to other parties that an action is legally valid. For example, an entrepreneur may seek advice about the probability of securing a patent on an invention and then show that opinion letter to potential investors to raise capital. Because the client will rely significantly on such an opinion, the standards for an opinion letter are high, and its format is fairly rigid.

In contrast, in an advice letter, you will communicate your analysis of a legal problem to a client in much the same way that you would use an office memorandum to communicate the analysis to a supervising attorney. Even if you cannot definitively resolve the legal issues in the analysis, you can evaluate the relative merits of the parties' claims and defenses, estimate the probability of success on the merits, and recommend a course of action or describe alternative courses of action. You can thus provide your client with valuable advice short of giving a definite opinion of the legality of certain actions.

In many law firms, only designated attorneys are authorized to issue formal opinion letters on behalf of the firm. Moreover, those attorneys tend to follow carefully developed forms when drafting their opinion letters, leaving little room for flexibility in format or creativity in analysis. Further examination of opinion letters is beyond the scope of this book. Instead, this chapter will explore the more common advice letter.

II. Purpose, Audience, and Writing Style

The writing style that you adopt for a document is partly a function of your intended audience and the purpose of your document. When you draft an office memorandum, you can easily identify your audience and purpose:

You will communicate a balanced legal analysis to an experienced attorney. When you draft an advice letter, however, your audience and purpose may be less clear.

For example, the legal experience and general sophistication of your audience may vary greatly from one letter to the next. One client may be new to his business, have no legal training, and have learned English only after recently arriving from a foreign country. Another client may be a sophisticated, experienced businesswoman with at least a rudimentary knowledge of the laws that affect her business. Still another client may be a corporation with an in-house counsel to whom you will direct your advice letter. You should adapt your writing style to suit the experience and legal training of your audience. In a letter to the legally inexperienced client described above, you should take special care to use plain, simple English and to avoid legal jargon. In letters to more experienced and legally knowledgeable clients, you can safely use legal terminology and assume familiarity with legal method. In each case, however, your goal is the same: to communicate clearly, not to impress the reader with the breadth of your legal vocabulary.

In some cases, your client may wish to share your advice letter with customers, partners, or other attorneys. If so, you should draft the letter with the needs of the secondary audience in mind. For example, if your law firm's client is a corporate manager, she may intend to discuss your advice letter with the corporation's separate, in-house counsel. If so, you may want to provide a full explanation of your underlying legal analysis or even attach a copy of the formal office memorandum on which the advice letter is based.

III. Format

You should adopt any format that suits your audience and the purpose of your advice letter. As a starting point, you can follow the basic elements of a reasonable format for an office memorandum:

Issues
Brief Answers
Facts
Discussion
Conclusion

With this format, your advice letter would

1. restate the questions that your client posed to you,
2. briefly summarize your conclusions,
3. state the facts on which your analysis is based,

4. summarize your analysis of the law and the facts, and

5. state your conclusions and your strategic recommendations.

If your advice letter is simple and brief, you need not use formal section headings to display the transitions between elements of your format. Instead, you can simply use sensible paragraphing to lead the reader from one element to the next. Indeed, some clients prefer to receive short advice letters in the body of an e-mail message, easily accessible to a client who is on the move.

On the other hand, if your letter is long and complex, you should use section headings, just as you would in an office memorandum or a brief. You need not use precisely the same format headings as you would for an office memorandum. One attorney used the following primary headings in an advice letter to introduce the issues, brief answers, facts, discussion, and conclusion:

Issues Addressed

Executive Summary of Conclusions

Background

Analysis (divided into subsections)

Recommendations

IV. Introduction and Statement of Issues

Immediately after the address and before the salutation of your advice letter, you should concisely state the general subject matter of the letter:

Clay Franks
Vice-President, Construction
GRT Developers
1212 Central Ave., Suite 2201
Boomtown, Calzona 81717

RE: TRI Corp.'s possible breach of contract on the Westcourt project.

Dear Mr. Franks,

In the first paragraph after the salutation, take a moment to build rapport with the client. Then, you should refer to your client's inquiry on this subject matter and state the issues that your letter addresses.

In some cases, your client will pose a general question that asks for strategic advice rather than legal conclusions: "Should we fire TRI and sue it for breach of contract?" If so, you might want to inform your client of the legal issues on which your strategic advice will depend:

Dear Mr. Franks,

It was a pleasure meeting with you the other day. You exercised good judgment to seek advice about the appropriate response to TRI's actions on this project. Specifically, you asked us at our meeting to advise you whether you should fire TRI from the Westcourt project and sue it for breach of contract. In formulating our advice on this matter, we have analyzed the following questions:

(1) Did TRI breach the construction contract by using Cohoes pipe rather than the Reading pipe called for in the architect's plans?
(2) If so, was TRI's breach "material," thus permitting you to cancel the construction contract and fire TRI from the project?
(3) If TRI has breached the contract, to what remedies is GRT entitled?

If you decide to introduce the primary parts of your letter with formal section headings, you could begin with "Issues":

Dear Mr. Franks,

It was a pleasure meeting with you the other day. You exercised good judgment to seek advice about the appropriate response to TRI's actions on this project. Specifically, you asked us to advise you whether you should fire TRI from the Westcourt project and sue it for breach of contract.

I.   Issues
In formulating our advice on this matter, we have analyzed the following questions:
A. Did TRI breach the construction contract by using Cohoes pipe rather than the Reading pipe called for in the architect's plans?
B. If so, was TRI's breach "material," thus ....
C. If TRI has breached ....

V. Brief Answers

Some attorneys will discourage you from summarizing your conclusions in brief answers near the beginning of your advice letter. They fear that your client will fail to appreciate or will even misinterpret your conclusions if he has not read your full analysis first. Like an assigning attorney reading an office memorandum, however, a client reading an advice letter is eager to reach the bottom line. You should not withhold it from him out of some misplaced concern that he is not ready to face it. On the contrary, the client may be so apprehensive about the conclusion, that he will not carefully read the letter, skimming until he reaches the conclusion. Moreover, mindful that he has paid for the entire letter, the client is nearly certain to read beyond the brief answers and to appreciate your full analysis. Thus, unless the letter is very short, or unless exceptional circumstances compel you to lay unusual groundwork before revealing an unfavorable conclusion,[2] you should satisfy your client's curiosity early in the letter.

If you use a simple format without section headings, you may briefly summarize your conclusions in a sentence or two immediately following your statement of the issues in the opening paragraph:

Dear Ms. Price:

Thank you for your telephone call the other day. In that call, you asked us whether you would be liable for damages if you discharged your head chef in retaliation for his testifying against you in a hearing of the state Food and Beverage Commission. As discussed more fully below, we conclude that such a discharge would not constitute a breach of your employment contract, but it would render you liable under the state tort law of "wrongful discharge."

In a more complex letter, you could state your brief answers under some appropriate heading, such as "Brief Answers" or "Summary of Conclusions":

Dear Mr. Franks,

It was a pleasure meeting.... Specifically, you asked us to advise you whether you should fire TRI from the Westcourt project and sue it for breach of contract.

I.   Issues
In formulating our advice on this matter, we have analyzed the following questions:
A. Did TRI breach the construction contract by using Cohoes pipe rather than the Reading pipe called for in the architect's plans?
B. If so, was TRI's breach "material," thus permitting you to cancel the construction contract and fire TRI from the project?
C. If TRI has breached the contract, to what remedies is GRT entitled?

II.   Summary of Conclusions
A. TRI breached the construction contract, because the architect's plans clearly call for Reading pipe and do not permit substitutes.
B. TRI's breach almost certainly is not material, because Cohoes pipe is nearly identical to Reading pipe in all important specifications. Therefore, you cannot cancel the contract.
C. GRT is entitled to the difference between the value of the Reading pipe and that of the Cohoes pipe, a difference that appears to be insubstantial.

In addition to providing these answers to the specific legal issues that you have formulated, you might add a sentence to your overview paragraph that summarizes your response to the client's general strategic question:

---

2 *See* Henry Weihofen, LEGAL WRITING STYLE 178, 199 (2d ed. 1980).

Dear Mr. Franks:

It was a pleasure meeting .... Specifically, you asked us to advise you whether you should fire TRI from the Westcourt project and sue it for breach of contract. In this letter, we summarize our legal analysis and advise you not to fire TRI or withhold its payments.

VI. Facts

In every advice letter, you should state the facts on which your analysis is based. By making a record of the factual premises of your analysis, you can protect yourself against criticism or liability if subsequently discovered facts render your legal analysis obsolete. Additionally, you should explicitly ask clients to correct or update the facts if they see any errors or haves received new information. Indeed, if a client has supplied you with the facts, you may want to disclaim responsibility for any fact investigation:

III. Facts

The advice in this letter is premised on the following facts, which you have supplied and which we have not yet independently investigated. If the following facts prove to be incomplete or incorrect, you should not rely on the advice in this letter without first consulting us. Please advise me of any corrections or changes to the facts stated in this letter.

VII. Legal Analysis

In the body of your letter, you should reach a conclusion on each issue by applying the relevant law to the facts. In a letter to a corporate client's in-house counsel or to a sophisticated client who has some legal knowledge, you can develop your legal analysis and cite to authority in much the same way that you would in an office memorandum. Other clients, however, will have little use for your in-depth analysis of authority or for legal citation. They would rather read a simplified summary of your legal analysis, and they are willing to assume that your underlying research and analysis has been thorough.

Thus, even if you have more fully expressed your analysis in another document, you may want to simplify the discussion in your advice letter. For example, as an initial reaction to a client's inquiry, you might draft a full office memorandum addressed to a supervising attorney. The memorandum will then serve as a basis for formulating advice to the client. In the advice letter, however, you need not analyze the legal authority with the same depth and formality that you found useful in the memorandum. Instead, you can more

simply and briefly convey your analysis of each issue by (1) abstractly summarizing the law with little or no citation to authority, (2) identifying the
relevant facts, and (3) stating your conclusion:

> Under state tort law, you are liable for damages if you discharge an employee
> for a reason that violates public policy. Legislation of this state establishes public
> policies of maintaining health standards in restaurants and encouraging witnesses
> to testify fully and truthfully at state administrative hearings. Therefore, if you
> discharge Chef Boyardi in retaliation for his testifying about violations of hygiene
> standards in your restaurant, you will be liable for violation of public policy.

In some cases, you can even leave the legal rule implicit by simply stating
a conclusion, after identifying the facts on which it is based:

> Your contract with Chef Boyardi does not commit the parties to a definite
> term of employment, and it does not restrict your right to terminate the contract.
> Therefore, under state contract law, you can discharge Chef Boyardi at any time
> and for any reason without breaching the contract.

If your client has some legal training or expects to share your letter
with another attorney, you may want to analyze authority to an extent that
approaches the depth of analysis in your office memorandum. Alternatively,
you can summarize your analysis in the letter and simply attach the office
memorandum on which the advice in your letter is based. In this way, the
client can rely primarily on the more accessible information in the letter, but
he also has access to your more thorough and formal memorandum if the
need for it arises.

Some clients may even prefer to receive short and simple advice letters
in the body of an e-mail message, to which they can easily gain access with
a laptop computer or handheld device while on the move. If a longer and
more formal legal document would be helpful as well, you can attach it to
the e-mail message. In some cases, however, you might have communicated
the analysis to your supervising attorney in a brief email memo, rather than
a formal office memorandum. If so, your advice letter to the client, even if
sent in the body of an e-mail, might be a bit longer, if necessary to explain
legal points that are readily understood by a fellow attorney but foreign to a
client without legal training.

VIII. Conclusion; Strategic Recommendations

In a final paragraph or section of your advice letter, you should summarize your subsidiary conclusions and offer your ultimate advice. If your

client's legal rights and obligations are unclear, do not hesitate to convey the uncertainty with words and phrases such as "probably," or "although the question is close, TRI probably committed a material because" or "although our client has some chance of success on her claim, we likely cannot prove ...." Even so, you should reach a conclusion, even if only a qualified one:

> Although the question is a close one, the noncompetition agreement probably is unreasonable in scope and therefore unenforceable as a violation of public policy. In particular, the geographic scope of the restrictions likely exceeds the area in which Exco has business interests now or in the foreseeable future. I recommend ....

Your ultimate advice likely will be strategic, such as a recommendation to change a term in a proposed contract, file a lawsuit, communicate a settlement offer, or refrain from discharging an employee. If the ultimate decision for the client is essentially a business decision, such as whether to purchase property for development, you should outline the legal consequences of the purchase but leave the business decision to the client. On the other hand, if the ultimate decision is more clearly tied to the legal merits of a claim or defense, such as whether to settle a legal dispute, you can more strongly recommend a specific course of action.

Be sure to fully articulate the merits of any recommendations so that the client understands the likely consequences, including nonlegal considerations, of alternative courses of action. For example, even though you determine that a client has a strong claim for breach of contract, you might recognize that your client and the breaching party have a long-standing business relationship that is worth preserving. If pursuing the claim would damage or destroy that relationship, an alternative course of action might compare favorably to a lawsuit.

Ultimately, the client must make the final decision. When advising a client to settle, for example, you should recommend a range of settlement offers within which your client can exercise some judgment to choose a position or to reject settlement altogether.

IX. Summary

In an advice letter, you should

1. use plain English whenever possible,
2. adapt your format and depth of legal analysis to your audience and your purpose,
3. restate the questions that your client has posed to you and identify the legal issues that they encompass,

4. briefly answer the issues,

5. state the facts on which your analysis and advice are premised,

6. discuss the law and apply the law to the facts to reach a conclusion for each issue, and

7. summarize your subsidiary conclusions and state your advice.

Exercise 10-1

1. Advice Letter without Section Headings

The following advice letter is addressed to a restaurant owner with no legal training. The author has used only paragraphing to signal the transition from one element of the letter to the next, and he has not cited to authority.

a. Identify the purpose or purposes of each paragraph in the letter.

b. At its current length and format, would the letter be suitable for delivery in the body of an e-mail message if the client has easy access to the Internet?

c. Research the problem and rewrite the letter so that it conveys additional information to a client with legal training. Specifically, cite to authority and briefly analyze the authority. If appropriate, divide the expanded letter into sections with section headings.

August 1, 2018
Leona Price
Hep Crepe Restaurant
123 Washington St.
Spinach Village, New Maine 10307

RE: Liability for terminating Chef Boyardi's employment

Dear Ms. Price,

Thank you for reaching out to our firm regarding your potential legal claim. You have asked us whether you would be liable for damages if you discharged your head chef in response to his testifying against you in a hearing of the state Food and Beverage Commission. As discussed more fully below, we conclude that such a discharge would not constitute a breach of your employment contract, but it would render you liable under the state tort law of "wrongful discharge."

Our analysis is premised on the following facts, as you have supplied them. Because a change in the facts may impact our analysis and conclusion, please contact us to correct any errors or to update us with any changes to the facts. The state Food and Beverage Commission has recently held hearings on violations of state health and hygiene regulations at various restaurants within the Village. The Commission requested your head chef, Anthony Boyardi, to testify at the hearings. Under examination by Commissioners, Chef Boyardi testified that employees have failed to control rat and insect infestations at Hep Crepe, resulting in continuing violations of state regulations. Because you view Chef Boyardi's act of testifying as disloyal conduct, you wish to fire him.

Your contract with Chef Boyardi does not commit the parties to a definite term of employment, and it does not restrict your right to terminate the contract. Therefore, under state contract law, you can discharge Chef Boyardi at any time and for any reason without breaching the contract.

Under state tort law, however, you will be liable for damages if you discharge an employee for a reason that violates public policy, regardless of whether the discharge would constitute a breach of contract. Legislation of this state establishes public policies in favor of maintaining health standards in restaurants and encouraging witnesses to testify fully and truthfully at state administrative hearings. Therefore, if you discharge Chef Boyardi in retaliation for testifying at the administrative hearings, you will be liable for violation of public policy. Your liability will include damages designed to compensate Chef Boyardi for his losses and may extend to additional damages designed to punish you for your intentional misconduct.

In conclusion, if you discharge Chef Boyardi in retaliation for his testimony, he will have a valid claim against you for damages. We advise you not to discharge him unless you are prepared to justify the discharge on other grounds. We recommend that you address the infestations in your restaurant, repair your relationship with Chef Boyardi, and capitalize on the continued popularity of your restaurant.

If you have any questions on this matter, please call me at (898) 123-4567.

Sincerely,

_____

Robert Linzer
for Avila and Celaya, P.C.
222 N. 3d St.
Spinach Village, New Maine 10307

2. Advice Letter with Section Headings

a. Compare the following letter with the one above. Describe each way in which the letters differ in style and format.

b. Assume in the letter below that your client, Clay Franks, is an Anglo-American with racist tendencies and that the opposing party's representative, Cal Dunlap, is African-American. Do those facts affect your analysis of the problem? Does the letter below adequately address the problems potentially caused by your client's racism without unduly offending him? Should you be worried about offending him?

c. The letter below is addressed to a client who has at least a basic knowledge of the law relating to performance and breach of construction contracts. Rewrite the letter so that it is appropriate for a client who has no legal training or knowledge. Specifically, summarize your analysis without citing to specific authority. If appropriate, eliminate the section headings and guide your reader through the simpler letter with good paragraphing and transition sentences.

Marcia Todd
Todd, Brown & King
1212 Central Ave., Suite 401
Boomtown, Calzona 81717
July 5, 2014

Clay Franks
Vice-President, Construction
GRT Developers
1212 Central Ave., Suite 2201
Boomtown, Calzona 81717

RE: TRI Corp.'s possible breach of contract on the Westcourt project

Dear Mr. Franks,

It was a pleasure meeting with you the other day. You exercised good judgment to seek advice about the appropriate response to TRI's actions on this project. Specifically, you asked us to advise you whether you should fire TRI from the Westcourt project and sue it for breach of contract. In this letter, we summarize our legal analysis and advise you not to fire TRI or withhold its payments.

I. ISSUES

In formulating our advice on this matter, we have analyzed the following questions:

A. Did TRI breach the construction contract by using Cohoes pipe rather than the Reading pipe called for in the architect's plans?

B. If so, was TRI's breach "material," thus permitting you to cancel the construction contract and fire TRI from the project?

C. If TRI has breached the contract, to what remedies is GRT entitled?

II. SUMMARY OF CONCLUSIONS

A. TRI breached the construction contract, because the architect's plans clearly call for Reading pipe and do not permit substitutes.

B. TRI's breach almost certainly is not material, because Cohoes pipe is nearly identical to Reading pipe in all important specifications. Therefore, you cannot cancel the contract.

C. GRT is entitled to the difference between the value of the Reading pipe and that of the Cohoes pipe, a difference that appears to be insubstantial.

III. FACTS

The advice in this letter is premised on the following facts, which you have supplied. We have not yet independently investigated the facts. If the following facts prove to be incomplete or incorrect, you should not rely on the advice in this letter without first consulting us.

GRT Developers is constructing a shopping center at the southwest corner of 27th Ave. and Marconi Way in Boomtown. As Vice-President of the Construction Division, you have hired TRI to install the plumbing system. GRT's contract with TRI incorporates the architect's plans, which you first transmitted to TRI in a letter soliciting its bid on the project. Those plans clearly call for the plumbing subcontractor to use Reading brand pipe for all plumbing: "All pipes in the plumbing system must be Reading pipe, in the sizes and grades specified in these plans, and no other brand pipe."

From the beginning, you have had difficulty working with TRI's foreman, Cal Dunlap. When TRI had completed about half of the plumbing on the project, you discovered that TRI had installed Cohoes brand pipe rather than Reading pipe. In a heated conversation with Dunlap, you demanded that TRI remove the Cohoes pipe, install Reading pipe, and compensate GRT for the resulting delay in construction. Dunlap agreed to install Reading pipe in the remainder of the plumbing, but he refused to replace the previously installed pipe. You now want to know whether you can fire TRI if Dunlap does not meet your demands.

Your own engineers have concluded that Cohoes pipe is equal to Reading pipe in durability and other relevant specifications. You do not know why the architect required Reading pipe, but you know that his brother-in-law is a sales manager for Reading Manufacturing Co.

IV. ANALYSIS

If TRI has breached the construction contract, GRT may sue it for all foreseeable damages caused by the breach, provided that GRT can prove the damages with reasonable certainty. *See Johnson v. Coombs Constr. Co.*, 345 Calz. 2d 331, 334 (1979). However, you may not fire TRI from the project unless TRI's breach is so substantial that a court would characterize it as "material," rather than "minor." *Lehman Brothers, Inc. v. Steenhook Enters.*, 401 Calz. 2d 112, 115 (1985). If a breach is only minor, you may not terminate the contract; instead, you must permit TRI to complete its performance, while reserving GRT's claim for damages resulting from its minor breach. *See id.* If you terminate the construction contract for only a minor breach, GRT will itself be guilty of the first material breach and will be liable to TRI for damages. *See id.*

A. Breach of Contract

The construction contract plainly requires TRI to use Reading pipe and no other. TRI has admitted that it used Cohoes pipe in approximately half of the plumbing. Therefore, TRI has breached the contract, and it is liable to GRT for foreseeable damages that GRT can prove with reasonable certainty.

B. Materiality of Breach

TRI's breach is material if it is so substantial that it either (1) robs GRT of the primary benefit that it expected from the contract, or (2) demonstrates that TRI is not competent to perform the work and therefore should not be allowed to continue. *See id.* at 116. Stated conversely, the breach is minor if TRI is competent to complete the contract and GRT can be fully compensated for its losses by an award of money damages that is small in proportion to the value of the entire contract. *See id.*

In this case, TRI's breach probably is not material under either branch of the test of materiality. First, GRT's primary benefit from the plumbing contract presumably is high-quality durable plumbing. Cohoes pipe is equal to Reading pipe in durability and other relevant specifications. The architect apparently required Reading pipe for personal reasons and not because it is superior to Cohoes pipe. Therefore, unless GRT has some special need for Reading pipe, it will receive its primary benefit from the contract even though half of the plumbing consists of Cohoes pipe.

Second, although TRI's use of Cohoes pipe shows that Dunlap departed from the architect's plans, we have no evidence that he has failed to follow more important specifications of the plans or that his crews have performed poorly in the actual installation. Dunlap probably knows that Cohoes pipe is equal to Reading pipe, and he may have decided not to take that architect's requirement seriously. Therefore, the events do not suggest that TRI is incompetent to perform Dunlap's promise to complete the installation of plumbing with Reading pipe.

In summary, a court likely would infer that your unhappiness with TRI stems more from your personal dislike for Dunlap than from problems caused by TRI's use of Cohoes pipe. Therefore, a court almost certainly will find that TRI's breach is not material.

C. Remedies

Assuming TRI's breach was only minor, you have no right to fire TRI from the project. Instead, you must permit TRI to complete its performance, and you may demand that it compensate GRT for any damages that result from its minor breach. If you are reasonably certain about the breach and the extent of damages, you may collect the damages yourself by withholding an appropriate amount of payments that GRT otherwise would owe to TRI. *See Johnson*, 345 Calz. 2d at 335. On the other hand, if you wrongfully withhold a substantial portion of TRI's payments above any amount that it owes GRT for breach, GRT may itself be liable for breach. *See id.*

Unfortunately, without further evidence that the choice between Reading pipe and Cohoes pipe will affect the value of your project in any way, you will have difficulty proving any damages. Therefore, we advise you not to withhold any payments owed to TRI.

V. CONCLUSION

Although TRI has breached its contract with GRT, the breach almost certainly is not material, and it probably did not cause any recoverable damages. In these circumstances, if you fire TRI from the project, GRT will be liable to TRI for breach of contract. Indeed, even withholding TRI's payments to cover damages caused by its breach is risky, because we have difficulty identifying any such damages.

We recommend that you work in a cooperative fashion with Dunlap to ensure the best possible performance of TRI's remaining duties under the contract. In the meantime, you might want GRT's engineers to calculate the damages, if any, the installation of Cohoes pipe has caused. If you find any damages, we will be happy to advise you about the best possible means of demanding compensation from TRI.

Please do not hesitate to call me if you have any questions about this matter. My direct line is (111) 232-3232.

Sincerely,

_____

Marcia Todd
for Todd, Brown & King

Chapter 11

Demand Letters

I. Purposes of a Demand Letter

With a demand letter, you may seek to achieve one or more of three goals. First, you may seek to persuade another party to take or cease some action. For example, you may send a demand letter to your client's commercial tenant in an office building, demanding that he stop entering into unauthorized subleases and that he pay past due rent.

Second, you may seek to revoke a waiver of rights to permit your client to assert those rights in the future. For example, even though your client's lease agreement clearly requires payment of rent on the first of each month, your client may have implicitly waived her right to demand timely payment by frequently accepting late rent payments over the previous year without complaint. If so, you can help your client reassert her rights by sending a demand letter that (1) revokes any implied consent, (2) demands prompt payment of rent strictly according to the contract for the remainder of the lease, and (3) warns of your client's resolve to pursue legal remedies for future breaches of the lease.

Third, you may seek to obtain information or concessions from the opposing party to help your client assert rights in the future. In such a letter, you do not really expect the opposing party to accede to your client's demand; rather, you hope to provoke a reaction that you can use to your client's advantage. For example, suppose that your client orally agreed to purchase goods from a supplier for a total price of $10,000, but the supplier has balked at performing. You know that your client will have trouble enforcing the oral agreement, because the Uniform Commercial Code generally requires such agreements to be evidenced in a writing signed by the party against whom enforcement is sought.[1] You might nonetheless send a letter to the supplier setting forth the terms of the oral agreement and demanding performance pursuant to those terms. In so doing, you may hold out little hope that the supplier will immediately perform as promised; instead, you hope that the supplier will either (1) respond by repeating its decision not to perform but admitting that it had entered into the oral agreement or (2) fail to respond within ten days of receiving the letter, thus implicitly adopting your letter's description of the agreement.[2] Either reaction to the demand letter will satisfy the Uniform Commercial Code's requirement that the oral agreement be evidenced by a signed writing, thus enabling your client to assert a contract claim.[3]

II. Audience, Tone, and Writing Style

The audience for your demand letter is the opposing party, his attorney, or both. Your purpose is to persuade the other party to take or cease some action or to otherwise modify her relationship to your client. In addition to establishing the legal and factual soundness of your client's claim, you will seek to convince the other party that acquiescence to your demand is a more positive outcome than the alternatives, such as litigation.

Of course, you should adopt a tone that will most likely achieve your goals. Your task is complicated, however, by the multiplicity of audiences and goals. For example, although your primary audience is the opposing party, his attorney, or both, your own client is an important secondary audience. Even if you think that a conciliatory tone will achieve the best results with the opposing party, your client may make it clear that she has hired you to take the strongest possible stance and to intimidate the opposing party. On the other hand, the community as a whole is a possible tertiary audience, because the opposing party may seek to gain public support by airing the dispute in the news media. If a particularly strident passage in your demand letter is published, adverse public reaction may hinder your client's ability or

---

1. *See* U.C.C. §2-201(1) (2011).
2. *See* U.C.C. §2-201(2) (2011).
3. *See* U.C.C. § 2-201(1), (2) (2011).

willingness to assert her claims. Thus, you should adopt a tone that is firm but not nasty.

Indeed, because a demand letter frequently is the first step in a process of negotiation, one author believes that the letter should "prime" the recipient in a positive manner, to encourage compromise and settlement.[4] Under that view, you might adopt a more collaborative approach if the value of your client's claim is uncertain so that you seek a cooperative process of mutual compromise. On the other hand, if your client's claim is quite certain on the merits and in amount, you might be less interested in compromise and more determined in your assertion of your client's demand for payment or other action that is clearly due.

Aside from tone, your style should be straightforward, businesslike, and professional. As is true in a brief, the most persuasive style in a demand letter is one that the reader does not notice, one that focuses the reader's attention on your demands, your justifications, and the consequences of his failure to satisfy the demands. Thus, you should write in plain English and avoid legal jargon or florid, distracting prose.

III. Format

You may adopt any reasonable format that will achieve the goals of your demand letter. At a minimum, your demand letter should include

1. an introductory sentence or overview paragraph,
2. a statement of the legal and factual support for your demands, and
3. a specific statement of the demands and the consequences of the opposing party's failure to satisfy the demands.

You need not divide a simple demand letter into sections; good paragraphing will suffice. If you divide a long or complex demand letter into sections, you should use whatever section headings suit the purposes of your letter.

IV. Overview

Immediately below the address and before the salutation of your demand letter, you should identify the general subject matter of the letter:

---

4. Carrie Sperling, *Priming Legal Negotiations Through Written Demands*, 60 CATH. U. L. REV. 107 (2010).

Arnold G. Hooper
Hooper Construction Co.
General Contractor
4094 Industrial Way
Fairbanks, New Maine 10713

RE: Damages for Delay in Completion of the Office Bldg. on Center St.

Dear Mr. Hooper,

In the first paragraph of your demand letter, you should provide any introductory information necessary to orient your reader. If this is your initial correspondence to the addressee, your opening paragraph should identify your representative capacity. Beyond that, the opening paragraph can provide such information as a general description of the relationships of the parties and an overview of your client's demands.

For example, the following opening sentence states the author's representative capacity and captures the reader's attention with a demand and the threat of a lawsuit:

Dear Mr. Hooper:

Our client, Dawn Development, Inc., has directed us to prepare legal proceedings against you if you delay further in paying the liquidated damages owed under the Center St. construction contract.

In contrast, the following opening paragraph in a settlement proposal develops the background and purpose of the letter more deliberately, and it introduces the demand for payment in a more conciliatory fashion:

RE: *Araiza v. Udave*

Mr. Phillips:

I met last Wednesday night with my clients, the plaintiffs in the suit against Max and Josephine Udave. All the plaintiffs are keen to press their claims. Nonetheless, they have agreed to make the following settlement offer: They will withdraw their suit if Max and Josephine Udave pay them a total of $10,000, conditioned on actual payment by noon on June 30, 2018. In light of my following evaluation of the case, I think you will find this offer to be quite reasonable.

V. Factual and Legal Basis for the Demands

A. Stating Your Legal Premises

Your explanation of the factual and legal justification for your client's demands may take many forms. In a routine collection letter, you can simply state the amount that is past due under an identified loan agreement, installment contract, or liquidated damages clause. In such a demand letter, the opposing party ordinarily will not dispute the general enforceability of such contracts, and you need not discuss the legal principles that make contractual obligations enforceable:

As you have conceded in correspondence with our client, your firm completed construction on the Center St. office building 22 days beyond the deadline in the Construction Contract dated September 8, 2017 (attached). This delay has caused Dawn Development to suffer damages, which you and Dawn Development reasonably estimated at the time of contracting would be $1,000 for each day of delay in completion. Accordingly, pursuant to the liquidated damages clause in section 15 of the contract, you are liable to Dawn Development for liquidated damages of $22,000. Our client has informally requested payment of these damages on several occasions, but has not received a satisfactory response from you.

In other cases, the fact or amount of the opposing party's liability may be more doubtful, prompting you to explain more thoroughly the legal basis for your client's demands. Such an explanation—at least if directed to the opposing party's attorney—can look very much like the legal analysis and application to facts in a brief. For example, the following passage justifies a demand for consequential damages stemming from a breach of contract:

In addition, the plaintiffs will be entitled to foreseeable consequential damages stemming from the breach. *See Southern Ariz. Sch. for Boys, Inc. v. Chery*, 119 Ariz. 277, 280, 580 P.2d 738, 741 (1978). Those will include the plaintiffs' expenditures on specialized accessories that were suitable only for the wedding and that some plaintiffs were unable to use. *See A.R.A. Mfg. Co. v. Pierce*, 86 Ariz. 136, 142, 341 P.2d 928, 932 (1959) (victim of breach entitled to award of damages for wasted promotional expenditures). Those members of the wedding party who could not fully participate in the wedding, the sole event for which the specialized gowns were ordered, can also recover damages for that lost opportunity. *See, e.g., Mieske v. Bartell Drug Co.*, 593 P.2d 1308 (Wash. 1979) (in UCC case, upholding award of $7,500 for emotional value associated with contracting parties' loss of home movies of significant events). Indeed, the opportunity to participate in the wedding formed the basis for the contracts for the gowns.

In all cases, be sure to determine whether any statute or regulation requires your letter to provide the other party with notice of specified legal rights, to use specific language in the demand, or otherwise to include certain information.

B. Audience

The appropriate level of formality of your legal analysis will depend on the sophistication of your audience. If you address your demand letter to the opposing party's attorney, or if you are certain that the opposing party will consult an attorney, you can reasonably cite to legal authority, as in the immediately preceding example. On the other hand, if the opposing party does not have legal training or legal representation, then you should express your arguments in terms that the party can understand. If you try to intimidate the opposing party with formal citations to authority, you might simply confuse or antagonize rather than persuade.

For example, the following excerpt of a demand letter to an insurance company's subrogation analyst assumes that the analyst has a sophisticated knowledge of business practices but has no formal legal training. The excerpt refers to three legal concepts: waiver, offer, and the "mailbox rule" governing the timing of acceptance. The author of the letter has tried to use these concepts in a persuasive manner without diverting the reader's attention to distracting citations:

Even if Mr. Upton's premium had arrived after expiration of the grace period, his rights were preserved in the conversation between him and Diane Campbell, assistant to Dee Boston, on March 12. In that conversation, Ms. Campbell notified Mr. Upton that his claim would be covered but that she would delay processing his claim until he paid his late premium. Mr. Upton stated over the phone that he would mail his premium. In effect, Ms. Campbell waived any condition to coverage that would require Mr. Upton to deliver the premium to her within the grace period. She thus made the date of her receipt of the premium relevant only to the matter of processing his claim. Alternatively, Ms. Campbell may have communicated a new offer of coverage that invited Mr. Upton's return promise to pay the premium. If so, Mr. Upton accepted the offer either over the phone or, under the "mailbox rule," when he placed his premium in the mailbox.

C. Avoiding Concessions, Admissions, and Waiver

A demand letter is not the proper place to make concessions or admissions that may come back to haunt you later. Therefore, if you choose to adopt a conciliatory tone, do so in a way that does not preclude you from taking a stronger position in the future. For example, suppose that your client demands compensation based on a strong contract claim and a weak tort claim. To maintain credibility and to avoid antagonizing the opposing party, you might invoke only the contract claim to justify your client's demands in a demand letter. If so, you should remain silent about the weaker tort claim or refer to it only vaguely. If you affirmatively concede the weakness of that claim in writing, you may hinder your ability to pursue it later if newly discovered facts enhance its potential merit.

You should also avoid ambiguous conciliatory language that might grant unintended rights to the opposing party. For example, in a letter demanding payment of a liquidated sum owed, you should exercise caution before explicitly stating that the amount is negotiable. Such a statement is unnecessary because the opposing party is aware of the possibility of negotiating a settlement that compromises the amount owed. Moreover, your statement of willingness to negotiate might be construed as an offer or promise to negotiate in good faith, to which the opposing party can bind you by accepting the offer or relying on the promise. To keep all your options open, state your demands in an uncompromising manner, even though you may be willing to compromise if the opposing party offers a reasonable settlement.

VI. Demands and Threats

You should not send a demand letter unless your client has a well-defined goal that you can formulate into a straightforward demand to the opposing party. Moreover, to maximize the chances of achieving that goal, you must provide the opposing party with an incentive to satisfy your client's demand. If the opposing party is fair-minded and your demand is just, your persuasive presentation of the legal and factual bases for the demand should help induce him to satisfy the demand. In most cases, however, you can provide the greatest incentive to the opposing party by threatening to take actions that would be less attractive to the opposing party than satisfying the demand.

Thus, you must clearly state both your client's demand and the actions your client will take if the opposing party rejects the demand. To ensure prompt action, you should set a specific date by which the opposing party must satisfy your client's demand or suffer the adverse consequences of the threatened action.

If the relief to which your client is entitled is uncertain, your unstated objective may simply be to initiate settlement negotiations. More specifically, you may desire to induce your opponent to advance the first realistic settlement offer, which might reveal something about her evaluation of the case or her client's interests. If so, your demand letter might state the maximum possible liability and threaten formal action unless the opposing party takes action to reach a settlement.

In other cases, your client may seek payment of a certain sum of money. For example, if your client is demanding the payment of amounts past due on an installment contract or liquidated damages clause, you should

- state the precise payment that your client demands;
- set a date by which the opposing party must deliver the payment to a specific address;
- depending on the circumstances, threaten to sue on the contract or take other appropriate legal action if the demand is not satisfied; and
- take care to satisfy any statutory or common law duties that apply to your transaction. For example, some attorneys or law firms may qualify as debt collectors subject to the provisions of the federal Fair Debt Collection Practices Act,[5] which will require some kinds of demand letters to disclose certain information and to refrain from making certain kinds of threats,[6] as illustrated in the final paragraph of the illustration immediately below.

The following excerpt from a loan collection letter illustrates the clarity, specificity, and directness for which you should strive. Notice that it identifies the risk of increased liability if legal proceedings are commenced: interest, costs, and attorneys' fees.

If you desire to avoid legal proceedings, you must submit $22,000 on or before August 4, 2018, in cash, cashier's check, or certified funds made payable to Dawn Development, Inc. You must mail or deliver the payment directly to:

Dawn Development, Inc.
Suite 11000, Financial Plaza
1901 South Alma School Road
Fairbanks, New Maine 10701
Attention: Kathy Growl

Take notice that time is of the essence. If Dawn Development has not received the above amount on or before August 4, 2018, it will immediately commence legal proceedings to collect the liquidated damages with interest, costs, and attorneys' fees.

. . . .

Unless you notify this office within 30 days after receiving this notice that you dispute the validity of any portion of this debt, this office will assume that this debt is valid. If you dispute the debt in a written notification sent to this office within 30 days from receiving this notice, this office will obtain verification of the debt or obtain a copy of a judgment and mail you a copy of the judgment or verification. If you submit a request to this office in writing within 30 days after receiving this notice, this office will provide you with the name and address of the original creditor, if different from the current creditor.[7]

---

5. 15 U.S.C. §§ 1692-1692(o) (2012).

6. For a helpful discussion of the Act's requirements, see Scott J. Burnham, *What Attorneys Should Know About the Fair Debt Collection Practices Act, or, the 2 Do's and the 200 Don'ts of Debt Collection*, 59 MONT. L. REV. 179 (2000).

7. With minor changes, this paragraph quotes from one recommended by author Scott Burnham as offering language that would satisfy some disclosure requirements of the Fair

To avoid any dispute about the opposing party's receipt of your demand letter, you should normally send the demand letter by registered mail or through a reputable delivery service that offers easy tracing of the letter. If same-day delivery is necessary for some reason, then you can consider hand delivery, faxing, or even attaching the letter to an e-mail. A fax or e-mail, however, is not likely to convey the sense of gravity and formality of an original letter delivered in hard copy.[8]

Finally, to preserve your credibility in future correspondence, you must confirm that your client is willing and able to back up its threats with action if your demand is not satisfied. As stated by one author, "Don't poke the bear unless you are ready for a fight."[9]

VII. Summary

In a demand letter, you should

- use plain English whenever possible;
- adapt your format and depth of legal analysis to your audience and your purpose;
- use an introductory sentence or paragraph to identify your representative capacity, provide an overview of the purpose of your letter, or orient the reader in some other fashion;
- state the legal and factual bases for your demand;
- state your demands, including the time and place for satisfaction of the demands, and threaten to take legal action if the demands are not met; and
- stay abreast of common law and statutory regulation of demands in your transaction, and comply with the law in your communications.

Debt Collection Practices Act. *Id.* at 190. It might be included, in an excess of caution, as boilerplate language in all demand letters that seek payment of money, even if its terms do not always apply.

8. *See* Bret Rappaport, *A Shot Across the Bow: How to Write an Effective Demand Letter*, 5 J. ALWD 32, 48 (2008).

9. *Id.* at 36.

Exercise 11-1

---

1. Collection Letter

Study the following collection letter and explain the purpose or purposes of each paragraph.

Scott L. Short
Stanley, Leeds & Cardon
100 W. Central Ave., Suite 2100
Fairbanks, New Maine 10701
July 21, 2018

CERTIFIED MAIL
RETURN RECEIPT REQUESTED
Arnold G. Hooper
Hooper Construction Co.
4094 Industrial Way
Fairbanks, New Maine 10713

RE: Damages for Delay in Completion of the Office Bldg. on Center St.

Dear Mr. Hooper,

Our client, Dawn Development, Inc., has directed us to prepare legal proceedings against you if you delay further in paying the liquidated damages owed under the Center St. construction contract.

As you have conceded in correspondence with our client, your firm completed construction on the Center St. office building 22 days beyond the deadline in the Construction Contract dated September 8, 2017 (attached). This delay has caused Dawn Development to suffer damages, which you and Dawn Development reasonably estimated at the time of contracting would be $1,000 for each day of delay in completion. Accordingly, pursuant to the liquidated damages clause in section 15 of the contract, you are liable to Dawn Development for liquidated damages of $22,000. Our client has informally requested payment of these damages on several occasions, but has not received a satisfactory response from you.

If you desire to avoid legal proceedings, you must submit $22,000 on or before August 4, 2018, in cash, cashier's check, or certified funds made payable to Dawn Development, Inc. You must mail or deliver the payment directly to:

Dawn Development, Inc.
Suite 11000, Financial Plaza
1901 South Alma School Road
Fairbanks, New Maine 10701
Attention: Kathy Growl

Take notice that time is of the essence. If Dawn Development has not received the above amount on or before August 4, 2018, it will immediately commence legal proceedings to collect the liquidated damages with interest, costs, and attorneys' fees.

Sincerely,

_____

Scott L. Short
Stanley, Leeds & Cardon

Notice: Unless you notify this office within 30 days after receiving this notice that you dispute the validity of any portion of this debt, this office will assume that this debt is valid. If you dispute the debt in a written notification sent to this office within 30 days from receiving this notice, this office will obtain verification of the debt or obtain a copy of a judgment and mail you a copy of the judgment or verification. If you submit a request to this office in writing within 30 days after receiving this notice, this office will provide you with the name and address of the original creditor, if different from the current creditor.

2. The Bad Example

Study the following collection letter and explain why it is less effective than the letter in Problem 1 above. Identify and describe each defect.

Green and Gain
120 West Washington
Phoenix, AZ 85003
April 1, 2018

Mr. and Mrs. Joe Smith
5555 North 55th Street
Phoenix, AZ 85055

RE: Delinquent Loan #9-1403726-841

Dear Borrower:

We are counsel of record for the Bank of Phoenix (hereinafter referred to as "the Bank"). Our client has informed us that you are behind in your home loan payments, and has asked that we write you on its behalf to request that you take some action to bring your loans current. We understand that you presently are approximately $2,500.00 behind in your payments.

Over the past several months, the few loan payments you have actually made have been consistently late. While the Bank was happy to take whatever it could get from you, it would prefer that you try to make payments on time. If you are having difficulty making your payments, the Bank would be happy to consider and, if reasonable, would agree to an extension of your loan, a modification of its terms, or a second loan to see you through whatever difficulties you may be experiencing. If you desire to pursue this offer, please call your loan officer or some other authorized representative of the Bank.

Please be advised, however, that the Bank has no intention of waiting forever for you to make good on your commitments. Frankly, in our experience the Bank has very little patience with deadbeat borrowers such as you appear to be. The Bank has ruined the credit of thousands of borrowers who, like you, did not take their obligations seriously. Hundreds more have been forced into bankruptcy. Moreover, the Bank is a large, powerful institution which can afford to hire big law firms such as this one, against which the average debtor has little chance of prevailing.

We spoke to your attorney about this matter over the phone this morning but found him to be uncooperative. We sincerely hope that you adopt a more constructive attitude and pay up.

The Bank therefore suggests that you make arrangements to bring the aforementioned loan current by paying the amount hereinbefore stated or making such other arrangements as you and said Bank may subsequently agree upon.

Sincerely,

_____

Bob Jenkins
Green & Gain

3. Settlement Letter

a. The settlement letter below is addressed to the opposing party's attorney in response to preliminary settlement discussions. It was written several months after suit was filed and shortly before a scheduled arbitration hearing. Explain the purpose or purposes of each paragraph. Precisely what does the letter demand? What action does the author of the letter threaten to take if the demand is not met?

b. Rewrite the letter so that it is appropriate for an unrepresented opposing party who has no legal training or knowledge. Summarize your analysis without citing to specific authority.

Charles Rehnquist, Esq.
333 S. Central Ave.
Phoenix, Arizona 85001
(602) 849-0101
June 2, 2018

Robert M. Phillips, Esq.
Kim, Phillips, Burley & Stewart
3301 E. Bethany Home Road, Suite B-111
Phoenix, Arizona 85012

RE: *Araiza v. Udave*

Mr. Phillips,

I met last Wednesday night with my clients, the plaintiffs in the suit against Max and Josephine Udave. All the plaintiffs are anxious to press their claims. Nonetheless, they have agreed to make the following settlement offer: They will withdraw their suit if Max and Josephine Udave pay them a total of $10,000, conditioned upon payment by noon on June 30, 2018. In light of my following evaluation of the case, I think you will find this offer to be quite reasonable.

I have no doubts about our ability to prove the claim for breach of contract. Indeed, your early correspondence and the defendants' answers to the complaint and interrogatories admit that Josephine failed to perform as promised. Even if she had acted in good faith and with best efforts, that would be no excuse for breach of the contract. Therefore, the defendants have essentially admitted to liability. The direct loss in value is easily computed: the difference between the value of each gown as promised ($900 each by your own correspondence) minus the value of the dress as delivered (we can prove that some are total losses).

In addition, the plaintiffs will be entitled to foreseeable consequential damages stemming from the breach. *See S. Ariz. Sch. for Boys, Inc. v. Chery,* 119 Ariz. 277, 280, 580 P.2d 738, 741 (1978). Those will include the plaintiffs' expenditures on specialized accessories that were suitable only for the wedding and that some plaintiffs were unable to use. *See A.R.A. Mfg. Co. v. Pierce,* 86 Ariz. 136, 142, 341 P.2d 928, 932 (1959) (victim of breach entitled to award of damages for wasted promotional expenditures). Those members of the wedding party who could not fully participate in the wedding, the sole event for which the specialized gowns were ordered, can also recover damages for that lost opportunity. *See, e.g., Mieske v. Bartell Drug Co.,* 593 P.2d 1308 (Wash. 1979) (in UCC case, upholding award of $7,500 for emotional value associated with contracting parties' loss of home movies of significant events). Indeed, the opportunity to participate in the wedding formed the basis for the contracts for the gowns.

All these losses are itemized in Count I of the complaint. They total approximately $20,000. Because the plaintiffs will certainly prove a breach of contract and will establish at least some of their alleged damages, they will also be entitled to an award of attorneys' fees, which could add thousands more to the total recovery.

Josephine's own theory of the case is that she breached the contract because she lost the ruffles. Coupled with her failure to warn the plaintiffs to obtain gowns from an alternative source, those facts should easily support the negligence claim in Count II. That claim provides even stronger support than Count I for an award of general compensatory damages, including damages for emotional distress.

Also solid are the claims for promissory fraud and consumer fraud in Counts III and IV. The consumer fraud statute prohibits use of deception, fraud, false promises, or suppression of material fact with intent that others rely, in connection with the sale of any merchandise. A.R.S. § 44-1522. "Merchandise" includes services. A.R.S. § 44-1521(5). Like the common law tort of promissory fraud, a claim under the consumer fraud statute will support an award of punitive damages. *See Schmidt v. Am. Leasco*, 139 Ariz. 509, 512, 679 P.2d 532, 535 (Ct. App. 1983). We should have little trouble proving a claim under either theory: The plaintiffs will offer abundant and vivid testimony describing the way in which Max and Josephine deliberately misrepresented that many of the gowns would be ready on time, thus inducing many of the plaintiffs to wait until the last minute and beyond, when in fact Max and Josephine knew that the gowns could not possibly be completed on time. In light of the recklessness or malicious intent associated with such actions, these claims potentially could add thousands of dollars in punitive damages to the compensatory damages detailed in Count I.

In sum, the plaintiffs are angry and confident. They are anxious to go to an arbitration hearing, and they are ready to enforce their judgment by attaching the Udaves' property. Indeed, I experienced some difficulty getting them to agree to propose this settlement offer. I can assure you that it is not a bargaining posture; it represents their current bottom line, before they have incurred significant legal fees. Despite their passionate views on this matter, however, they have compromised their full claims substantially. The $10,000 figure represents 50% of the compensatory damages for Count I, without costs or attorney's fees, and without any punitive damages.

This offer remains open until noon, June 15. Please call or write to me before then if your clients wish to settle.

Sincerely,

_____

Charles Rehnquist, Esq.

4. Response to Demand Letter: Demand for Withdrawal of Claim

The following letter responds to a demand letter from an attorney for Framer Insurance Co. addressed to Michael Upton. Mr. Upton caused an automobile accident, resulting in injuries to Eileen Bradley, who was insured by Framer. Framer paid Ms. Bradley's claim for $10,000 in losses and medical expenses arising out of the accident. Framer then demanded that Mr. Upton reimburse Framer for Framer's payment to Ms. Bradley. Mr. Upton, however, claimed that he had liability insurance from Framer and that Framer thus was obligated to assume the cost of his liability to Ms. Bradley. The primary matter of dispute between Framer and Mr. Upton was whether Mr. Upton had validly renewed his insurance contract with Framer despite Framer's assertion that it received his late premium payment only after expiration of the policy's grace period.

a. Although it responds to a demand letter, the letter below is itself a demand letter, albeit a subtle one. What does it demand? What action does it implicitly threaten if the demand is not met? Should the author have stated the demand and threat more strongly?

b. Who is the audience for this letter? Assuming that Marilyn Branscomb is not a lawyer, would she likely consult with Framer's attorney, Jon Drake, before deciding whether to drop Framer's claim against Mr. Upton? If so, should the author have advanced a more formal legal analysis with citation to authority?

Charles Rehnquist, Esq.
333 S. Central Ave.
Phoenix, Arizona 85001
(602) 849-0101
January 28, 2018

Marilyn Branscomb
Subrogation Analyst for Framer Insurance
P.O. Box 3108
Mesa, Calzona 89211
Policy No. 881347 94

Dear Ms. Branscomb,

I represent Michael Upton in his claim for coverage under the above policy. I write in response to Jon C. Drake's letter dated January 7 to Michael Upton, in which Mr. Drake requests Mr. Upton to indemnify Framer for Framer's payment of claims to Eileen Bradley. I address this letter to you because Mr. Drake directed Mr. Upton to contact you. I'm sure that everyone hopes to resolve this matter before either party must incur the enormous legal expenses associated with litigation.

Mr. Upton is unwilling to pay the claim because he claims liability coverage under his policy and thus expects Framer to satisfy Ms. Bradley's claims. Mr. Upton recognizes that his insurance policy requires actual receipt of a late premium before expiration of the grace period. Even so, Mr. Upton is certain that the post office in fact delivered his premium within the three days remaining in the grace period, and he doubts Framer's claim that it received the premium a full week after it was posted five miles away. A jury would have the same doubts. Once Mr. Upton proves to a jury with his testimony and that of a witness that he posted the letter three days before expiration of the grace period, the jury will not likely believe that the letter took longer than the standard one to three days for delivery.

Mr. Upton is confident of his ability to prove his version of events before a jury, particularly in light of his previously communicated willingness to submit to a lie detector test. Of course, if litigation or other inquiry reveals that anyone within the Framer organization sought in bad faith to deny Mr. Upton coverage by covering up the facts, the resulting issues would transcend the relatively small dispute now before us. Thus, you should consider the possibility of a counterclaim to any claim that Framer might consider pursuing against Mr. Upton.

In sum, Mr. Upton is prepared to prove that he owes Framer nothing because Framer had a contractual duty to provide him insurance coverage for his liability to Ms. Bradley stemming from the March 12 accident. If Framer drops its claim, Mr. Upton will be happy to cease any further inquiry into possible claims he might have against Framer based on bad faith or other misconduct that Framer may have engaged in.

Sincerely,

_____

Charles Rehnquist, Esq.

Appendix

In a legal method and writing course, you can best master a challenging writing assignment by preparing for and accomplishing your task in at least three separate steps. First, you should acquire information about the topic of your assignment by reading assigned portions of a descriptive text, such as the main text of this book, and by attending classes in which a professor lectures and leads class discussion. Second, you must become an active participant in the educational process by analyzing assigned problems and preparing legal documents, such as case briefs, office memoranda, and briefs. Third, you should welcome constructive criticism from professors or peers, and you should thoughtfully react to their editorial comments by deciding which have merit and by revising your draft accordingly.

Along with the exercises in the main text, these Appendix assignments provide you with the problems and other materials you need for the second step of the educational process: your active participation in research, analysis, and writing. The exercises in the main text are suitable for class discussion or for in-class writing exercises. They include policy questions, invitations to critique sample documents, an essay examination, and composition problems.

This Appendix includes "problems" like the "exercises" in the main text: They provide further opportunities to think about and discuss fundamental questions of legal method and writing. Although a professor could make these problems the subjects of formal writing assignments, they are primarily designed for individual review or for class discussion.

The "assignments" in this Appendix, on the other hand, are take-home assignments requiring formal written documents. They ask you to analyze a problem and draft a document such as an office memorandum or a pretrial brief. Many of the assignments requiring formal documents provide all necessary materials and require no supplementary research. Others, particularly the more complex ones, provide you with little or no authority and require you to perform all necessary research in the library.

The assignments that require research will inspire different analyses depending on when you perform them and what authorities have been issued at that time. For example, statutes or judicial decisions issued after the publication of this book might radically alter the nature of the issues originally intended to be raised. Or your professor might set an assignment in the state in which your law school is located, making that jurisdiction's laws mandatory. Because your analysis of the problem in that assignment will depend on the law of your state, the assignment may be more interesting in some law schools than in others. For all these reasons, your professor might perform some "fine tuning" of some of the assignments by modifying the facts or otherwise adjusting the problems to avoid unintended difficulties raised by intervening laws or the laws of a specific jurisdiction.

Appendix

Pleadings and Pretrial Motions:

Assignments for Parts I and II

Assignment 1. Revision of Sample Complaint

Critically evaluate the following complaint for substance and style. In this actual complaint, the names of the parties and attorneys have been changed, and the text is single-spaced to conserve space in this book.

a. Specificity of Allegations

Identify the fact allegations that are especially detailed and redraft them to achieve greater generality. What are the advantages and disadvantages of each version?

b. Simplicity

Discard clichés or jargon in the sample complaint and replace them with simple, plain English.

c. Request for Relief

Each count in the sample complaint includes a request for punitive damages, as well as compensatory damages. Would a court be likely to instruct a jury that it could award punitive damages on the first count, for breach of contract? What tort, if any, does the second count allege?

IN THE SUPERIOR COURT OF
THE STATE OF ARIZONA
IN AND FOR THE COUNTY OF MARICOPA

Georgia Anne TUCKER,
                    Plaintiff,

            v.

James CLYDE,
                    Defendant.

No. CIV-9X-79

C O M P L A I N T
(Breach of Promise; Tort)

Plaintiff alleges:

I

This is an action for money damages exceeding $1,000.

II

Plaintiff is a resident of Cushing, Oklahoma. Defendant is a resident of Morris, Oklahoma. Defendant has caused an act to occur in Maricopa County, Arizona, out of which this cause of action arises.

COUNT ONE
(Breach of Promise)

III

At all relevant times, both Plaintiff and Defendant were over the age of 18 years, and in all respects capable of entering into a marriage contract.

IV

Plaintiff and Defendant were introduced and became acquainted with each other in September 1983. On or about December 8, 1983, Defendant proposed marriage to Plaintiff, and Plaintiff accepted. On January 17, 1984, the proposal and acceptance of marriage were reaffirmed when Defendant purchased a diamond engagement ring for Plaintiff.

V

Plaintiff and Defendant discussed their marriage agreement from time to time and on a great many occasions too numerous to mention herein. In the course of these discussions, Plaintiff and Defendant confirmed plans to be married in Hawaii on March 10, 1984.

VI

In January and February of 1984, Plaintiff and Defendant came to Phoenix, Arizona, for the purpose of locating and purchasing a home for their future marital residence. Defendant purchased a house located at 6052 East Cortez Drive, Scottsdale, Arizona. In addition, in preparation for the marriage, Defendant opened bank accounts, charge accounts, and utility service accounts in the names of James Clyde and Georgia Anne Clyde.

VII

At the insistence of Defendant and in reliance on the agreement to marry, Plaintiff gave up a profitable business as a hair stylist in Cushing, Oklahoma; borrowed and spent the sum of $12,000.00 to refurbish her residence in order to facilitate its sale; listed her residence for sale with a real estate agency; leased her residence to Defendant's son; withdrew her children from school; and moved her household possessions and her children from Cushing, Oklahoma, to Scottsdale, Arizona, at great expense and inconvenience.

VIII

On March 1, 1984, after having moved to Scottsdale, Arizona, Defendant presented to Plaintiff a prenuptial agreement that, among other things, listed the State of Arizona as the domicile of the parties and that provided for execution of the agreement in Maricopa County, Arizona. Plaintiff refused to sign the prenuptial agreement as written; however, despite Plaintiff's refusal to sign the prenuptial agreement, Defendant again renewed his promise to marry Plaintiff.

IX

On March 8, 1984, Defendant, Plaintiff, and three of Plaintiff's four children flew to Hawaii for the purpose of consummating the marriage, which was scheduled for March 10, 1984.

X

At approximately 8:00 A.M. on the morning of March 9, 1984, Defendant informed Plaintiff that he would not go through with the wedding. Since that date, Defendant has refused to carry out his promise to marry Plaintiff.

XI

On March 9, 1984, Defendant, Plaintiff, and Plaintiff's three children returned to Scottsdale, Arizona, where Defendant left Plaintiff and her three children in the house that was to have been the marital residence. On March 22, 1984, Defendant demanded that Plaintiff and her three children vacate the Scottsdale residence; for lack of other accommodations, Plaintiff was forced to return to Cushing, Oklahoma.

XII

By reason of Defendant's breach of promise to marry, Plaintiff has been deprived of Defendant's support and care for herself and her children, and of the commensurate standard of living that she would have enjoyed had the marriage been consummated. In addition to the foregoing, Plaintiff has suffered, and will continue to suffer, the following damages: a loss of past and future income as the result of Defendant's insistence that she give up her business; economic loss as the result of monies expended for refurbishing her residence in preparation for sale; economic loss resulting from the move from Cushing, Oklahoma, to Scottsdale, Arizona, and from Scottsdale, Arizona, back to Cushing, Oklahoma; and mental pain and anguish, wounded pride, mortification, humiliation, shame, and disgrace, which has directly impaired Plaintiff's health.

XIII

Defendant's actions in breaching his promise to marry were intentional or taken with reckless disregard for the rights of Plaintiff.

Plaintiff therefore requests judgment as follows:

1. past and future lost income in an amount to be determined at trial;
2. out-of-pocket expenses in an amount to be determined at trial, but not less than $12,000;
3. mental pain and anguish in an amount to be determined at trial, but not less than $10,000;
3. other compensatory damages in an amount to be determined at trial;
4. reasonable attorney's fees;
5. punitive damages in an amount to be determined at trial; and
6. such other and further relief as the Court deems just and proper.

COUNT TWO
(Tort)

XIV

Plaintiff realleges and incorporates into this count paragraphs I through XIII.

XV

Defendant stated to friends, relatives, and acquaintances of Plaintiff that Plaintiff and Defendant were engaged, that Plaintiff and Defendant were moving to Scottsdale, Arizona, and that Plaintiff and Defendant would be married on March 10, 1984.

XVI

After Defendant informed Plaintiff that he would not go through with the marriage, Defendant promised Plaintiff that he would provide her with the financial means to relocate wherever she desired so that she would not have to return to Cushing, Oklahoma, where she would experience the humiliation, shame, disgrace, pain, and anguish of explaining Defendant's failure to fulfill his marriage promise.

XVII

Defendant, after making the above-described promise to Plaintiff, forced Plaintiff to move out of the residence located in Scottsdale, Arizona, and refused to provide any financial assistance except transportation expenses to Cushing, Oklahoma.

XVIII

Defendant's actions in providing only transportation expenses for Plaintiff's return to Cushing, Oklahoma, were extreme and outrageous, were intentional, and were done with full knowledge of the emotional consequences to Plaintiff.

XIX

Plaintiff has suffered grievous mental pain, anguish, mortification, humiliation, shame, and disgrace; Plaintiff's mental and physical health has been impaired.

Plaintiff therefore prays for judgment as follows:

1. compensatory damages in an amount to be determined at trial, but not less than $12,000;
2. punitive damages in an amount to be determined at trial; and
3. such other and further relief as the Court deems just and proper in the premises.

Dated May 21, 1984   TICKER, STRANGER & NEAR

By _____
    James R. Near
    Joseph A. Hammer
    900 East Camelback Road
    Scottsdale, AZ 85281
    Attorneys for Plaintiff

Assignment 2. Drafting an Answer

Review the sample complaint in Assignment 1 above or the revised version prepared by you or by a classmate. The defendant, James Clyde, is prepared to prove that Georgia Anne Tucker repudiated the marriage agreement when she refused to sign a written prenuptial agreement, that he never renewed his promise after Tucker's repudiation, that Tucker called off the wedding, and that he suffered severe disappointment as a result. Draft an answer on behalf of Clyde.

Assignment 3. Drafting a Complaint

> ### Introduction to the Dispute: Office Memorandum
> ### Multiple Issues
> ### Jurisdiction: State in which your law school
> ### is located, or as dictated by your professor
> ### Open Library

You are an associate with the law firm of Roberts and Cray. Partner Susan Cray asks you to prepare an office memorandum analyzing the claims of Charlotte Rembar, a potential client. The following is a transcript of your interview with Rembar. Fill in "20ZZ" with the current year, "20YY" with the year before the current year, and "20XX" with the year before "20YY." Alternatively, you can use the dates provided in the sample motion for summary judgment at the end of Chapter 5.

Associate: I understand that you have a problem with your employer.

Rembar: My ex-employer—he fired me November 20YY; that's my problem.

Associate: Did he tell you why he fired you?

Rembar: It was pretty obvious—he cut me off because I wouldn't go to bed with him.

Associate: Start from the beginning. Tell me about your job and your employer.

Rembar: I worked for Alexander Hart. He owns Comcon, a local computer consulting firm; they help businesses determine the best computer system for their needs, and they create custom computer programs for them. Alex is a real genius, and he hires the best consultants to work for them, so his business is booming. I started working there January 1, 20YY.

Associate: What was your position with the firm?

Rembar: I was one of his consultants; I designed computer systems and developed programs. I graduated from Stanford with honors in May 20XX with a degree in computer programming; this was my first decent job in the computer industry.

Associate: How many of you work at the firm?

Rembar: Alex works in the field himself as a consultant, and he had six of us working also as consultants. Other than that, he's got a secretary and a part-time accountant.

Associate: Is that his full work force? Has it ever been bigger?

Rembar: As far as I know, that work force represented substantial expansion for him from previous years; his firm has never been bigger.

Associate: Tell me about your termination.

Rembar: Well, Alex had an eye for me since the day he hired me. He was always flirting and asking me out on dates. I always thought of some polite excuse not to go out with him; I didn't want to offend him, but I don't like him that much, and I didn't think it would be good for our working relationship to get involved in dating. It started getting worse last fall, and near the end of October, 20YY, he called me into his office at the end of the day and flatly propositioned me. I refused, and he fired me.

Associate: Precisely what did he say, and how did you respond?

Rembar: First he asked me how I liked my job and my pay; I said I liked it fine. Then he said that he was in love with me and that he wanted me to go home with him that night and sleep with him and that I wouldn't regret it if I did. I didn't know what to say—I was so shocked. I think I just stood there with a stupid expression on my face for a few seconds; then I told him I had to go to a Halloween party, and I ran out of his office.

Associate: Did he fire you then?

Rembar: Not at that meeting. I was so distressed, I could hardly eat or sleep the whole weekend. I was worried about how we were going to maintain a decent working relationship if he was infatuated with me. I decided to talk to him about it the next morning, but I never got a chance. When I arrived at work, Alex called me into his office and told me that he didn't need my services any longer and that I had one week to clean out my office. I was literally speechless. I just walked out to my car and cried and cursed him. I got my last paycheck a week later.

Associate: Were you upset for a long time?

Rembar: Oh yes. I had trouble sleeping for a month. I was so nervous and depressed that I couldn't attend normal social functions. And I felt guilty—and stupid. I thought that I could have avoided all this if I had been more assertive in the beginning and told Alex more clearly that I wasn't interested. I started seeing a doctor and a counselor so that I could cope with it. I guess you've probably handled bigger problems than this, but I felt like my world was coming apart. This was my dream job—I was making $5,000 a month doing work that I love. When Alex fired me, I didn't know how I would ever explain it to other employers in job interviews. Luckily, I told the truth to the personnel manager at IBM, and she believed me. I started working there at the same salary in early January, 20ZZ.

Associate: How was your performance at Comcon?

Rembar: Great. I was the newest consultant, but I was better than two or three of the more experienced ones.

Associate: Did Alex ever praise your work, either orally or in writing?

Rembar: Sure. In my first month, he said I was learning fast. And in August, he complimented me on a particularly good job I did with one account. But he never put anything like that in writing.

Associate: Did he ever complain about your work, either orally or in writing?

Rembar: Never.

Associate: Do you want your job back at Comcon?

Rembar: No. I'm happy at IBM, and I don't want to ever work for that worm again. But I went through a lot of pain, and I think he owes me something for it.

Associate: Did you have a written contract of employment with Comcon?

Rembar: No, we just orally agreed that I would provide the consulting services for a starting salary of $60,000 a year. But he gave me a little policy manual to look at when I interviewed for the job. I've got a copy of it right here.

Associate: Did he say anything when he gave it to you?

Rembar: Yeah, he said that he believed in treating his consultants like professionals and that he could offer me better benefits and working conditions than I would get at the bigger firms. He encouraged me to read the policy manual to confirm that. He obviously wanted to give the appearance of a class operation so that he could attract the best consultants; he made a lot of money off of us.

Associate: I think that's all I need. I don't have authority to take your case; I'll have to report to the partners and get a decision from them. I'll get back to you by the end of the month. If we don't take the case, I'll help steer you toward some other attorneys who may be interested. In the meantime, read this explanation of our fee system and call me if you have any questions.

POLICY MANUAL
for Employees of Comcon

I. Introduction

The success of Comcon lies in its ability to recruit and retain the best employees available nationally. To promote a stable and productive workforce, Comcon provides attractive terms and conditions of employment, including those set forth in the following policies.

II. Salary

A. *Initial Salary....*

B. *Change in Salary....*

III. Holidays, Vacations, Sick Leave

A. Holidays....

B. Personal Leave....

IV. Termination

A. Probationary Employment

Each employee will work on probationary status during his or her first 60 days of employment. During this probationary period, Comcon reserves the right to terminate the employee for any reason or for no reason at all.

B. Nonprobationary Employment

Comcon reserves the right to terminate the employment of any employee who is not performing satisfactorily.

Based on the analysis in your office memorandum, determine what claims you could allege in good faith, and draft a complaint for an action in state court on behalf of Charlotte Rembar. You may assume that both parties agree Ms. Rembar has received notice of right to sue by the appropriate state agency under Ariz. Rev. Stat. Ann. §1481.D, or a similar statute in the jurisdiction in which your professor sets your assignment. You may also assume that your complaint meets all applicable limitations periods for any claim that you allege.

Assignment 4. Motion for Summary Judgment

Review (1) your Office Memorandum and Complaint in Assignment 3 above, and (2) the sample motion for summary judgment at the end of Chapter 5 of the main text. Do you agree with the decision of Hart's attorney to concede for purposes of summary judgment that the employee manual stated terms of Rembar's employment contract with Comcon?

Now imagine that the second sentence in Section I of the Comcon Policy Manual (Exhibit A of the materials supporting the motion) instead stated the following: "To promote a stable and productive workforce, Comcon endeavors to provide attractive terms and conditions of employment, as reflected in the following policies." On these terms, would you still concede for purposes of summary judgment that the employee manual stated terms of Rembar's employment contract? Add a section to the argument of Hart's memorandum in support of his motion for summary judgment, arguing that the employee manual did not state contract terms under the statutory standard but instead set forth Comcon's current polices, to which it was not contractually bound.

Assignment 5. Opposition to Motion for Summary Judgment

Review (1) Assignment 3 above, and (2) the sample motion for summary judgment at the end of Chapter 5 of the main text.

Prepare materials opposing Hart's motion for summary judgment, or opposing a similar motion on Hart's behalf supplied by your professor.

In preparing your opposition, you may assume the following premises or developments:

a. Your firm filed a complaint alleging four claims for relief: (1) breach of a promise of job security, (2) violation of the Arizona Civil Rights Act, (3) wrongful discharge in violation of public policy, and (4) infliction of emotional distress. In his answer, Hart denied that Rembar's contract contained any provisions for job security and denied the allegations of sexual harassment. He alleged that he discharged Rembar for poor performance.

b. Rembar stands by the information she provided in the initial interview, set forth in Appendix XX, and she is willing to swear to it in an affidavit. Your independent fact investigation has revealed some corroborating evidence from Leslie West, Alex Hart's secretary during Charlotte Rembar's tenure at Comcon. In a recent interview, West revealed that she and Rembar developed a close friendship and that she was distressed to learn of Rembar's discharge. After Rembar filed suit, Hart became irritable and unpleasant to work for; West voluntarily quit her job at the end of the year after Rembar's discharge. She has offered to support Rembar with trial testimony and statements in an affidavit. The following is an excerpt from your interview of West:

> *West:* That was on Halloween last fall, 2017. I saw Charlotte leave the office in tears at quitting time. The following workday, in the afternoon, Mr. Hart told me to process the paperwork to terminate Charlotte's payroll at the end of the week. When I said that I had thought Charlotte was one of his best consultants, he said, "Her consulting isn't my problem—it's her stuck-up attitude." I asked him what I should put down on the paperwork as the reason for her termination, and he said something like, "I don't care what you put—just say that she has a negative attitude."

c. Through discovery requests, you have obtained copies of the contents of Rembar's employment file at Comcon. The file includes only a few insignificant notes and the two payroll action forms attached to Hart's motion for summary judgment.

d. In responding to the Motion for Summary Judgment, you may assume that both parties agree that Ms. Rembar has received notice of right to sue by the appropriate state agency under Ariz. Rev. Stat. Ann. §1481.D, or a similar statute in the jurisdiction in which your professor sets your assignment, and you need not address that issue. You may also assume that your complaint met all applicable limitations periods for any claim that you alleged.

Assignment 6. Motion to Exclude Evidence

Review Assignments 3 and 5 above. Assume that you have successfully opposed Hart's motion for summary judgment and that the trial judge has scheduled a pretrial conference.

You are concerned about some embarrassing evidence that Hart has obtained through the discovery process. While a freshman at Stanford University, Rembar posed nude for a two-page spread in *Hustle and Bustle*, an adult magazine; some of the poses would strike the average juror as lewd and tasteless. Rembar explained that she posed for the pictures on a dare and that she didn't realize until later how lewd and revealing they would be. She regrets her decision to pose, and she insists that the pictures do not reflect her current personality or style of relating to friends or colleagues.

Hart probably learned of the magazine spread through one of Rembar's freshman college classmates or professors. In a discovery request, Hart requested confirmation of the event, along with a copy of the out-of-print magazine. Pursuant to your state's counterpart to Federal Rule of Civil Procedure 26(c), you objected to the request on the ground that the information requested would be inadmissible at trial and that its production would result in annoyance, embarrassment, and oppression. The trial judge, however, compelled discovery on the ground that the information sought, whether or not admissible itself, might lead to the discovery of evidence relating to a claim or defense. *See* Fed. R. Civ. P. 26(b)(1); *Kidwiler v. Progressive Paloverde Ins. Co.*, 192 F.R.D. 193, 199 (N.D. W. Va. 2000).

You now seek an advance ruling barring any reference to the magazine spread at trial. Draft a motion to exclude the evidence before trial.

INDEX